IF YOU'RE IN

MY OFFICE,

IT'S ALREADY

TO   LATE

# IF YOU'RE IN MY OFFICE, IT'S ALREADY TOO LATE

*A Divorce Lawyer's Guide
to Staying Together*

JAMES J. SEXTON, ESQ.

HENRY HOLT AND COMPANY NEW YORK

Henry Holt and Company
*Publishers since 1866*
175 Fifth Avenue
New York, New York 10010
www.henryholt.com

Henry Holt® and ® are registered trademarks of Macmillan Publishing Group, LLC.

Library of Congress Cataloging-in-Publication Data

Names: Sexton, James J., author.
Title: If you're in my office, it's already too late : a divorce lawyer's guide to staying together /
   James J. Sexton, Esq.
Description: First edition. | New York : Henry Holt and Company, [2018]
Identifiers: LCCN 2017050059 (print) | LCCN 2017042566 (ebook) | ISBN 9781250130785
   (Ebook) | ISBN 9781250130778 (hardcover)
Subjects: LCSH: Divorce. | Marriage. | Spouses. | Interpersonal conflict.
Classification: LCC HQ814 (print) | LCC HQ814 .S43 2018 (ebook) | DDC 306.89—dc23
LC record available at https://lccn.loc.gov/2017050059

ISBN: 9781250130778

Our books may be purchased in bulk for promotional, educational, or business use. Please contact your
local bookseller or the Macmillan Corporate and Premium Sales Department at (800) 221-7945,
extension 5442, or by e-mail at MacmillanSpecialMarkets@macmillan.com.

First Edition 2018

Designed by Meryl Sussman Levavi

Printed in the United States of America

1  3  5  7  9  10  8  6  4  2

*For Mom, Casey, and Nate "The Great"*

*She insists she's in love with me—whatever that is. What she means is she prefers the senseless pain we inflict on each other to the pain we would otherwise inflict on ourselves.*

—PADDY CHAYEFSKY, *Altered States*


*Negotiations and love songs are often mistaken for one and the same.*

—PAUL SIMON, "Train in the Distance"

Everything in this book is factual. Names and identifying details have been changed to preserve my license to practice law.

# CONTENTS

# INTRODUCTION

### *Take the Path They Didn't*

This is a how-*not*-to book.

How *not* to fuck up a good relationship or marriage.

If you're married, the goal of this book is to keep you out of my office. Better still, the goal is to help you have a marriage in which the idea of coming to my office would only ever be the most momentary of fantasies when your spouse does something boneheaded.

If you're not married, the goal of this book is to keep you from heading toward the mistakes and bad choices that my clients and their romantic partners have made that brought someone like me into their lives.

As a divorce lawyer who has facilitated the demise of more than one thousand unhappy marriages (and counting), I observe the things people typically do to ruin their relationships, to stifle their happiness and that of the person whose well-being they once cared so much about. Year by year, couple by couple, I can't help but take it in. I'm not a therapist, but almost every day at work, women and men describe to me, in total candor and painful detail, all the behaviors that they or their partners engaged in to turn a relationship born of the best intentions into a steaming pile of shit. The miscommunication, the noncommunication, the deluded communication, the self-absorbedness, the changing when stability was called for, the not changing when evolving was called for . . . I've had a ringside seat to countless ruined or doomed-from-the-start relationships.

After two decades of performing this profoundly intimate service for so many ex-spouses-to-be, as well as for people in myriad other relationship permutations (e.g., living together; having a child in common), the sheer bulk of these observations has turned into a wisdom of sorts. Not long ago—about the time my own marriage was dissolving—I started to think that there was practical value in sharing what I had learned; that people in marriages and other romantic relationships who really want things to work in the long term might be at least as well served by the not-to's as by the words of those who claim to know the "secret" of creating a "strong" or "good" relationship, those mystical truths that fill so many magazines and books.*

Let me say right here: In my practice, I have not gained insight into what makes a relationship "good," and I won't really opine on the subject. It may be, quite simply, that from where I'm sitting, there appear to be countless ways that something can be good but a finite and more easily identifiable set of ways things go bad. In my professional life, I do not see the good marriages, the great marriages, the solidly pretty okay marriages. The people in those marriages never set foot in my office. I know that—just as an oncologist is aware that not everybody has cancer, though everyone who comes to see him does.

No, everybody is *not* fucking everybody. (Most divorce lawyers adopt this dark worldview pretty quickly.) No, *not* everyone is cheating their spouse out of money or trying to use the kids as leverage to minimize child support obligations. I am guessing—though I believe this is an educated guess—that in the good relationships, the ones I don't see, many of the recommendations I make throughout this book are already in use, resulting in incredibly rewarding, enduring unions. I know this: In twenty years of practice, I have never—not once, not ever—met a person who was cheating on their spouse and who also appeared genuinely in love with that spouse. I have never met a happily married

---

* As a divorce lawyer who got divorced, I have learned at least as much about love and honesty from the latter condition as from the former.

person—not once—who was involved in massive financial impropriety. If you know you've got something special, you don't out of nowhere start behaving in ways to jeopardize that.

But do you really want insights into love and romance and successful partnership from a divorce lawyer? Yes, and here's why: The therapists and women's magazines and television and radio "experts" (I'm looking at you, Drs. Laura and Phil) who claim to offer the keys to a great relationship have shared them for decades—and somehow my business and that of my colleagues is still booming. If there's a shortcut to the happy marriage, somebody would have found it by now.

Maybe we need a different approach to the challenges of marriage, commitment, long-term happiness, monogamy, and the rest. Because as a species we certainly seem to suck at it. Maybe if we focus on how we break things, we can figure out how to keep them from breaking.

I did not set out to write a how-not-to book. My original aim was to give a candid, witheringly honest look into the world and perspective of a divorce lawyer, especially the parts of that world that most people don't normally see and hear, much as Anthony Bourdain showed us what being a chef is *really* about. Not the make-believe. I didn't want to hold anything back.

The more I wrote, though, the more I realized that there was utility, not just drama, in the unique view I had of relationships:

- Virtually all the unions I see are damaged beyond repair.
- I have heard the stories of these relationships in their entirety, from promising beginning to unhappy end.
- I am given virtually unprecedented access to even the tiniest details of these stories. (In many ways, I am privy to more of a person's true life than any therapist: I am told what you tell your therapist + your accountant + your best friend + your financial advisor + your parole officer + your spiritual leader + [if you're a parent] your child's school guidance counselor or shrink.)

- I am tasked with an act of reparation/improvement that demands yet more brutal honesty (if I am to help my client build the best next steps).

I thought, *Why not leverage what I've learned to provide value for the many, many people who will never set foot in an office like mine?* I was motivated to do this for two reasons, the second of which you'll laugh at: One, I'm a realist and, two, I'm a romantic. (I am. I'll explain more in Chapter 1.) A new book emerged, though it still includes just as many of the revealing (and, I hope, entertaining) details of the life of a divorce lawyer.

I have not watered things down. As I just wrote, I'm a realist. Show me a divorce lawyer who is not a realist, and I'll show you someone who is no longer a divorce lawyer.

What I say may sometimes sound pugnacious, nihilistic, perhaps offensive. I believe it takes great courage and hard work to make a relationship last, and to make a good relationship even better. I believe it's preferable to confront what may not be working so that you can make your strong marriage or relationship stronger (or yourself stronger). I believe this is far better than the illusory comfort provided by not confronting issues, pretending there are none, and letting that denial gradually and inevitably drag things down, then trying to yank the relationship back up to where it had been. I believe in living in the real world. A friend once emailed me a clip of an episode of *Real Housewives of Some American City,* and one of the wives, to prove how solid and secure and "divorce-proof" her marriage was, boasted that, "In our house, we don't use the D-word." My honest opinion? That's just fucking stupid. The existence of divorce is out there whether you acknowledge it or not. I may decide we won't "use the C-word" in our house, but it doesn't mean no one's getting cancer.

I'm not so arrogant (some who know me may take issue with that assessment) as to believe that following the advice in this book will turn a bad relationship into a good one. Nor is this book just about steering (more) clear of divorce. It's about life outlook. It's not so much "I don't want you to divorce me" but "I want you to be happily married to me." Those are two totally different ideas. You're not interested in white-knuckling it through until death does one of you part. You're interested in having the best, most mutually enriching, joy-filled, good-sex-filled life with someone who wants to stay married to you. A marriage that makes you both better people, on a continuing basis. Isn't that what you signed up for, or thought you had?

It's not even about marriage. It's about meaningful connection. That's something I learn over and over and over. Ask most people to name the two top reasons for divorce, and they'll almost always guess correctly: cheating and ruinous money issues. But those are never the reasons for divorce—rather, they're the symptoms of a bad marriage. Lack of meaningful connection and proper attention and enduring affection led to those lapses, not the fact that someone in Accounts Payable happened to be wearing an incredible outfit one day when the weather turned warm. (Damn you, Heather!)

This is a how-not-to. How *not* to stifle your happiness. How *not* to stifle your partner's. How *not* to sabotage the connection that made you want to get into a romantic relationship to begin with. If you think you see occasional contradictions in the advice that follows, you're right. Marriage is full of contradictions. Same with love. Same with life. But there are some basic truths that can't be contradicted, some actions you can absolutely take. The pillars. If I enunciated them in five or six bumper stickers, though, I wouldn't have a book. I'd have five or six crappy bumper stickers.

And you'd still have a relationship that's not as fulfilling as it could be.

My profession has made me pragmatic, but it hasn't taken away my faith in the power of love. If anything, it has shown me how deeply we all yearn for connection and romance. I never set out to learn what makes a relationship strong. But I have witnessed, up close and always personal, what makes it weak. No single raindrop is responsible for the flood. But if you look hard enough, you can reverse engineer, pretty easily, how the flood came, and when the first drops started falling.

Let's try to find, and keep, some clear blue skies.

# HE SAID, SHE SAID:
# A QUICK WORD ABOUT
# PRONOUNS

My clients are a diverse group. I represent old people, young people, white people, black people, brown people, those with kids, and those without. While the overwhelming majority of my clients have been heterosexual women and men, I have helped many same-sex couples dissolve their long-term, live-in relationships; now that the U.S. Supreme Court has made marriage equality the law of the land, I expect I'll be representing increasing numbers of gay men and lesbians dissolving actual marriages. (It will take a while to see whether gay and lesbian couples are better at staying married than straight couples; it would be pretty hard for them to be worse.)

To keep things as readable as possible, I use the term "husband" and "wife" to describe the parties to a heterosexual divorce action. I am aware, however, that at this point these terms are heteronormative, perhaps inaccurate, frequently undesirable. Still, an endless stream of references to "one spouse" and "the other spouse" becomes quickly confusing. I trust that you will accept my apologies for taking this literary liberty.

IF YOU'RE IN

MY OFFICE,

IT'S ALREADY

TO  LATE

*Chapter 1*

# WHAT IS THE PROBLEM
# TO WHICH
# MARRIAGE IS THE SOLUTION?

If you've thought long and hard about what marriage means, congratulations: You're different from many of my clients. (That may be one reason they're not still married.) I'm forced by professional necessity to think deeply about marriage. I get to analyze it, though in its broken, Humpty-Dumpty-after-the-fall form, from so many angles—the psychological/emotional, the sexual, the financial, the parental, the practical/logistical. If we can stand back for a moment from an institution so rich with powerful associations—many very good, some not so good—it's helpful to recognize that *marriage is a technology*. Like every technology, or tool, it solves certain problems, intentionally, and creates new problems, unintentionally.

What is the problem to which marriage is the solution? Take a minute to think about it. Or three. Is it the problem of being alone? Nope. You can find ways to not be alone without being married, nor does being married solve the problem of loneliness all the time, or for many people, even most of the time.

Does marriage solve the problem of being uncommitted to anyone? No; you can feel committed to people and not be married. You're certainly committed to your children, your biological parents, your coworkers, your religious community, even your softball team (bonus points if it's a softball team associated with your religious community).

What about the problem of not getting enough regular sex? Come on. Sex is everywhere. From Tinder to Grindr, it's in the palm of our hands anytime we want it (no pun intended). And countless married people will tell you that marriage is not, in fact, the solution to the problem of not having a satisfying sex life. Rather, it's often the primary cause. Being married doesn't guarantee a regularly accessible, satisfying sex partner any more than living near a restaurant guarantees being well-fed.

No matter how much you love love, if you want to stay in a marriage or long-term commitment and, more important, if you want to keep it vital, you're strongly advised to acknowledge that the relationship solves certain problems while causing others. What problems does it inadvertently create? Lots of people, including many of my clients, were or are reluctant even to ask this question. Or maybe they asked it but, confronted with the answer, failed to do anything about it.

This appeal to be clinical may seem jarring. After all, marriage is the triumph of faith over reason. That's not just a divorce lawyer talking—I mean, look at the statistics: 56 percent of American marriages end in divorce. (The divorce rate for first marriages is a bit under 50 percent; with each subsequent marriage, the divorce rate increases, hence the over-50-percent total.) Let's say another 5 percent hang on for the kids' sake. (The percentage is considerably higher than that, but let's say 5.) Say another 5 percent hold on for religious reasons. (Eternal damnation is a terrifying, powerful incentive!) Say 2 percent hang in just because the sex is still phenomenal, though nothing else is. We're up to 68 percent of marriages that either end because of unhappiness or continue unhappily. *Two in three.* If I told you that when you walk out the door there's a two in three chance you'll get hit by a falling bowling ball, would you ever leave the house? Would you at least wear a helmet? In 2010, Toyota discovered a .003 percent failure rate on a vehicle they produced with certain brake pads; the company immediately recalled the vehicle as unsafe. So here's an institution that fails roughly 70 percent of the time, yet remains a legal, wildly popular endeavor and multibillion-dollar-per-year industry, regardless of the massive financial and emotional costs of failure. As a divorce lawyer, you sometimes ask yourself, Is *any* married person happy? Is *anyone* happy in a committed, long-term, nonplatonic relationship? (Yes, they are. I don't want you to think I believe it's an enterprise doomed to fail from the start.) Given a divorce rate of 50-plus percent, meaning the two people strolling down the aisle are "more likely than not" (a legal term) to someday end up in a matrimonial law office, and given that divorce almost always causes profound harm to the parties and their infant issue (kids), *one could reasonably argue that the act of getting married is legally negligent*!

Okay, that's depressing—but it's the preamble. Now for the encouraging part. While divorcing parties are generally not inclined to work at making things better for their partner—often to their own detriment, too—those in decent marriages or relationships *are motivated precisely to do so*. Both parties can and probably will work toward improving and deepening the relationship, so long as they identify what needs improving and they carve a clear path to doing so. Because it's better to stay in love, to stoke existing love, than to slowly fall out of love and try to find it again. The process is something that you control, and that the person you love controls. How great is that? My incredibly astute former office manager, Annmarie, believes that the marriage contract should be renegotiated every seven years. Agree with her or not, the idea shines a light on the need to stay conscious and motivated and excited, on a very regular basis, about this unbelievably important, consuming relationship to which you're committed. I can't count how many times I've heard some version of this sentiment from clients, particularly wives who were cheated on: "But I was perfectly happy with our miserable life!"

So that you don't think my work has totally jaded me: I'm a romantic. Don't laugh. I get misty-eyed at weddings, every time, during the ceremony and the toasts. (I don't bother to dissuade those sitting next to me who assume I'm tearing up at the prospect of future business.) How do you *not* get choked up looking at the two of them up there, as public and operatic as can be, staring at each other unbroken for so long? The moment the bride appears, I always look to the groom, whom almost no one is watching. This is (supposedly) the first instant he's seeing her in her wedding gown. At that moment, he's more in love with her than anyone is in love with anyone else in that big room. Every wedding I go to, I want so badly for it to work for those two.

Whenever I help to facilitate the demise of an especially long-standing marriage, there's a moment, usually right before the final dissolution, when I am overcome by a desperate urge to see the wedding album. I want to climb up to their attic or open their closet, dig out the album in its cardboard box in the corner, dust it off, and make my way slowly through its pages. I want to see my client and their ex when they were completely in love and nothing mattered but each other. When the idea of "grounds" and "alienation of affection" and "interlocutory order" and "grandparent visitation" and "community property" and "irretrievable breakdown" and a litany of depressing Latin terms would have been laughable, unimaginable, so "Not us!" When the parties' "infant issue" or "the child of the marriage" (as I call them in written pleadings) was just yellow-highlighted possibilities in a book of baby names. I want to see the faces of the newlyweds on that day, one image after another, in mutual bliss. (Maybe I want it so badly, have always wanted it so badly, because as kids, my sister and I were forbidden to look at our parents' wedding album: If we did, Dad, a former pilot in Vietnam, would start to cry, because so many of the groomsmen and other young men in the photos, buddies from the Naval Academy who also became pilots in Vietnam, were dead.)

I want to see that album because inside so many bad marriages is something good and hopeful that, at one time, was absolutely salvageable.

I'll be candid: I'm secretly a pretty sensitive soul. I love puppies. I adore my kids. I love courtship and holding hands and music and sunsets and Russian poetry. Dammit, I've seen *Love Actually* fifteen times. I love love.

I do not, however, believe in fairy tales.

I don't believe in a false sense of security, or in adult make-believe, or in lives as they're portrayed on social media. Honesty and candor are critical for healthy outcomes, relationships, and lives. That shouldn't be a shocking revelation.

Sadly, most of my clients didn't get the memo.


Marriage is a technology.

When you got married, or if and when you think about getting married, did you or will you think about what you expect to get out of it? Did you ask yourself, *"What is the purpose of marrying this person?"* Yes, you're crazy about her or him, and love love love being in their presence . . . What roles, specifically, will you play in this person's life, and they in yours? What do you get in exchange for doing this?

What's the job description of marriage?

Marriage is tricky; any long-lasting relationship between two partners is tricky; maintaining romantic love can be tricky. I have learned, over and over, that marriages and other committed relationships fail for two fundamental reasons.

1. You don't know what you want.
2. You can't express what you want.

End of story.

No, not end of story. It gets more microscopic. The roots of relationship failure are many. You're dishonest with yourself. You're dishonest with your partner. Expectations are out of whack. There's passivity or lack of appreciation. The dynamic between what one wants, needs, and feels entitled to is strained, strange, and ever-changing. The list of specific possible problems is long, but most of them fall into the two broad categories above.

Over my years doing what I do, I have made just these sorts of diagnoses about clients after I've heard the intimate details of their story, their ex-to-be's story, and the state of their disunion. But except in rare situations, I never dispense to them my pearls of relationship wisdom, such as they are. It's not because I'm in the business of dissolving marriages rather than fixing them. Nor is it because if I succeeded at the latter, I'd put myself out of business.

I say nothing because if I did, it would be a complete waste of my time and theirs.

By the time a person sets foot in a divorce lawyer's office, the marriage is beyond repair. By that point, one or both parties are so invested in the conflict that it's too much to back out of. In all my years, not once have I talked a client out of divorcing, or felt that she or he wanted to be talked out of it. Circumstances may *delay* the visit: Individuals who would otherwise hurtle toward divorce are slowed from initiating the process for all sorts of reasons, from economic recession ("We'll lose the house if we split now—the bank is our common enemy"*) to holiday season (things fall relatively quiet in my office between Thanksgiving and New Year's; then, the week of January 2, visits to divorce law offices spike, as unhappy, resolution-fueled spouses are seemingly shot from a cannon) to the children's alleged best interest (one client of mine made her appointment after waiting patiently until the very day her youngest turned eighteen). Once they walk through that door, though, it's over. If they hesitate in hiring me, it's not because they're having second thoughts about the marriage: They're tire-kickers, just deciding if I'm the right attorney for them or if someone else might be better.

Now, I *do* dispense advice, constantly, that's useful to my clients in their broken situation. I'm there to help architect or sculpt the next stage of his or her life. (My clientele is equally split between women and men.) Their conflict is the clay; together we must mold it into a future that's optimal—psychologically, professionally, financially, emotionally, and residentially. How do we make that happen? What are the logistics, concessions, and stipulations? What will strengthen my client's resolve as quickly as possible, allowing them to work toward their own happiness? To arrive there, it's my job to help bury what's dead, not to convince the client that the marriage still has a beating heart.

---

* Months later, no matter the state of the mortgage or the prime lending rate, husband and wife return to the real enemy: each other.

That does not mean that what I know about marriages and relationships is useless (hence . . . this book). For my clients, yeah, it's too late. The timing of divorce is much like the timing of hospice care. Ever since I was a college undergraduate, I've volunteered to do hospice care. At first I did it because it was a great way to make a little money while mostly reading or sleeping; eventually, I recognized it as the single most bracing, perspective-giving, eye-opening activity a human being can engage in. When you provide hospice care, your first thought about a new patient is usually something like *Okay, to start, you're going to die. There's nothing we can do about that. And unfortunately, it looks like you're going to die pretty soon. If you had come in a month ago, we probably could have made the last thirty days a lot more pleasant and functional for you. But you're here now and it's good that you got here. Because starting right now, we can make things better for whatever time you've got left in this unfixable situation.* Then it's compassion and clear-headedness—getting to work providing company, medicine, ice chips, a laserlike focus on comfort and dignity, and so on.

Same with divorce: My first thought about many new clients is something like *If you had come to me* before *your spouse served you with papers,* or before *you moved out of the house and into a new apartment, thus giving your spouse de facto custody of the kids and putting us behind the eight ball on any future custody claims, I could have helped more—but we'll do the best we can.* Then it's compassion and clear-headedness—getting to work providing legal advice, financial advice, a laserlike focus on dignity and securing what my client needs. And though my client has a future, the marriage does not.

But this book isn't trying to save those past saving. It's for all those in good marriages/relationships, or reasonable ones, or at least not-terrible ones. For them, fortunately, it's *not* too late.

More than half of marriages may end in divorce, but I suspect that the number of individuals in great, good, or okay marriages or partnerships far exceeds those in the ready-to-divorce-or-break-up category. And just like my divorcing clients and what awaits them, married couples and those in ongoing relationships want a good outcome *and* need a good process to get where they want to go. This book is about the process and the insights that can make a good thing—or a once good thing—better.

In handling so many finished marriages, maybe the number one thing I have learned is this: From the outside, no one knows anything about anyone. *No one. Nothing.* It doesn't matter who's giggling and holding hands or who's arguing too loudly at Starbucks. It doesn't matter who's loaded (with money, I mean) or who always struggles to pay the bills. (My experience has taught me that money, like any tool or technology, is an improved means to an unimproved end: It offers real solutions to imaginary problems and imaginary solutions to real problems.) And you really, truly never know who's sleeping around. (But why must it be that those who get caught by their spouses sending naked photos or videos of themselves to their lovers are never the ones you might enjoy seeing naked? My entire office is curious about that one.) And to anyone who believes that social media has made our lives and feelings more genuinely transparent to the outside world, ergo allegedly better, I respectfully disagree: The typical Facebook family vacation post or romantic getaway post is Grand Kabuki Theater, viral delusion, more concealing than revealing. Among my clients who are rabid Facebook users, and whose marital breakups may have been hastened by Facebook, there is zero correlation between how they look in their photos—happy or miserable, alone or nestled in the bosom of family, in Prague or at Disney World—leading to their appearance in my office. (You'll see in Chapter 19 what I *really* think about how Facebook fucks with your happiness.)

Yet life and marriage and love are not totally unsolvable mysteries. In dissecting the circumstances and retracing the steps that culminate in a distressed woman or man sitting across the table from me in my conference room, sharing their heartbreak, anger, disappointment, confusion, and fear, I have come to understand a few strategies and refreshed viewpoints that might work for those who are still in love and working toward common goals, and which could be implemented for positive effect. I grant that certain individuals are simply bound to divorce or break up, no matter how much relationship insight they're exposed to, and that some unions ought to be dissolved as quickly as humanly possible. But the great majority of the insights I have accumulated, I believe, have the potential to help those in marriages and relationships, from the strong ones to the less solid, to make their lives better, fuller, happier, more in their control. These behavior tactics may also improve closeness and connection in other relationships—with one's kids, friends, other family members, even colleagues.

Yeah, I know: I'm no marriage counselor. Pitchers should stick to pitching, not hitting. Bald men don't make persuasive hairbrush salesmen. What makes me think these insights could actually help?

I believe in utter candor and honesty. It'll be for you to decide if any of this works, not for me to persuade you that it does. As Charles, the Hugh Grant character in *Four Weddings and a Funeral,* humbly states in his best-man toast to a new bride and groom, "I am, as ever, in bewildered awe of anyone who makes this kind of commitment." Me too. And maybe, though my day job is to help bury the marriages and unions that didn't work, I love the possibility of helping the ones that *do* work to get better.

## Chapter 2

# STORYTELLING:
# THERE'S AN ARC THERE,
# SOMEWHERE

From the moment I entered law school, I wanted to be a divorce lawyer. That made me an outlier: Divorce law is usually something you end up doing, not that you tack toward. When people who practice divorce law discuss the trajectory of their professional lives, they almost always use that phrase, "ended up."

"I was working for a small firm when I got out of law school and ended up doing some divorce work and I was good at it."

"I did tax work for a few years and took a position outside the city so I didn't have to commute when my children were in grade school. The lawyer I ended up working for was a divorce lawyer."

It's not a good thing. When you use the phrase "end up," it's not to describe how you found yourself someplace good.

"I went out to that bachelor party and ended up in a Tijuana jail."

"I made a left instead of a right and ended up in the Bronx."

It wasn't that way for me. I didn't end up a divorce lawyer; I wanted to be one from the first day of Fordham Law School, an institution widely regarded as a boot camp for trial lawyers. Most of my classmates wanted to be corporate lawyers, public interest lawyers, district attorneys, public defenders, or, if all else failed, law school professors.* There

---

* A saying at my law school: The A students will eventually teach the B students to work for the C students. My own professional experience has done nothing to challenge the validity of this saying.

was one other guy, out of 373 of us, who also wanted to be a divorce lawyer even as a first-year student. (He became one, too. A few years ago I had a case with him and took a certain pleasure in getting a key piece of evidence suppressed in his case against my client. He got a B+ in that class and I got a B.)

Why was I so keen on being a divorce lawyer?

I enjoy being around people. Tax attorneys don't get so much of that.

I like the aspect (sort of a hero/savior wish, I admit) of helping people to rebuild lives that have been really badly damaged, of helping to clean up and organize something that looks and feels like an impossible mess.

I find divorce law exciting because it is the closest thing to "law without a net": The emotions are so raw, the personal stakes so high. It really, truly matters how you navigate each interaction, from how confrontational you are with opposing counsel to how gentle you are with the client. You aren't just a cog in a giant machine serving a client you will never meet. You are a key player in a chess match where every move impacts the available options you have and the other side has— and there are real-world consequences, things like where people live and when they see their children.

There's another major reason I wanted to go into divorce law: I love stories. I love telling stories. And I love learning about people not only from the stories they tell but also from what stories they deem worth telling.

Everyone's got a story. People going through divorce, however, tend to have more dramatic stories than most, or at least they're obliged, for the sake of their own best (or less bad) future, to share their saga in graphic detail so that their lawyer can understand their new reality. (That's part of the reason I wrote this book: Everyone kept telling me that the cases I dealt with every day were, though quite often painful, too compelling not to share.) As my client's advocate, I have to tell the judge a good story about my client's life, so that we can get the best possible settlement. I tell the judge the tale of a marriage from the perspective that most favors my client, blurring and obfuscating aspects that are less flattering to her. (How to explain the undeniably unflattering aspects of my client's situation? There's lots of "She's only human, Your Honor, like you and me. . . .") Like a novelist or screenwriter, a divorce attorney looks for the moments that compel. I often feel that getting the more favorable deal comes down to this: Whoever tells the best story, wins.

I also have to tell a story *to* my client, about himself or herself. Clients are unlikely to come ready with their own narrative because, typically, at the first visit to my office, they see that life is anything but ordered and functional, and certainly hasn't led to a happy ending. Finding meaning and coherence in a client's story—not to mention a dash of uplift—is work. There are a lot of scenes and characters to get through. Some episodes do not fit neatly. Many times, it takes a while even to unearth the real story. Often it's a story about the future, since the present (and past) have produced such unhappiness. In my job, I am always telling stories.

I was representing Carl, an ex-cop and a real tough guy, who'd discovered that his wife, Janet, was having an affair with her Pilates instructor. They had two daughters: Eva, thirteen, and Maddy, eight. Given Carl's sense of humiliation, I could see that we were moving toward real nastiness in the custody litigation. I asked for a four-way meeting—Carl, me, Janet, and her lawyer—and told Carl to bring a framed photo of Eva. When everyone was seated, I set the picture on the conference room table for all to see.

"Look, before we begin," I said, "I just want to say one thing. There's going to be a wedding someday, and it's going to go one of two ways. It's either going to be the wedding where Mom and Dad have to be kept on opposite sides of the reception hall because if they pass each other by the shrimp boat one of them is going to mutter something to the other, and soon they'll be bickering and silverware will be flying, on their daughter's supposedly happiest day. We've all been to that wedding. It's not a fun place to be.

"Or it's going to be the other kind of wedding. Where everybody stands there smiling for the pictures, and maybe at some point during the wedding, Mom and Dad even find themselves standing next to each other, and one says to the other, 'You know what? We screwed up the marriage, but we did a pretty good job with the kids.' And maybe they have a toast. And maybe they even have a dance. But their daughter has a lovely wedding and a lovely start to a new chapter in her life—because her parents loved her more than they hated each other." Pause for effect. "So before we begin, let's just keep in mind that what we do, right now, here at this table, is going to determine what that wedding looks like for Eva. We'll be able to draw a straight line from this table to that day. It's up to you two what that looks like."

The framed picture of Eva and that little speech gave Carl a chance to be a different person from the one he started out being in that room. You-bitch-you-ruined-my-life Carl was overruled by Loves-his-daughters-more-than-anything Carl.

Divorce is the marriage story that ends abruptly and unhappily. But everyone, including those in very good marriages or relationships, has to tell stories—believable stories—about their own lives, to themselves. And even in very good unions, with their day-to-day demands and course corrections, it can be as hard to see the contour of life as it is to see the curve of the earth. Without that vision, though, small digressions and conflicts can make us lose perspective, or lose faith in the reason we fell in love with our partner in the first place: because she or he offered not just a beautiful present tense but also a happy (imagined) ending (future), too.

When I tell the stories of people's marriages, I do it from a partisan perspective, for a specific purpose: to write the story of their divorce and hand them the pen so that they can then begin to write the story of their post-divorce life. In many contentious cases, the client whose lawyer tells the better story, wins.* What if my client was the cheater? I can tell a

---

\* About 20 percent of the divorces I handle are highly contentious, but the percentage goes up every year—so either people in general are getting more unreasonable, or the subset of people who walk through my door have heard that I'm good at handling tough cases.

tale of neglect by the spouse. Human beings crave attention and affection and, absent that, we seek it where we can procure it—right, Your Honor?

As I figure out that story with my client, I make them do something pretty unpleasant: be defensive about the relationship. That's something that those in solid marriages and relationships generally don't do; no one's pushing them to defend or explain it, so they don't. When they do talk about their relationship, they mostly describe the good things—where they first met, how they fell in love, and so on. The story will include a fair amount of covering up. That's not to say that every relationship is, at its core, a farce; not at all. But we tend not to share the stuff that's said (or not said) in the car on the ride home from that party, or the reason we didn't go away this Christmas, or how we managed suddenly to find a way to send Davey to private school. That stuff isn't part of the story you tell anyone else, or sometimes yourself. Oh, and for true, NSA-level coverup? Just look at the story we tell when we're first meeting and falling in love. The level of dissimulation on a first date is through the roof. We dress in a way we don't normally dress, talk in a way we don't normally talk, hold ourselves a certain way, curate our histories, all an elaborate, dissembling show. It's fair to say that if you find yourself facing a stranger at a bar or a party, anything that comes out of their mouth or yours, at least for the next five minutes, is unadulterated fiction.*

Have you ever been out to dinner with friends when someone asks how you and your romantic partner met? It's a pretty predictable choice for polite dinner conversation. More than once in my life I've been in that position and told the tale of how I came to be sitting next to whoever was there as my date. There's something terribly romantic about telling the story of how we met, even when the story isn't particularly remarkable. Perhaps storytelling forces us to reflect on our experiences and condense the most important parts into a larger narrative. It makes

---

* The comedian Nikki Glaser calls this character transformation "Spanx for your personality."

us look, at least for a moment, to what's most important and compelling, and where it all fits in the larger narrative of our lives.

Try it. Sit down and write the story of how you met your partner or, if that story isn't particularly remarkable, then the story of your first date or a special vacation you took or a particularly fond moment in your relationship. Storytelling is powerful even when you're the only audience for what you have to say.

If you had to tell the story of your marriage, what would it be? Stories remind us of how we got where we are and, in the process, remind us of who we were, are, and aspire to be. I can't help but wonder how it might benefit people to reflect on the story of their marriage while it's still going on, not just when it's necessary to formulate a strategy to end it. So many couples, when they're writing their wedding vows or wedding toast, incorporate the story of how they met. They know the power of that tale to inspire sighs of pleasure from the audience; the power to swell their own hearts with feelings of joy and connection. If these narratives inspire us, why don't we tell them more frequently as time passes? The power of storytelling can be harnessed by all of us, every day, to build the bonds that connect us to our partner.

## Chapter 3

# HIT SEND NOW

Justice deferred, they say, is justice denied.

The same can be said for honesty: Wait too long to deliver the truth, to your partner or yourself, and the truth curdles, turning a whole lot messier. I wish I could say this next story is a one-off, but it's so common in divorce, sadly, that we've coined a name for it in my office: "the Ocho."

Cynthia, a teacher and a mother, enlisted me to help with her divorce from Mac, a firefighter. She told me the story of how she ended up in my office. Six years earlier, she'd given birth to Landon, a beautiful boy. Despite the joy of his arrival, though, behavior that had characterized the marriage before Cynthia and Mac became parents, such as loud arguments and Mac's frequent heavy drinking, only got louder, more frequent, heavier. Even after more than three or four years of this, Cynthia still didn't want to acknowledge all the problems in her marriage—and who could blame her? Did she really want to go from being a married mother of a young child to being a divorced mom living on a teacher's salary and some alimony and child support?

Rather than discuss how bad things had gotten and work together to repair them, she and Mac steadfastly avoided their problems. Instead, Cynthia talked him into having a second child. That would improve things, right?

Sleep deprivation aside, there's a rush of optimism that arrives along with a pregnancy and the birth of a new baby. New Baby fills the room. Someone new to talk to and about! Friends and family offer congratulations. Everyone offers support. Conversations about issues that may previously have seemed unsolvable start to feel a little more promising, even resolvable. At a minimum, a new baby demands action (e.g., crib assembly, house baby-proofing) and focus that give the couple something to look at and tend to other than the difficulties of the marriage.

Cynthia had convinced herself that having this baby was a good idea for her marriage, if only because with a new baby she would have even less opportunity and energy to think about and deal with what wasn't working in her relationship with her husband. You sleep better when you're beyond exhausted, don't you? When you're not getting along well, adding dirty diapers and a couple of middle-of-the-night feedings will clarify things for the better—right?

It won't surprise you that, in the long run, the arrival of a second beautiful baby, Anthony, did zero to make the big problems go away.[*] Now, with a six-year-old and a one-year-old, Cynthia was in my office to begin divorce proceedings. When there's one child in a divorce, the custodial parent receives child support equal to 17 percent of the other parent's gross income. If there are two children, the amount is 25 percent. Technically, that second child is worth 8 percent more in gross income. "The Ocho," as we call him or her.

Eight percent more child support. That's what a lack of candor gets you.[†]

I have seen over and over how marriages break, in large part thanks to a lack of honesty and candor. It's important that when a potential client shows up in my office, he understands right away, painful as it is, that

---

[*] If the strategy of shoring up a troubled marital situation with another child *does* work—and I acknowledge that it can—that mother or father won't be showing up in my office.

[†] That's not to mention another possible downside of having a maybe-this'll-save-the-marriage kid: If such a couple *does* stay together, and spend years treating each other terribly, that's one hell of a burden for that second-born (or third-born) to bear when it comes out that he or she was a marital Hail Mary pass. Because everything, eventually, comes out.

denial, self-delusion, and convenient overlooking cannot continue, not if I'm to do a proper job on his behalf. Self-delusion may be a luxury abundantly available to the unhappily married; those going through a divorce simply can't afford it (at times, quite literally).

So at our first consultation, I make sure that potential clients know that "hyper honesty" makes for a better divorce experience. As they sit across the table from me in my conference room, a box of tissues and a bowl of candy within arm's reach, I offer roughly the same soliloquy every time:

"Before you tell me anything about yourself, I want to tell you a few things that anyone sitting in that chair needs to know. And I want to tell you these things before you tell me anything about yourself or your case so you know I'm not tailoring what I say to match up with what you want to hear. When I first started practicing law, I found myself, at the end of cases, thinking, 'I wish I had told the client this or that,' and I started forcing myself to say this stuff to clients the first time I met with them. So over the years this has transformed from a two-minute spiel to a ten-minute rant. I apologize in advance. But if you don't mind, please let me say what I need to say and then I'm going to shut up and listen to what's happening in your life. Does that work for you?"

I pause for a moment. No one has yet objected at that point.

"I'm a divorce lawyer. That's all I do. I don't do wills. I don't know how to do a closing on a house. If you slip and fall, I can help you up but I have no idea how to go about suing the person who tripped you. Divorce. Custody. Child support. Prenups. Postnups. That's what I do and all I do. And because of that, I represent all kinds of people. I represent people whose spouses have a drinking or drug problem and I represent people who have a drinking or drug problem. I represent people who are victims of domestic violence and I represent people who are perpetrators of domestic violence. I represent people whose spouses are cheating on them and I represent people who cheat on their spouses. I represent people who say, 'Help me, my spouse is hiding money in secret bank accounts,' and I represent people who say, 'Help me hide money so my spouse won't find it.' I represent people who are, by any objective standard, amazing parents, who want to get custody of their children so they can ensure that the kids' best interests are protected, and I represent people who are, by any objective standard, atrocious parents, who want to get custody solely to minimize their child support obligations and torture their soon-to-be ex. And I do my absolute best to help all of the people I just listed accomplish those goals. All of them. My absolute best. Without judgment. I'm not here to be anyone's moral compass."

I let that sink in for a second.

"I'm not telling you this to warn you that you're in the presence of a sociopath, though every good divorce lawyer I know has been accused of that at least once. I tell you because I want you to know, before you tell me anything about yourself, that I'm not in the business of judging you. It's not my personal proclivity and it's not what I do professionally. I'm here to get a result for you as a client. You don't know me from a hole in the wall and you're about to tell me the most intimate things about your life. And all I can say is: Tell me the truth. You have no reason not to. Nothing you say behind this door is ever leaving this room without your agreement. So be honest with me. Otherwise, if you give me inaccurate or incomplete information, I'll be giving advice about a person who doesn't exist, and that's not useful to either of us. I'm asking you humbly to tell me what you need to tell me. I'd rather know it and not need it than need it and not know it. You're paying for advice based on my experience and knowledge. It's the only thing I have to sell. The candy's free."

The last line usually gets a nervous laugh.

It doesn't take a huge leap to see that total candor makes not only for a better divorce but also for a healthier relationship.* Because of the drumbeat in my professional life of Lack of Candor = Impending Marriage Disaster, I think it would be wise for couples to employ a form of hyper honesty in any relationship they want to keep healthy.

---

* One of the upsides of divorce: radical honesty afterward. My ex-wife and I joke that when we discuss anything important—our sons, money issues, concerns regarding our interactions with each other— if I wonder for even an instant whether she is being completely truthful, or she wonders the same about me, I (or she) will say, "I have no reason to lie to you. What are you gonna do, divorce me?"

Let's call it Hit Send Now. A commitment to a specific form of radical honesty.

If your partner does something during the day that bothers you even a little, within a couple of hours—or minutes—write him or her an email or text about it. Don't censor yourself. Don't obsessively read and reread the email or text. And then, *against all your instincts as a human being who, like most human beings, has a people-pleasing streak,* just press Send. Then and there.

Hit Send Now. It's the opposite of asking someone out when you were younger and hesitant, but just as scary—and just as potentially rewarding.

You want your partner to know how you feel, truly and without delay. You don't want to start filtering that feeling, reassessing it, rationalizing it, questioning it, and ultimately burying it. If you feel it, you feel it, right? That way, your "From now on, I really prefer your great gazpacho without cilantro" doesn't become, five hours or two weeks later, "You don't know or care to know what I like and, you know what, I never really liked your mother!"

And have your partner do the same with you. Insist on it. And be prepared to take it.

It's a way to address and resolve small problems immediately, before they mushroom. It says, "This is exactly how I feel right now." You can express your feelings in an email or text, maybe a phone call. I advocate for email, because the format allows the recipient to digest what's being communicated and to reread it as the content sinks in; even better, you can make the subject header "Hit Send Now," to give your partner a *little* emotional preparation—a little advance warning that this is one of "*those*" emails," related to something that may require reflection and, thus, maybe shouldn't be opened while eating lunch with friends or right before going into an important work meeting.

Try not to second-guess the wisdom behind the message's content or the burst of id that made you send it. It's not terrifying that you can't take it back: It's thrilling. You're sticking up for yourself and making the relationship stronger. You have the power to do that instead of stewing for the rest of your life over whatever upset you. And the more you send a communication of this kind (and it's not as if you'll be sending them multiple times a day, or daily, or even weekly), doing it becomes like emotional muscle memory.

A few examples of Hit Send Now, to get the tone and kind of topics I'm suggesting:

> *When we were out with friends the other night, you said some stuff about my sister that sat with me the wrong way. Either I misunderstood you or it stung that you meant what you said. Either way, I feel like you needed to know it blipped on my emotional radar and not in a good way. I've thought about it a few times since and just wanted to put it out there.*

> *I'm really craving some alone time right now. I'm not sure why. But I think it might do me good to get out for a few hours solo or go away for the weekend.*

> *If I've been a little off this week, I'm sorry. I've got a lot going on at work. I don't really want to get into the nuts and bolts of it so that's why I didn't bring it up—but I didn't want you thinking it was something to do with us, or something more than what it is. I'll be okay.*

My clients often try to explain to me why they feel what they feel, or why they did what they did. I appreciate that desire. But having listened to people attempt to explain away the stupid things they've done (or pay me to do it for them), I observe that many of our acts and feelings are inexplicable even to us, never mind to a judge. Maybe that's part of what complicates our staying connected to another person. If it's hard to navigate ourselves or explain ourselves to ourselves, how can we expect to do it for another person? Or expect them to do it for us? Yet without that explanation, it's even more difficult to maintain connection, particularly in a world where there's so much stuff (temptation, distraction) creating disconnection.

Hit Send Now is a way to share how you're feeling *without attempting to explain it*. You feel how you feel. And those feelings have repercussions both short- and long-term. They inform how we relate to our spouse or partner on a day-to-day basis. They create habits that build intimacy or distance. We owe it to ourselves and our partners to share the building blocks of our inner lives before those little blocks create a wall that separates us from them.

I don't claim to know if there's a solution to this or that particular problem, but Hit Send Now is a way to level the playing field between you and your partner, giving you both the same information about what you're feeling and what, big or small, might be making you feel that way.

The most dangerous lies are the ones we tell ourselves. The unexamined life may not be worth living, but it appears to be incredibly popular, at least from where I'm sitting. People don't mean to lie to me most of the time. Who would lie to their divorce lawyer? It's ridiculous. I'm bound by rules of total confidentiality. I've heard nearly every form of perversion, deceit, and atrocious human behavior under the sun, and spent countless hours trying to cover up or clean up such behavior. Yet people lie to me all the time, primarily because they don't realize they're lying. They've been lying to themselves for so long, they don't even know they're doing it.

They lie about how they've behaved as a parent. They lie about how they've behaved toward their spouse. They lie about what they're capable of doing in the future, and about what plan makes sense for the day-to-day reality of their lives. They lie about what their financial prospects are and what obligations they will or won't be able to handle. They lie about what was said to them (or at least, they remember it in a self-serving way) and they lie about what they said (and did) in response. Sometimes they lie even when confronted with a recording. Their recollection of their past behavior is often partially accurate, which is a kind way of saying that it's inaccurate.

We are not honest, or fully honest, with ourselves or others, for very understandable human reasons. Honesty is hard to express. It hurts to speak honestly and it hurts to hear honesty. (When an angry client yelled at me, through tears, "You lost me custody of my kids!" it was all I could do not to respond, "Really? Your being on heroin had nothing to do with it?") We want to protect ourselves. We want to protect others. We don't want to be vulnerable or appear mean. We want to make other people, particularly intimate partners, happy and content, and want them to feel they are making us happy and content. It's a game of make-believe that nobody ever wins.

Still, lack of honesty hurts more than it helps. It creates new, usually bigger problems. I'd estimate that what exes argue about, 90 percent[*] of the time, is not directly what they're arguing about. Hit Send Now is designed not to keep arguments from happening but to make sure that you're actually arguing about what you're arguing about. (For more on how to argue, see Chapter 32.) Is this really about whether he can handle the kids on Tuesday night? Or is it "Why have you taken my youth from me?" Is this really about whether bacon should be cooked until it's crispy or taken out of the pan while it still has some give to it? Or is it about "Why do you make me feel so incompetent and self-conscious?"

Hit Send Now is meant to combat or neutralize the natural inclination of so many of us to not express the true nature of what we're feeling. And—no small bonus—it makes you feel much more as if you're living in the moment, because you're expressing yourself in the moment. It's a hack for maintaining authenticity, for both you and your partner.

They say that the truth is the easier path. I believe that. And I believe that path is laid, brick by brick, *as you're walking it*—not miles later, when you turn around to look back at the ground you've just covered, and certainly not when you turn around to look back at the ground you've just covered and realize that you're totally, utterly lost.

---

[*] I'm kidding, of course. It's 98.7 percent.

## Chapter 4

# YOU CAN BE RIGHT OR
# YOU CAN BE HAPPY

Two of the most troubling expressions heard in the divorce trade are "soulmate" (if the concept of soulmates didn't exist, I'm certain we'd have far fewer divorces and unhappy relationships) and "fifty-fifty." So long as you're getting what you need, why must it be half? Who gives a shit? It's what you need, right? That's all that should matter.

I deal with people caught up in calculating what they believe they're entitled to based on what their ex is getting. They're keeping a tally (external *and* internal). Blame, fault, and righteousness are perceived as zero-sum games: The more one party possesses, the less the other has, and vice versa. I represented a mother hell-bent on sticking it to her ex and giving him as little time as possible with the kids, even though he was a good father. She was more interested in being right—or, anyway, in showing her ex that her position had merit and his didn't—than in what was genuinely right for her kids, not to mention for herself. It was my role to tell Diane, "Look, you don't want him just being Disneyland Dad, right? Where every time the kids visit him it's all fun, and you're the taskmaster? We need to force him to have some time with them where he has to put them to bed, he has to get them to school on time."

Healthy couples know how to disagree with each other: They're not so worried about being right, or about being more right than their partner. Being right is not the most important takeaway, and is often precisely the obstacle to resolution.

Even in healthier relationships, though, it can be deceptively easy to keep an internal scoresheet. He (1) leaves his socks everywhere, (2) always finishes off the last of the milk, (3) is consistently fifteen minutes late . . . and you don't do anything like that. So you're up 3–0, right? If things are truly solid, though, you'll tell yourself that that's bad math because he is (1) supportive, (2) monogamous, and (3) reliable . . . and one would think those three positives far outweigh the three negatives. I have never in court heard one party say, "My husband cheated on me!" to which the other party retorted, "But my wife leaves her socks everywhere!" to which the judge interjected, "I grant full custody to Mr. Jones. Keep this sock-dropping monster away from these children. Dismissed!"

Divorcing couples usually have legitimate gripes, true—but it's also a trademark that every negative of their partner counts for 25 points, every positive, half a point. Confirmation bias creeps in when you're unhappy and primed to think that your partner's always the cause.

In most divorces, or marriages heading in the direction of divorce, there is all manner of scale-tipping, meaning little to no balance: balance of fault, balance of agency. Or there's an insane, narcissistic need to be right every time—*every single time*! Or there's a need to get even. Or a desire for mutually assured destruction. It's exhausting for me to witness. And more exhausting, of course, for them to keep score.

There's a fairly easy way to apply, in your own relationship, what I've learned from my clients—by doing the opposite. It's also fairly low risk and easy to road-test without sacrificing much of anything. The next time your partner says, "I'm sorry I did [fill in really stupid thing]"—and it was genuinely a stupid thing your partner did, like not listening to you or not giving credit to your perspective—instead of pointing out how very stupid it was, why not respond with "I'm sorry, too"—which, in my experience, nine times out of ten, will completely disarm your partner.

"Wait—*you're* sorry?" they might say.

"Yes, I'm sorry for the way I handled it," you'll say. "I'm sorry if I didn't see that you were in a bad place. I'm sorry I didn't realize what you needed from me in that moment and let the conversation go down the road it did."

What you do with that kind of reaction—and what your partner should, ideally, do back—creates balance. Balance of fault. Balance of virtue. Balance of investment in the relationship. I doubt I need to point out that balance is one of the key components of a healthy relationship—or that, as mentioned above, I don't see much of it in my line of work.

What I do professionally has taught me an enormous amount about what is possible personally. Being a divorce lawyer, or any kind of lawyer, quickly drains you of the arrogance that you can always be simultaneously successful *and* virtuous; it has taught me that good relationships require deep compromise—yes, to the point that even an important value or two is sacrificed.

It's natural to want to win the argument, to want our individual perspective validated. I don't blame anyone for wanting to be heard and acknowledged as right. So many of us spend time each day arguing with drunk uncles on Facebook and yelling on Twitter at celebrities we'll never meet. When it comes to the person you love, you can concede once in a while.

Which is more important: having your perspective on an issue validated and the ego gratification of being right, or the feeling of connection that comes with being both understood and understanding? Which is more important: the feeling that you won the argument or the feeling that you're winning at the larger game of love and companionship? (Yeah, I stacked the deck on those.) Do you want to be the friend who goes to the movies and yells at the screen, "That's fake! Animals can't talk!"? You might be right, but all your friends hate you.

You can be right or you can be happy.

I know what the healthily-in-love individual would choose. I've seen what the divorcing individual too often chooses. Marnie, an office manager for a medical group practice and a devoted mother of two, had an affair with her boss, a cosmetic surgeon who was also married. When the affair was discovered, she ended it, but the pain she had caused her husband, Lucas, could not be erased. Marnie and Lucas went to a mediator to help them sort out and finalize the terms of the dissolution of their marriage.*

Marnie hired me to review the agreement. While the agreement wasn't grossly unfair, it was definitely lopsided in Lucas's favor. I told Marnie I could easily get her a better agreement in court, one that would more than make up for the extra money she'd spend on legal fees. But that didn't seem the most important point I needed to make to her.

At times, a client may be more in need of personal advice than legal advice. The personal and the legal are often at odds. Legal advice? Incredibly simple: Cut it in half. Use Wednesday as the overnight. Trade the pension for the equity in the house. That's the simple stuff.

Personal advice? Not so simple. But this was the time for it.

"Marnie, may I offer some personal advice?" I asked. "In Lucas's eyes, you're never going to make up for what you did. You cheated on him. He thinks you're an awful terrible atrocious whore. If you think you get absolution by giving him a larger share of your assets . . . you won't. You're not going to find forgiveness from an unequal division of assets or by agreeing to waive your right to the timeshare in Mexico. You're not going to gain absolution by taking three fewer years of alimony. You're just going to have trouble paying your rent and he's still going to resent you and be mad at you for cheating on him. If you want to go with this agreement just to get it done and over with, fine, I understand. But really identify what you're feeling and why you're doing what you're doing. Because you're not a horrible person. You're imperfect.

---

* Mediation is a much less adversarial process that many couples use to divorce, rather than traditional negotiation between attorneys or litigation in court. The role of a mediator is generally to help the couple identify the issues that need resolving and come to a mutually acceptable resolution. A mediator friend of mine has a bumper sticker that reads, MEDIATORS DO IT UNTIL EVERYONE IS SATIS-FIED. It's a great approach; unfortunately, it requires of both parties a maturity and willingness to compromise that are rare in the emotional minefield of a marriage that's ending. After a successful mediation, each party typically hires a "review attorney" to go over the final agreement that codifies, in writing, the terms they have agreed upon. Most mediators have a list of mediation-friendly attorneys they can trust to review the agreement, discuss the pros and cons of it candidly with the client, and not blow up the deal reached in mediation just to generate counsel fees in litigation.

You're human. You had an affair, like many people do. There's a reason the behavior made the top ten in the Bible. They made those commandments about stuff that people did then and still do thousands of years later. I'm not your father-confessor, but you did what you did, and whatever you give Lucas now won't undo that. So ask yourself: 'With this agreement, am I going to have what I need? Will it be enough?' If the answer is yes, then fine. This is your decision to make. But if you're looking to set things right by screwing yourself, and wearing a hair shirt, you're heading down the wrong road. You can't fix this by hurting yourself."

I apologized to her, in case I'd overstepped.

"No," she said, slightly teary-eyed. "It's the most valuable thing anyone has said to me through this process."

Marnie was more concerned with being right or, truthfully, with being less wrong, than with being happy, which entailed getting what she needed financially and could legally procure from the settlement, to better secure her future. And as hard as happiness is to achieve, true righteousness is virtually impossible. Because couples breaking up are so often perpetual fighters, there's almost always at least one party, often both, who can't walk away from a fight unvictorious or unsettled. Almost always they pursue this strategy to their own detriment. Their happiness is the collateral damage of being "right."

Shoot for resolution rather than full satisfaction. Stop worrying about being right.

*Chapter 5*

# EXPECTATION VS. REALITY

We divorce lawyers know the reputation of our profession, and it's not pretty. People are free to say what they want, of course; cold-bloodedness is often ascribed to your average divorce attorney—quite often correctly, and, frankly, it's exactly what our clients need from us. I'd suggest that lawyers generally are cold-blooded, since law school tends to beat the humanity out of you.

When something incredibly significant is happening in your life, you don't want the professionals who are providing guidance to be emotional about it. You want focus. Sure, ideally they would understand that you're having some intense feelings, and they might present things tactfully, in a way that controls for that—e.g., repeating important points because everything is flying out of your head as soon as it's said to you—but you don't want them emotionally invested. That's not going to help.

People also tend to think of divorce lawyers as dishonest. I don't think that's accurate. I'm not sure why some people equate the ability to do a difficult job in an emotional situation with being dishonest (or snake-like, or immoral). The two have little to do with each other. The ability to be ice cold when needed and the tendency (or ability) to lie effectively aren't related to each other, as far as I can ascertain.

As a technician, you are taught to keep your eyes on the facts as they are, not as you wish to see them. A good divorce lawyer—or cop or shrink or accountant—quickly learns to see people as they are, not as we wish they would be. Several years ago, when the saga of Tiger Woods's adulteries dominated the news, many of my friends wanted me to huddle with them in their disbelief. I was having none of it. If you do what I do, you know all too well about "aberrant" behavior, from your roster of clients present and past.

He's physically abusive.

She doesn't come home some nights.

He infected her.

She hates the kids.

He keeps a rubber vagina in the closet.

She swipes the inhaler from her twelve-year-old son to give to her new lover, also an asthmatic, whom she claims doesn't have health insurance and thus needs it more.*

The third in the love triangle is a nun.

False domestic violence charges are made to get the husband thrown out of the house and gain a tactical advantage in the financial aspects of the case.

And on. And on. And on.

When a client comes in for a consultation and, after my little opening soliloquy, says, "You're not going to believe what I'm going to tell you . . ." or "This is going to be a new one for you . . . ," my interior monologue is something like, *Really? Because unless you're a nun who's fucking your cousin while married to a hit man for the Russian mob who has liquidated all of their drug money and converted it into Nigerian currency that you've transferred to your tattooed bisexual lover who happens to be a sitting judge, you're not making a blip on my shock radar. If you're about to tell me that you caught your spouse cheating with the babysitter, I'm going to have a hard time not falling asleep in my chair. I get stranger things than that in the box with my breakfast cereal.*

Politics aside, I admire something that former New York City mayor

---

* The new lover died of an asthma attack a month later, so I guess she really *did* need it more.

Rudy Giuliani once said, as told to me by a friend in law enforcement, (so I can't quote verbatim). Giuliani, performing his regular mayoral duty of swearing in a new class of police recruits, told them: "It's a tough job, don't be a screw-up, don't get caught with your hand in the cookie jar, you're gonna get drunk, you'll most likely get a divorce."

There's the world we want to live in, and the world we live in.

Where do you make your home?

Does your unrealistic worldview fundamentally undermine the possibility of improving your relationship? More specifically, do you live more in the World of Expectation and Hope than—for lack of a better term—the Real World? If so, can that be changed?

It's rare and tough, but ultimately necessary and liberating, to be honest about your situation, yourself, and the flawed clay we're all made of. From my experience, well-meaning people don't live in an unreal world because they're delusional; they do it because they mean well. They want the best for everyone, including themselves. Let me give an example, from numerous custody cases. Very often the parent sitting in my office will say—here's that troublesome phrase again—"I want fifty–fifty custody." I hear that phrase a lot. "I want at least fifty–fifty time."

No, they don't.

I don't know any married people with children who actually monitor the ratio of time they spend with their children as compared with the amount of time their spouse spends. Once upon a time, in another chapter of my life, I was a married man with two young children, and I never reflected on the week and thought, *It was a good week with the kids, but I had them only 43 percent of the time as compared to my wife's 57 percent. I'm going to need to make up that 7 percent sometime this month.* "Kids, I need you back here for exactly ninety-five minutes of catch in the front yard. Billy, get the timer!"

For people in functional parenting relationships, there are really only two amounts of time you're spending with your children: Enough, and Not Enough.

Divorce changes all that, and brings more sharply into focus the time you aren't spending with your children. I think that's at the root of the fifty–fifty obsession; when I dig deeper in conversation with a person telling me that they "want fifty–fifty time" with the children, it quickly becomes clear that they don't want it, nor do they need it, nor could they engineer a schedule that truly provided them with the 50 percent of the children's time they're asking for.

What they're *really* saying—to take the case of quite a few fathers (though increasingly this reasoning applies to mothers, too)—is "I want enough time with my children to be a very involved dad, not one of those visiting uncle–type dads, a fun playtime person who sees the kids every other weekend."

This is admirable and understandable. And it's one of those situations in life when it's important to be honest about what you're actually capable of doing.*

In intact relationships, as in divorce, it's important to be honest with yourself about your real, actual capabilities. Clients tell me what they want; I try to balance it against what they're entitled to. And there's almost no limit to what people might want, while there are rather concrete limits to what they're entitled to; thus, the former must ultimately be driven by the latter. I try to get people to "live in truth" when it comes to their targets. I try to get them to avoid goals that are conclusions, that are destinations instead of steps to get there.

If I were to ask a hypothetical client what he wants, and he said, "I want to be an involved father," I'd praise him, and then say that that's way too vague. After all, there are "involved" fathers who are deployed in Iraq right now and haven't seen their children in person for more than a year. Do you want to go to Iraq? What do you really mean?

"I want to have a schedule with my children that enables me to spend both casual relaxed time with them (like weekends) and active 'heavy lifting' parenting time doing things such as homework with them (like Wednesday nights)."

---

* This is a whole other issue, but the jury's still out on whether it's ideal for kids of divorce to split their time equally between two homes. A significant body of mental health literature suggests that when you have two equally shared homes, in essence you really don't have any home, and end up feeling kind of homeless—though of course, each child is different.

That's real. That's tangible. For my purposes, that's also a lot easier to sell to the other side in a divorce case.

Or take this hypothetical: You're a mom, you're getting divorced, and your soon-to-be ex-husband, who has generally abdicated most of the day-to-day parenting responsibilities to you, makes the following pitch: "I want equal time with the children. I'm their father and I deserve equal time. I'm just as important to them as you are, and I'm not going to be treated like a second-class parent. They're my children, too. I want fifty percent of the time with them."

Compare that with the clarity and reality of this: "I think a schedule that requires both of us to share the heavy lifting of parenting time is important for the children to develop a balanced relationship with each of us. I don't want them to see me as a 'fun' parent they do fun things on the weekends with and you as the 'no-fun' parent who makes them eat their broccoli at night, do their homework, and brush their teeth before school. I don't want them to see either of us as the hero and the other as the heavy, and even though I've always trusted you to do the majority of the difficult parts of parenting, like homework and doctor's appointments, now that our family dynamic is shifting because of the divorce, I want to step up and share some of that work with you."

I won't bother to quiz you on which is more likely to elicit a positive response, and which is more likely to end in arguments and/or litigation.

Now let's take the lucky person who is *not* walking through the door of my office. If I met this person, and they were to declare, "I want to be in a happy relationship," I would ask, "What does that mean?" I would want them to clarify. Can you try that again?

"I want to be in a relationship where I have companionship during the most enjoyable times (to share the joy) and during the most difficult times (to give me support)."

I'd say they were getting a bit warmer, though still not there. But they've described something at least a little more tangible.

Why wait until you're getting divorced (or heading in that direction) to be honest with yourself about what you're capable of in your relationship with your spouse and/or your children? Why not look closely at certain key areas in your marriage and give yourself an unflinchingly honest progress report as to what you're actually doing? While you're at it, maybe you can compare that totally candid report against an equally honest, tangible set of goals that aren't made up of conclusory statements lacking in measurable meaning.

"I want to be more present in my marriage."

What the hell does that mean? It's a conclusion. It's a destination, not a path to get there. How about something more tangible, like "I want to stop playing with my phone when my spouse is talking to me" or "I want to do more activities on the weekends with my spouse."

Those are two great examples of ways to be "more present" in your marriage, and they're tangible and measurable.

"I want to feel closer to my spouse."

Again—I know what you mean, but I have no idea how you could measure it and I'll bet that, with five minutes of reflection, you could give me a list of tangible, clear, and measurable behaviors that would produce that desired effect:

"I want to have mutually satisfying sex with my spouse at least twice per week."

"I want to remember to compliment my spouse at least once per day and, ideally, to have him compliment me."

These are both behaviors that would likely result in "feeling closer" to your spouse.

Be honest with yourself, deeply and painfully honest. Admit to yourself what you're good at and what you're not good at. Admit to yourself how much time you have to devote to the goals you're trying to achieve as a parent or partner, and what you're doing with that time. Be honest about the aspects of partnership and/or parenting that you enjoy and the ones that you loathe (or maybe could take or leave).

## Chapter 6

# TIGHT GRIPS AND LOOSE ARMS

Charlotte, whose divorce was one of the very first I handled when I started my own practice, was angry. Paul was her husband of more than thirty years, a highly regarded trial lawyer, a serious man. A man accustomed to being an expert and telling people what to do.

He advised his wife that he wanted a divorce *while he was sitting on the toilet.*

It was a typical Saturday morning. They woke up early. She pruned a few things in the garden. She made the two of them scrambled egg whites and whole wheat toast for breakfast. They discussed their respective weekend tennis plans at the country club and which permutation of foreign-engineered vehicles it would "make sense" to take there. Then he called her into the bathroom where he was sitting on the toilet, and told her that he had "really been meaning to talk" to her "about the marriage" and that he was "really not happy anymore" and thought it "would make sense to go our separate ways."

He didn't even provide a courtesy flush.

Paul, it turned out, had been sleeping with a considerably younger woman, a paralegal at the firm. Clichéd middle-aged male behavior or not, it devastated Charlotte and caught her completely off guard. Small comfort that it was, she got her first measure of revenge by taking his precious antique tennis racket collection, dumping it in the empty swimming pool in their backyard, squirting lighter fluid on it, and making a bonfire.

More than once during our conversations I heard Charlotte lament, "He took my skinny years!"

As I learned of their life together, I heard about the out-of-town legal conferences/junkets he attended; he often invited Charlotte, but she always stayed back with the kids. I heard about how Paul kept getting away, occasionally adding golfing trips with buddies, but Charlotte never did the same with her friends (though Paul encouraged it), even after both of their children were off at boarding school and then college.

Charlotte, now in her sixties, had married in the late 1970s, when the institution was radically changing, but she had led a very traditional life. And maybe it didn't have to be *that* traditional.

Who knows what would have become of Charlotte's life had she put herself, and not her narcissistic husband, higher on her list of priorities. In my interactions with him, Paul left me wondering whether the women who slept with (or married) him had ever met any other men, or were aware that men come in more charming, less repulsive models.

And, not to blame the victim here, but I couldn't help but wonder, what would have become of Charlotte's marriage had she been more adventurous, more open to doing things on her own, or doing more and different things with Paul, so that she broadened her own horizons and theirs together?

You don't have to come from an earlier era to fall into that trap. I've handled recent divorces of women and men in their early thirties who are doing the same thing: letting themselves be changed, to an unhelpful degree, by marriage and commitment.

Jaclyn was a travel photographer when she married Matt, a financial analyst for a private equity firm. They met in Barcelona, walking on La Rambla. She was shooting photos of seafood in the outdoor markets; he was looking for lunch while on a break from a meeting with the upper management of a Spanish-owned hotel chain. They bonded over their shared love of langoustines and Catalan red wine. They married impulsively in Las Vegas less than a year later and had two children in rapid succession. Within a year of the birth of their second child, Jaclyn was increasingly unhappy, not only with the marriage, but with the person it had, in her view, transformed her into.

Before she and Matt moved in together, Jaclyn was a free spirit. She had a small apartment near Madison Square Park in Manhattan. She went to yoga a few times a week, played in a dodgeball league during the summer months, kept in touch with her college friends, and made a point of seeing as many movies at the Tribeca Film Festival each year as she could get tickets to. "Six months after I married Matt," she shared with me, "my life was unrecognizable."

Jaclyn had never really intended to change so much of herself. It happened the way that one of Ernest Hemingway's characters says he went bankrupt: gradually, then suddenly. Her life before Matt didn't require things like "entertaining clients" or "corporate dinner parties," but suddenly she was thrust into that world and, wanting to maintain the collective good, adjusted her life to make room for new demands. When the children arrived, they were an even greater change—a welcome and wonderful one, but a further redistribution of her energies.

Jaclyn and Matt were splitting up in part because of Matt's financial irresponsibility (he had a gambling issue he hadn't shared with her until the house was in foreclosure) and in part because the marriage didn't do what they hoped it would do.

When they got married, they had both hoped, as many marrying couples do, that the marriage would help them find a deeper connection to each other and also to themselves. That they would, through intimacy, deepen their connection to both the "me" and the "we" in the relationship. In fact, the opposite happened: The expectations they placed on themselves as a function of the marriage (and that, to some degree, our culture places on people who get married) were antagonistic to their own sense of self and the habits and hobbies that helped them, for lack of a better term, like themselves.

If you don't use a muscle, it gets weaker. If you're in spouse mode or parent mode all the time, don't you eventually forget about the "I"?

(I realize they're not completely distinct.) And eventually get less good at being it? You just become a resentful, worse version of yourself.

Proximity, both physical and psychological/emotional, is an important element in good relationships—you know, the nearness of you. But the occasional lack of proximity is critical, too. Being physically away from your spouse for a period; being away from your spouse while you, and they, gather valuable new experiences that can be brought back and shared with each other; and being away, together, from your normal routine (home, work, kids) are obviously valuable. You can't end every night with, "Oh, I forgot to tell you that crazy story about when we both sat next to each other and watched Netflix until just now."

I've had a number of clients who divorce after the children head off to college; they've told me that the reason they were happy—or at least moderately content and able to stay married for many years—was that during the child-raising years, they (or their spouse) traveled a lot for business, which gave each of them an abundance of "me time" and left them frequently looking forward to the return of their spouse so they could catch up and share what happened during their time apart.

Again, this is not a revelation. You already know the messages at the core of this: Make time for yourself. Don't lose your identity in your marriage or in becoming a parent. I'm not here to regurgitate the obvious.

But I would like to point out just how often this issue, in one form or another, is at the root of so many divorces. The husband or wife (depending on who I'm representing) inevitably brings up the fact that they didn't take enough dedicated time away from each other, or at least from their set life together. "I can't believe Roxanne and I didn't go away with our friends, back when we still felt connected and I still trusted her," lamented Owen, a computer programmer, on the day we finalized his divorce after two years of protracted custody litigation. Roxanne had left him for Todd, a chef at what had been their favorite local restaurant. (It's no longer Owen's favorite restaurant.)

"I can't believe I let this happen to me when I had seen it firsthand in my parents' terrible marriage," said Owen. "It was worse there, I think, because my dad never seemed to have any identity at all before the divorce. He was just this silent grumbling figure on the couch. It was only after the divorce that he started to have all these hobbies and interests. . . . I never realized, until I discussed it with him after Roxanne and I split, that all of that stuff was stuff he loved before the marriage but, for whatever reason, he let go when he decided to make my mom and my sister and me his priority." This was one of those moments where I felt it was more my role to listen than to attempt to dispense advice. I do a lot of talking in the courtroom, and a lot of listening on the benches just outside it. Owen continued, "But still, I told myself it would never happen to me. And then I got married and somehow got it in my head that for the marriage to live, part of me had to die. It just so happened it was my hobbies, and my passions, and my personality and the things that made me interesting . . . and then it was my marriage."

Of course, we *do* need to change in a long-term relationship. We do so willingly; ideally, we do so enthusiastically. We give up sleeping with other people. We start to share our living space and our daily routine. Our perspective becomes more long-term and we start to think about developing the "we" instead of just walking the path solo.

Yet sometimes we end up mothballing important, joy-bringing parts of us—the dancer (our partner doesn't like to dance), the fisherman, the museum-goer, the aspiring yogi, the film buff, the person who travels or who doesn't count calories on Saturdays. Part of this is a function of adulthood, not just of coupling, but how much of it is really required, and how much of it is a prison of our own making?

What would my clients say to those who might listen—or, more poignantly, to their former selves, though it's too late to salvage the marriage?

This, in essence, is what I hear them saying:

You stay interesting to your partner by staying interested in things outside your life together.

You stay interesting to *yourself*—therefore better equipped to stay interesting to your partner—by stepping outside the marriage, from time to time, to find satisfaction. Your spouse can be a lot of things for you without being everything. Why the hell did we start trying to have one person be everything? Who thought that was a good idea?

Make girls' night out or boys' night out a very regular thing. There's always an excuse not to. Find a good excuse to not give yourself an excuse to miss it. You don't wake up one day, like Jaclyn suggested, and find yourself "unrecognizable" without taking countless tiny steps farther and farther away from who you were at the start.

Don't be afraid to be selfish, even once you've become a parent— *especially* once you've become a parent.

If you never fully allow yourself to unplug from being married, you never fully recharge. If you don't step away from the "we" to reconnect to the "me," you eventually find yourself far from shore (sometimes too far to get home) and lose both.

I've studied, trained in, and competed in the martial art of Brazilian Jiu-Jitsu for about a decade. It started out as a way to get stress out during my own divorce and ended up becoming my favorite hobby and passion. Unlike karate or tae kwon do, both of which focus on striking (kicks and punches), Brazilian Jiu-Jitsu emphasizes ground fighting (grappling) and the use of principles of leverage and angles to allow a smaller, weaker combatant to incapacitate a larger, stronger one. I've had a sixteen-year-old girl whom I outweighed by a hundred pounds throw me across a room and hold me in submission until I was forced to tap out or risk having my arm snapped. It's a martial art based on principles that demonstrate that neither strength, nor size, nor speed is needed to be powerful.

When I first started training, I, like most new students, would hold on tightly to my opponent in the hope that my firm grip would give me power over his movements. I learned, quickly and painfully, that this is simply false. When you hold tightly to another person, you lock yourself to them, giving them the ability to move you simply by moving themselves. I would grab my opponent's sleeve to give me control over his arm, only to learn very quickly that I had simply sacrificed the mobility of my own arm, yielding control over the rest of my body to my opponent.

I learned a basic principle: Just because you are holding something doesn't mean you are controlling it.

Again, during my years as a white-belt beginner, I mistakenly believed that if I could evade my opponent's grasp, I could prevent him from gaining any advantage or leverage over me. Time after time, I would charge at a more experienced opponent, convinced that if I merely evaded his gripping my hands or feet, I could get past him and obtain superior position; time after time, I found myself flying through the air, grabbing at an arm or leg that was moved out of my reach with precision and technique. I was the cheese in a trap designed to make me throw myself off balance or move in the direction my more seasoned adversary wanted me to go. He was throwing me without ever laying a hand on me. In essence, he let me throw myself.

I learned a second basic principle: Just because you aren't holding on to something doesn't mean you aren't controlling it.

I see so many individuals in my office who were, during the marriage, terrified of losing their spouse and, to prevent it, tried to control him or her closely—*very* closely. Some extreme examples: the client who put a GPS tracking device on his wife's car so he could see where she was going every night (usually the grocery store or the gym); the client who put spyware on her husband's phone so she would get duplicates of every text he sent or received during the day; the client's husband who refused to allow her to spend time with "bad influences," such as her recently divorced sister, for fear that she might embrace ideas about getting divorced.

There are more routine examples, like the client who wasn't "allowed" to go to the International Fly Fishing Expo because it would require an overnight stay without his spouse. Not, mind you, that the two of them enjoyed spending time together so much that they didn't want to travel without each other; but because his wife wasn't interested in attending a fly-fishing expo with him, and didn't have anywhere similar that she wanted to go alone, she felt it was "unfair" that he would have a "night off" from the marriage or children without her having one, so "case closed." There was the client who was made to feel foolish that she wanted to join a local CrossFit gym because her husband, an Army vet, felt it was "silly" to need "all that stuff" when you could "just as easily get into shape" through push-ups, sit-ups, and running.

Many individuals who hold on tight to their partners have good intentions. Some don't. With the majority, it seems fairly obvious that the need is born of insecurity; their actions can seem, on some level, understandable and forgivable.

But after years of such control, the would-be dominating party ends up losing control over the other, precisely the situation the former was hoping to avoid. And then they end up losing so much more.

As in Brazilian Jiu-Jitsu, merely holding on tight, rather than holding on effectively, simply does not work, and can suffocate the relationship. Possessiveness often manifests in one party discouraging the other from going out into the world. And yet, apart from hyper-religious marriages, in which such control/submissiveness is often very much part of the covenant (I won't delve here into such unions), discouraging your spouse from having, say, that regular girls' night out or boys' night out is a profoundly dumb idea. In fact, not only is it dumb to discourage it; it's dumb to not actively *encourage* it.

This is what someone who has facilitated the demise of more than a thousand marriages has learned:

- If you think the only thing keeping your spouse with you is your refusal to allow him or her to see that there are any compelling alternatives in the world, here's some bad news: Your spouse sees what else is out there. They don't need to leave the house for that.
- If you think the only thing keeping your spouse from sleeping with other people is restricting his or her access to other people they might want to sleep with, here's some more bad news: If your spouse wants to sleep with someone else, they will. At work. Or

while you're at work. In the car. Or outside a bar. They'll do it in the broom closet of your children's school, with the janitor. (Not a made-up example; I cross-examined the janitor.)

Encouraging your spouse to play a regular round of golf, or hit the gym, or get her nails done, or get that drink with his old college roommate, or go away for a weekend, is almost always a winning relationship strategy, for two reasons:

One, remember when I wrote (of course you do, it was three paragraphs ago), "If you think the only thing keeping your spouse with you is your refusal . . ." Yeah, that. "Letting" them do their thing imparts a sense of trust in them.

And two, maybe more important:

The person who comes back to you is a better version of the person who left.

I think of my own current relationship: When I am away for many days from the woman in my life and come back to her, she always smells particularly great, and it's not because she's wearing some new fragrance. It's the familiar scent of her, newly appreciated. It's the satisfaction and resolution of the longing born of her absence. She's happy to see me, and I am happy to see her.

Whenever I am doing Brazilian Jiu-Jitsu (which I aim to do as often as my middle-aged body and busy professional life allow), I feel like the best version of myself: intense, physical, competitive, challenged, fully engaged, respectful, learning, present, connected, part of something bigger than myself. I'm bettering myself and cultivating space in my life for myself.

Consequently, when I'm done with a morning of training, and I've showered, and I arrive home, I come back to my relationship (and my parenting and friendships, too, but those aren't the point here) as one of my favorite selves. She can feel it and I love that she can feel it. And I want her to be, as often as possible, her best self.

The marriage vows ask us to forsake all others. They do not demand that we forsake all the other good things we can be. Then, we're just two boring people in a boring marriage, and most likely still scared and insecure.

In a relationship or marriage, we possess great agency for our own happiness; by exerting that agency, we have great power over the happiness of the union. For those in love, there is so much opportunity for finding and making happiness, so long as you keep finding and making new meaning above and beyond the daily, sometimes mundane life you lead.

My current Brazilian Jiu-Jitsu instructor, Paul Schreiner, often tells students that they need to develop "tight grips and loose arms." He means we need to learn how to "hold on loosely" in a way that keeps control over the key area we are trying to hold ("tight grips") but allows for movement and adjustment depending on how we move around in response to the hold ("loose arms").

I can't think of better relationship advice.

Divorce represents a massive, ultimately terminal loss of control.* You lose control of your spouse. You lose control of many other important relationships (especially the one with your children—though a parent's grip on children is perpetually slipping, divorce or no divorce). You lose control over aspects of your day-to-day life—where your money goes, where your time is spent, where you get to live, where you don't get to live anymore.

It's scary to let go of your spouse. It's scary to let go of illusions about

---

* For some people, that loss of control is simply unacceptable. One client, Anton, was okay with almost every aspect of his impending divorce but one: His ex, who had slept with only a couple of guys before she met him a decade before, and whom he felt he had taught all kinds of things in bed, would now be free to use that education with someone else. Never mind that Anton and his ex were barely on speaking terms anymore. After countless hours trying to explain to him that there was nothing that could be done within the legal system to get an order directing that his ex-wife be prohibited from dating new men until his children had left for college, I was actually getting close to acquiescing to his request that I make a motion to the court seeking precisely that relief. (I get asked to make this motion on average about once monthly, by men and women both.) I decided I wasn't willing to do it: You can't restore your credibility with a judge once you lose it by making frivolous motions. "I don't know what to say to you, Anton," I had to tell him. "The court doesn't have the authority to force her to wear a chastity belt after the divorce is finalized."

your marriage, marriage generally, or even yourself. But perhaps that scary letting-go and the resulting loss of control may, ultimately, prevent the massive loss of control that comes with complete relationship breakdown. Perhaps by letting go, you'll find yourself establishing a much stronger grip.

## Chapter 7

# READING MINDS AND
# ACCEPTING APPEARANCES

Elizabeth—early forties, dark-blond hair, striking blue eyes, pearl earrings, expensive pale-gray suit tailored to show off her SoulCycle build—sat across the table from me in my conference room. My staff and I had met her in person two minutes earlier, in the reception area of my office. Everything about her was crisp and efficient: She came through the door exactly one minute before our scheduled appointment. We shook hands. She introduced herself by her full name, with a stiff spine and as much formality as possible.

I asked, somewhat routinely, if friends ever called her Liz or Beth. She barely angled her head as if to say, "Why would that be relevant?" or maybe "Enough foreplay, let's get on with business." "Elizabeth," she said.

"Okay, Elizabeth it is," I said.

Sometimes, in getting a difficult conversation started, I appropriate (okay, steal) a line that the plastic surgeons in the TV drama *Nip/Tuck* use on their prospective clients—"Tell me what it is you don't like about yourself." I change one word: "Tell me what it is you don't like about your spouse." But as an icebreaker, that didn't feel right for the vibe Elizabeth gave off.

"By the time someone is sitting in that chair across from me, their marriage is either over or in a very fragile state," I said to her. "Which one applies to you?"

"My marriage situation became untenable nine days ago, Sunday the twenty-second," Elizabeth said, unafraid to maintain steady eye contact. "We were in the kitchen and Douglas said, 'What would you like for breakfast?' And I said, 'A divorce.'"

She pressed her lips together slightly, as if she thought maybe I needed to absorb things. I did not. I'd done enough divorces that very little shocked me.

She took a measured breath. "Douglas did not seem to understand. Then he said, 'You're kidding.' And I said, 'No. I've prepared a spreadsheet of what I'm taking.'"

I nodded. Despite her demeanor, I didn't know if I believed that the ax had dropped on Douglas quite so neatly. Everyone has trouble recounting accurately; when the topic is something as emotionally charged as marital breakup, and the storyteller is one of the players, memory gets even fuzzier. So I wasn't sure Elizabeth had delivered the news quite that neatly and unemotionally and, well, *coldly.*

"That's the way the conversation with Douglas happened?" I asked.

"Yes, that's how it happened," she said, with a hint of annoyance at my doubt. She broke eye contact, reached into her buttery leather Fendi bag, and pulled out a small silver device. "I recorded it in anticipation of potentially needing it later for litigation purposes."

I listened to the recording later. Yes, that was exactly how it happened. The pause before his "You're kidding" was brutal. The guy was legitimately expecting to hear "Poached eggs," and got "A divorce" instead. No wife. No eggs. Rough day.

I shouldn't have been surprised by the precision and preparation. Elizabeth was a well-paid executive at an information technology firm, managing a large team of analysts. She had to be organized, no-nonsense. During the three times we met in person—there were also numerous phone calls and emails—she never once smiled. The next time I saw her, a Monday, I opened by asking how her weekend had been; again, she all but ignored the question.

Once, during financial negotiations, Excel spreadsheets proposing various distribution scenarios were going back and forth between counsel.

I sent Elizabeth a short email (a few sentences) telling her that attached to the email was a proposed spreadsheet from opposing counsel, that the numbers were lowball, but that she should review it and the two of us would schedule a call or meeting to discuss how to best respond. In the final paragraph, I wrote, "Keep in mind, this is merely a proposal from the other side and, ultimately, may not bear any resemblance to the settlement we achieve. Don't let it rattle you that he's making such a low opening offer. That's not an uncommon strategy in cases of this kind."

She wrote me back a few hours later:

> Confirming receipt of the email and attached proposal. I've sched-
> uled a call with you for tomorrow from 3:00 to 3:30 p.m. to review.
> I'll email you my comments this evening so you can review before the
> call. Please don't waste time in your communications explaining to me
> how negotiations work. I'm an executive at a Fortune 500 company.

Okay. Duly noted.

Having learned my lesson, I dispensed with any attempts at the virtual handholding that many clients need at junctures during the divorce process. I briefly considered dispensing entirely with pleasantries and normal human interactions such as saying hello when I entered the room to meet with her.

The closest Elizabeth came to sharing vulnerability was during a lunch break at her deposition; we sat in a small juice-and-salad bar, and she was discussing her answer, on the record, earlier in the day, regarding a promotion she had received at work. She spoke about her professional life and how men below her chafed at the notion of a female boss, while those on her level treated her differently from their male counter-parts. She told me how the increased salary and stock options came at a significant personal cost, as she had been put in charge of men older than she, with longer tenure at the company, and she knew they resented her for it and would be happy to see her fail at her position. She won-dered whether they might even torpedo their own individual and collective performance to prevent things from going well on her watch, now that she was their manager. She talked about how the past year, since she took the promotion, had been the hardest of her life.

In all our conversations, opposing counsel told me that Douglas claimed to feel utterly blindsided by Elizabeth's request for a divorce. They must have repeated the " 'What do you want for breakfast?' 'A divorce' " story fifty times, and they made a point of injecting it into every court conference. Even the judge actually referred to us during one of our conferences as "the breakfast case." Opposing counsel steadfastly maintained the position that Douglas had absolutely no clue that Elizabeth was so unhappy.

Elizabeth, in turn, was surprised by Douglas's cluelessness. She was sure that he, or anyone, could have seen she was extremely discontented, that she was lonely even while with him, that she felt disconnected from any common interests or passion for each other. Her conversations with her husband were solely about work. She felt as if they were colleagues in the business of running a household.

"In the months or years leading up to that breakfast conversation, did you tell him that?" I asked her.

"No, not exactly," she said. "But he should have known."

It was an ugly case that dragged on for a year and a half. The combination of no kids and lots of money makes for a toxic brew: It frees the participants to concentrate on torturing each other. Douglas had a sizable IRA, as well as three million dollars he'd recently inherited from his mother's estate, but because he was retired—he was more than a decade older than Elizabeth—and had, he said, no earnings, he wanted her to pay alimony. When I deposed him, I intended to show that he was being greedy. On the stand, he quickly turned long-winded. When Elizabeth was on the stand, she maintained her composure. (No surprise there.)

The trial took three days. At the end of the last day, we struck a deal that, after all the back-and-forth, both sides could live with. As we hammered out details about how to distribute certain vested and unvested tranches of stock options provided to Elizabeth by her employer, a law student intern from my office, Christina, scrambled between the large conference room, which Elizabeth occupied, surrounded by folders filled with bank statements and account information, and the smaller conference room with Douglas and his lawyer and the iPad that showed scans of countless spreadsheets dividing their assets in every conceivable permutation. "Shuttle diplomacy," we call this back-and-forth; I mostly stood in the hallway, periodically pulling my opposing counsel out of the room, away from his client, trying to negotiate the best deal possible in the plainest "just us lawyers talking" terms, and then sending him back into the room to get his client's approval or popping my head in to ask my client quick questions. ("Can he have the Hockney from the living room if he gives in on the two Richters from the dining room? I think I can get him there.")

After the deal was finalized and the warring parties had gone, I left the courthouse to head back to my office with Christina. On the ride there, she told me that Elizabeth was very upset—with me.

"Wait, what?" I asked Christina. "With *me?*"

First, I was shocked that Elizabeth was capable of displaying emotion, any emotion. Second, I was shocked that she was experiencing a human emotion strongly enough to express it to another human being.

"Yeah," said Christina, "she said she felt you were really cold to her throughout the process. She said you never asked her at any point how she was doing."

I was dumbstruck. I consider the best and easiest (most natural to me) part of my job the relating part, understanding where my clients are emotionally and psychologically, and what they need right then. I can usually talk people off the ledge, calm them, help them to manage the tumult. Yet I'd failed completely at it with Elizabeth. After noting her business-like demeanor—this was a person, after all, who'd prepared a spreadsheet of the division of marital assets even before asking for a divorce; someone who'd made an audio recording of the breakup conversation—and hearing that at work she constantly dealt with men treating her differently from male colleagues, the last thing I wanted was to give even the slightest appearance of patronizing her. She *seemed* okay, therefore she *was* okay.

Disappointed in myself, I wondered: Had there been a way to give her what she needed, to ask her a form of "How are you holding up?" without being condescending?

I called Elizabeth. I got her voicemail and left a message of apology. I never heard back.

As angry as she may have been at me, I realized we were both guilty—not of the same thing, exactly, but of related lapses that almost always lead to resentment and friction, and often to breakup.

Elizabeth had the misplaced belief that others could read her mind.

I had the misplaced belief that appearances are truthful. Given what I do for a living, I should have known better.

Actually, her husband and I were guilty of the same thing, if he was to be believed. Elizabeth didn't appear to be miserable, and however much of a gasbag Douglas may have been, he was genuinely shocked that she was unhappy enough to ask for a divorce. How could he have known what was coming, and maybe have done something to change the course? Well, Elizabeth could have told him. But she didn't. She was deeply unhappy, and so she assumed—no doubt with building, perhaps even blinding, resentment—that he could just feel it coming through her pores. If he couldn't? Well . . . *he should have known*.

The takeaway of this story is, sadly, not unique. Not even close. I'd say a good two-thirds of the divorces I handle, maybe more, are marked by some degree of disbelief, usually mutual disbelief. I find it somewhere between poignant and tragic that, for all their eventual hyper-honesty, the divorcing husbands and wives I represent assume so often, for the final unhappy years of their marriage, that their spouse could hear what they *weren't* saying. And not only that their spouse could hear the main gripes they weren't stating, but they could also hear the nuances behind those gripes. Which they also weren't expressing.

People can't hear what you don't say.

No one—not even individuals in really happy couples, or with exceptional hearing—can hear what the other person isn't saying.

It's easy to look at couples on the verge of a breakup and nod about their lack of communication: "Well, of course they broke up—they long ago stopped communicating frequently and effectively." But that could also be Monday-morning-quarterbacking. Flip the sentiment and it makes just as much sense: "They don't communicate frequently and effectively, so of course they're bound to break up."

Checking in is scary when we're not sure what's on the other end, or when we *are* sure that it's going to be a critique of us or of a situation we helped to create. But fear and denial are not strategies. No team ever won the Super Bowl by ignoring videotape of what the other team was better at, crossing their fingers, and hoping for the best.

Everything comes out eventually—everything. Most divorce is not the result of one betrayal or other huge fuck-up; it tends to be death by a thousand paper cuts. Things are phenomenal, great, good, okay, not-so-good, and then they drop off a cliff to awful. "How did we get here? Can we ever get back?"

One reason to get it all out is to make things unpleasant sooner rather than later, because the later unpleasant is *way* more unpleasant. (See "Hit Send Now.") The other reason is so that the real problem can be discovered before it gets buried. We try so hard not to chip the glass that we shatter it. We try so hard not to cause our spouse mild irritation with a difficult conversation that we inadvertently create a major issue in our relationship that never gets fixed and that leads to much larger problems. (See, um . . . "Hit Send Now.")

I'm not suggesting that Elizabeth and Douglas, who had to eat marital breakup for breakfast, ought to have stayed together, or even could have. But who knows where their marriage would be right now if she had let him know, periodically, what she needed from him, that she was not happy with things, and told him what those things were. Who knows where they would be if Douglas had checked in with Elizabeth enough—prodded her, if that's what it took—to learn whether he was holding up his end of their bargain and whether their union was nourishing to her. No doubt my professional relationship with Elizabeth would have ended less abruptly had I checked in with her, at the risk of a few more icy looks.

Those dissolving their relationship have a huge advantage over those who are still in an active relationship: They can be totally blunt and honest. Why lie any longer? This thing is over. There's no reason to try to keep the other person happy. They're unhappy with you anyway.

Those in love often have a weakness: They may believe they magically know each other's feelings and understand their mood changes. Of course they do! How could they not? They're in love! They're soulmates!

No, you *don't* understand what's going on. Neither does your partner. Does that sound cold and cruel? Maybe. To me, it's an important reminder that we disrespect our partners when we refrain from asking what we clearly don't know about them, when we don't bother to confirm, or upend, what we're so sure we do know.

Maybe you go months without monitoring how much is in your bank account, or days without looking at your teeth; I highly doubt it. I can't tell you exactly how often you should check in on your relationship. (As much as you check the thermostat? Fill your car with gas?) The most technical I ever get is *early and often; often and early*. Because, however great you think you are at mind reading, at guessing what an expression or lack of expression means, my years of hanging around folks who are finally confronting the fact that their relationship did not go as planned have taught me this:

Your partner can't hear what you don't say, and vice versa. Ignorance is rarely bliss for long. If you care enough about your relationship to want to keep it, be sure you're checking in with your partner on a regular basis.

No, you are not good at mind reading. No one is. There is no such thing.

## Chapter 8

# EVERYONE'S FUCKING
# THE NANNY

Gemma and Noah's was the kind of collapsed marriage I see lots of. (In truth, it's the kind of marriage *anyone* can see lots of; it's just that the parties in such a marriage only reveal its truth to their respective divorce attorneys. Up to that point, they can still keep up the fiction.) Routine, semi-efficient, often boring, kids busy with school and after-school, while often being cared for by the nanny or baby-sitter; the home stays tidy thanks in large part to the nanny or housekeeper. Mom is stay-at-home or working part-time. Mom and Dad have sex once every couple weeks or so.

Is it happy? Put it this way: It's not unhappy. Or, correction: Gemma feels a tepid happiness. She's okay with stasis. It's punching in for work on Monday.

But then Noah starts sleeping with the nanny, who's twelve years younger than Gemma.

This is not a news flash. Men sleep with the nanny all the time. My colleagues and I call it the Nanny Fascination. (Okay, probably we could use a cleverer name.) As I write this, I am handling four nanny-related divorces. Jude Law, Arnold Schwarzenegger, Gavin Rossdale: You are not alone.

Nor is the psychology complex. The nanny is there for the kids, is good with them, the kids probably care for her, too; the nanny helps take care of home life and generally fits into the domestic environment, while also leading a life outside the home—and, because she's very often younger, hers is a life we imagine to be more exciting. Like the wife, the nanny is defined by the kids—but to a much lesser extent. In time, the husband sees the nanny as a younger, earlier version of his wife.

There is a saying that "everything in life is about sex, except for sex, which is about power." The power component of the Nanny Fascination cannot be discounted. The power differential between the husband and the nanny is huge. The nanny is subordinate to the husband, who is, in that dynamic, the boss of her. She follows his directions, and his decision-making authority is generally not open to questioning. There's also no reciprocity required in the relationship: The transaction is simple. The nanny cares for the children and the husband gives her money. The husband isn't required to fulfill her emotional or familial needs as he would be with a spouse, nor is he required to indulge her complaints or moods unless he feels like it.

This is in sharp contrast to the typical relationship between husband and wife—and the contrast may appeal to many men. In discussing the problems of their marriage that led to divorce, men often complain to me about the ways they felt their wives negated or discounted their decision-making authority, made them feel incompetent or sorely lacking in control. Men have also told me frequently how their wives were "impossible to please," which, after a little further inquiry, I typically understand to mean that they craved some exchanges with their spouse free of buried meaning. If he was making a lot of money, she was upset he wasn't home and resentful that he was distracted by work. If he was present and undistracted, she was upset that they weren't making enough money or couldn't purchase luxuries they might have otherwise afforded. If he wanted more sex, he was demanding. If he didn't request sex, he was making her feel unattractive. The straightforward, transactional nature of the nanny's expectations of the husband may, quite understandably, feel refreshingly uncomplicated compared to the challenges of navigating an actual relationship with an equal partner.

In my experience, that's very often who the nanny is—and very often *all* she is: pieces of the wife that the husband hasn't seen, or seen well, or that have been obscured for a long time. The nanny may be easily impressed with the husband, which makes the husband feel good. The nanny has enough regular contact with the husband and the family to initially appear safe (which is nice) but not so much as to feel predictable (which is also nice). The one real advantage the nanny has over the wife is that she has an *obligated* life outside the home. She goes out. Maybe she goes to school. She has an array of external influences. She's in flux.

The wife may also be in flux. But it's harder for the husband to see that because, as they say, whoever discovered water wasn't a fish. If you want to know if you've gained weight, don't ask someone who sees you every day; ask someone who hasn't seen you in six months. Changes are often gradual and imperceptible, even—sometimes especially—over the long term.

And honestly, many women, once they become mothers, allow their identity—also very understandably—to be consumed by their role as caregiver. Motherhood is intense and all-consuming. It impacts a woman's mind, body, and soul. The vast, vast majority of mothers will say that there is life BC (before children) and AC (after children). It's hard to keep going out every night when there's now a tiny person who came out of you *who will literally die if left unattended.*

I realize it may be politically incorrect to ask my next question: How can the wife become more like the nanny? It's politically incorrect and outrageous because, well, *why* should the wife have to be anyone but who she is? And why should she have to be more like—of all people!—the nanny?

I hear all that—but my business traffics in the brutal math of love and connection. So I hope you'll indulge my asking the question.

First, encouragingly, I don't think the Nanny Fascination is a function of youth. I've seen photos (some more explicit than I would have preferred) of the various nannies that my clients (or their spouses) have slept with. They aren't always younger. They aren't always more attractive.

Second, to judge by what I hear from straying husbands and strayed-upon wives, the remedy for the Nanny Fascination would probably not have taken that much work. Examples that they have shared (if wistfully, because it was after the fact) suggest that the remedy requires you, the wife, to go out occasionally with friends, without your husband.

That you take care of yourself (e.g., do yoga, get massages, read books, go to movies and galleries, travel solo).

That you remember to have time for yourself, separate from the kids.

That you remember that, while you're a mother, and very likely a mother first and last, you are also a woman, and those are not the same thing. A couple of Junes ago I found myself drawn to an essay on Jezebel.com titled "This Father's Day, Remind Your Partner Where the Baby Came From," by Kathryn Jezer-Morton. I was sure, from the title, of what its (obnoxious and unnecessary, I had already imagined) message was going to be: *"Hey, it's Father's Day, but instead let's give a shout-out to mothers, without whom there would be no fathers blah blah . . ."* Only that's not at all what the essay was about. It was a reminder to mothers to remember their sexuality. Because—another non–news flash—men really want sex. Women do, too. And the reason you're a parent, plain and simple, is that you had sex.

Daniel, one of the nanny-fascinated, soon-to-be ex-husbands with whom I'm working, said very bluntly about the nanny, "I fell in love with a younger version of Molly." I couldn't help but think there was something terribly sad and unaware about that: He didn't see the nanny on her own terms, but only as she contextualized what he thought of his wife.

You know who else is a version of your wife? Your wife!

There may well be a bigger, nanny-free issue here: After all, the day after your wedding, and for every day thereafter, your husband was in love with a younger version of you (just as you were in love with a younger version of your husband). And while only a fool would not acknowledge that the needs of the individual and of the relationship evolve with time, it's worth remembering that we're often comparing our present-day partner with another, maybe more generally exciting version of that same person. So do what you can to make the contrast less stark. Your spouse's reaction might surprise you—and even if it doesn't improve your relationship with your spouse, it might improve your relationship with yourself. I'm sure there are pieces of that younger version of yourself that it might be fun to dust off now and then, pieces that *you* haven't seen in a long time. As my mother often told me, "Everything in moderation—including moderation."

Alternatively, you can vow to never, under any circumstances, hire an attractive baby-sitter. It's just going to make everyone sad. Trust me.

## Chapter 9

# GRATUITOUS TIME-OUT: AND YES, I MEANT *EVERYONE* IS FUCKING THE NANNY

Do not expect to gain much, if any, insight from this next story. I tell it mostly to show that the nanny's life, or the nanny herself, or all that she represents, is not solely an object of male lust.

Katy is divorcing Tom. They have two young kids, ages eight and three. They have a live-in nanny from Russia, named Natalya. One day, Tom shows Natalya photos and videos of himself and Katy. In the pictures and videos, Tom and Katy are naked, and often having sex.

"You know, Katy really wants a threesome," Tom tells Natalya.

Natalya, not surprisingly, is deeply troubled by the conversation. She's also concerned about getting fired if she doesn't satisfy the implied desires of her host family—so one day, when Tom is out of town on business, Natalya makes a pass at Katy. After all, Tom told Natalya that that's what Katy wants, but that Katy is not comfortable bringing it up herself.

Katy recoils at the come-on. She tells Natalya that, for employee and employer, this is outrageously inappropriate. Natalya, freaked out that she has now put her job in far greater jeopardy, apologizes profusely to Katy, telling her that she did it only because of what Tom had shown her and told her.

When Tom returns from his business trip, Katy confronts him.

"What the fuck did you do?" she asks. Tom apologizes, telling his wife that he thought it would be okay, that she would like it.

Two months pass.

One night, the three of them stay up together talking until very late, well after the kids are asleep. Too much wine is consumed—and they end up having that threesome.

This new arrangement continues on a regular basis for almost three months, at which point Katy tells Tom enough is enough.

She's leaving him.

For Natalya.

Katy and Natalya are now together, as a couple. I represent Katy. We're in the midst of working out custody and visitation issues.

## Chapter 10

# MARRIED PEOPLE:
# PRETEND YOU'RE NOT

Because I'm legally obligated to figure out a defense for almost any marital behavior, including how one manages as a parent, I tend to be more forgiving of mothers and fathers than others are (including themselves). Once, I found myself making an argument before Judge Reynolds in the morning—"Your Honor, my client's ex's plan to move twenty miles away would substantially impair his meaningful access to his children: no longer will he be able to just stop by baseball practice, or share an ice cream cone"—and then, in an afternoon session for a different client, found myself arguing, I kid you not, before the exact same Judge Reynolds—"Your Honor, my client would be moving all of thirty-two miles away, not exactly a herculean distance. Driving time is often the closest thing to quality time that we have, a chance to chat and catch up . . . to enjoy the ride together. I'm sorry if this child's father wants to be a father only when it's convenient and doesn't want to participate in transporting the child to activities, but that's not my client's problem. . . . These children aren't going to be scrubbed and brought to him for inspection like the Von Trapp children in *The Sound of Music,* Your Honor. . . . With texting, emailing, and video-chatting, there are ample opportunities for him to enjoy additional connection with the children on a daily basis should he suddenly decide that's something he wants to do. . . . It's not where you live, Your Honor, it's *how* you live." As this second argument crescendoed, I was amazed that I managed somehow not to laugh at myself or blurt out an apology. I kept waiting for the judge to tell me to shut up for gross intellectual hypocrisy—or perhaps to applaud me for Olympic-caliber shadowboxing.

Perhaps it's ironic (perhaps not) that parenthood, which fundamentally concerns your devotion to another human being, is often a more clear signature of who *you* are, both to yourself and to others, than anything that might seem more self-directed—your job, your passions, your home.* Custody cases are complicated further by the fact that partners who are breaking up rarely agree about how good or bad each is as a parent.

Having been both a parent who's married and a parent who's divorced, I can offer a very concrete suggestion for happy spouses who are bringing up kids:

Pretend you're divorced.

People behave differently when they're around their kids and when they're not. (Duh.) A unique feature of divorce that married people don't get to experience: You have your kids for a couple of days, or maybe half the week, and get to truly focus on them; then you get to not have them for several days, and let another part of yourself breathe. This is, in some ways, the best of both worlds.

Why can't parents in a happy or stable marriage leverage this idea? "This is my weekend with the kids, so you go be someone who doesn't have a spouse or kids—go to a museum or the movies or get away, or if you want to hang around the house reading a book, then do that, knowing that I'm the parent in charge and the kids are okay and you're on your own."

Suppose you suggested that to your partner. Then the next weekend, or one weekend a month—however often you agree on—you switch. "Custodial rotation" forces people alternately to see themselves as adult parents and as just plain adults. I can't think of any good reason why divorced people should have all the fun. How many married partners

---

* For some people, particularly men, the size of their bank account is the most telling signature of who they think they are. For some people, particularly women, the attractiveness of their home is most emblematic.

would be happier, or actually happy, with such an arrangement? If you tried a custodial rotation for a month, what would you lose?

Or, at a minimum, create more frequent, extended pockets of free time during which one spouse cares for the children, and the parent who doesn't have "custody" at that moment is given explicit permission and encouragement to enjoy guilt-free time. I'm not talking about something that happens on a birthday or special occasion, but rather about building into the fabric of one's family life a structure that actively encourages each parent to enjoy both time focused on the children, and time focused entirely outside of the children.

If it seems wildly speculative of me to guess that committed couples might really enjoy such an arrangement: It's not. I see a version of it, all the time. While waiting to get divorced, couples with children often continue to live together—"temporary nesting" is the legal term—and the judge will advise Dad to make himself scarce one weekend, Mom the next, back and forth, until the action is scheduled for trial. In the months leading to litigation, the spouses often find that they're getting along well. While that may not be entirely because of custodial rotation, I can't help but feel it plays some part.

There are other tangible benefits to enjoying a custody rotation rather than a full-time parenting schedule. People don't like talking about the benefits of divorce (it seems indelicate) but my personal and professional experience, particularly in the world of parenting, has been very positive:

- When parents rotate custody, for instance under the increasingly popular 2-2-3 schedule (two nights with Mom, two nights with Dad, then rotate the weekends), they can easily schedule personal and professional obligations, and they have a good excuse to focus, guilt-free, on one or the other. In a society where divorce is not uncommon, people are fairly accepting of being told, "I don't do late meetings on Monday nights—I've got my kids—but how's Wednesday?" When you've got the kids, you can focus fully on them and tell the rest of the world to wait. When you don't have the kids, you can focus on work and be secure in the knowledge that the kids are with the other person who, at least theoretically, likes them as much as you do.

- After a few years of a custodial-rotation life, transitions like a child's heading off to college are far less daunting than they might have been if you were accustomed to having that child with you full time. When our elder son went off to college, my ex and I checked in on each other for the first few weeks, both joking that it didn't feel as jarring as we had expected. "It feels like he's at your place," my ex said, and I felt the same. Over the years we'd grown accustomed to the sensation of having our children with us sometimes and away from us at other times, and we'd developed an emotional security and confidence in their return.

- The time your children spend with their other parent gives you a great opportunity to reconnect with yourself, make fewer compromises, recharge, and refocus. You can curse without worrying about your kids imitating you and getting sent to the principal's office on Monday. The depth of our love for our children, and our willingness to sacrifice for them without having it feel like a sacrifice, often lead us down paths where we lose sight of who we are as individuals. A little time away from our kids helps us reset our sense of self and return to parenting refreshed.

- As parents we are tasked, in so many ways, with modeling behavior for our children that will serve them in their own lives as adults. To teach your children, by example, the importance of maintaining an individual identity outside of one's role as a parent or spouse seems to me a tremendous gift. This may not be readily understandable to your child when they are disappointed by your temporary absence while you're attending to yourself. But as experienced parents know, countless lessons of childhood are appreciated only after the child has grown up. If you and your spouse can model, for your children, a functional relationship that makes time for both the pleasures and the demands of spouse, children, and self, doesn't that bode well for your children's own long-term relationship happiness?

The above are the benefits to the parent who *doesn't* have the children during a particular stretch in the rotation. There are equally important benefits to the parent who's with the kids:

- A custodial rotation reminds you to be fully present with your children and give them your attention during a scheduled period of time. When I was married, I tended to think, "I can see the children anytime I want," so I never set specific times to be with them. Once I was divorced and started to see my children on a set schedule, I made that time specifically about parenting and no longer had the "They're always around" attitude, which, in fact, had made me less likely to focus on them.
- The children can focus on one parent at a time. They can enjoy the unique qualities of each parent, free from the influence of the other. Children get to learn a more detailed version of the parent they are with: e.g., "Here's what Dad likes to eat; here's what Mom likes to eat," rather than "Here's what Mom and Dad were able to agree upon both eating."

Why can't any or all of those benefits be enjoyed on a part-time basis by those in healthy, intact relationships? Why do so many people let the difficulty of raising children cause disharmony in their relationships, split up, and only then, after the marriage is over, create a system of parenting that might be less stressful? If you try custodial rotation in the context of a stable relationship, one of three things will happen: You'll both enjoy it and see some reduction in your individual or collective stress levels (win-win); you'll both *not* enjoy it, and decide to abandon it, perhaps with a better appreciation for your status as full-time parents (win-win); you'll find that one parent enjoys it, and the other doesn't, in which case you compromise and let the parent who enjoyed it have it from time to time, or you don't compromise and things may go south (tie–lose–sort of win because necessary to adapt anyway–sorry).

## Chapter 11

# GO WITHOUT OR GO ELSEWHERE

If you're going to sign what amounts to a legally binding contract for sex with only one person for the rest of your life, you need to feel you can speak candidly to that person about your needs and desires. You simply have to. You owe it to yourself. You owe it to your partner. If you don't express your desires (or if you feel as if you *can't*), then you've created a dynamic in which, to put it plainly and painfully, *the only person you're allowed to sleep with does not know how you want to be slept with.* You have not clearly shared what you need with the one person with whom, under traditional Western rules governing contemporary marriage, you're allowed to assert that type of need.

Consider, if you will, the foot.

Feet have never held sexual interest for me; the term "foot fetish" just seems kind of . . . Well, as I'm by nature and training not judgmental, I'll just say that feet are not my thing, and leave it at that. I'm a pretty standard heterosexual male and find women appealing for perhaps more predictable reasons.

Yet while feet don't do anything for me, they do for quite a few people out there. Some people are really, *really* into feet—like, feet are what they think of when they think of sex. There's a subculture of foot fetishists, and an entire vocabulary for describing one's own feet or the feet of those with whom one desires interaction.

"SWM w/long, smooth, clean peds into SWF w/short or long, high, natural peds for rubbing and mouth play."

Nothing in my three years of law school quite prepared me for the above. My client was surprised when she intercepted a response to this personal ad on her husband's iPad, after one of those incessant but seemingly unnecessary Apple "updates" that serve little discernible purpose but to make every device in your house suddenly start beeping and, more important, cause previously unwitting individuals to suddenly and accidentally receive iMessages from their spouse's lover.

I knew what "SWM" and "SWF" meant from reading the personals in the back of the old *Village Voice,* but after some Googling and assistance from UrbanDictionary.com, I came to understand the rest of what my client's husband was communicating: identifying himself as a straight white male with long toes that were smooth (not hairy) and clean (odorless). He was looking for a straight white woman with short or long toes (no preference) but with high arches and "natural" (not recently pedicured) toenails. The desired activities to be performed with (or on) the feet included rubbing and massaging them, and sucking and licking them. One of my associates, who to my surprise was versed in foot fetish culture, corrected me during our weekly team meeting and discussion of the case, noting that "mouth play can also include biting and/or nibbling of feet and/or toes."*

Many of us are ignorant of this subculture, and regard the feet of our sexual partners as nothing more than the implements they use to walk to and from the bed, where we focus on other body parts. But what if we're in love with a person who loves feet in that other way? What if we're in love with that person and don't at first know that they feel that way? To put it plainly: If the one woman I was madly in love with confided in me, "Listen, I'm really into feet," then I would do everything in my power to respond to that need.

---

* I have never looked at that associate the same way since. There's nothing shocking about a foot fetish but the level of specificity was surreal to me. There's a big difference between someone who says "I like coffee" and someone who says "I prefer a mountain shade–grown Peruvian blend brewed in a French Press." This was the foot fetish equivalent of the latter.

Do I "owe" this woman I love a fully committed foot love experience? Suppose I learned of this fetish only after we were dating, or even after we'd been sleeping together for several months and only then did she feel comfortable enough to share this fact, this sexual need, with me—would I, *should* I, still be on the hook for her pedal stimulation?

That misses the point. The fact is, if feet were that important to the woman I loved, and if she were the only person I was going to sleep with for the rest of my life, and if I was supposed to be the only person *she'd* be sleeping with for the rest of *her* life: I could probably fake my way through foot stuff well enough to scratch that itch for her.*

Because the truth, as I've seen across hundreds and hundreds of failed marriages, is this: Presuming that your own sexual need is important to you, if you say nothing to your partner to alert him or her, then either you're going to go unfulfilled or you'll try to get that need filled with someone else. For those in a traditional committed relationship, neither option is remotely palatable. My experience as a divorce lawyer has taught me a number of cardinal truths about relationships. Chief among them: No one likes being deprived. Not far behind that biggie is this one: It *never* helps the original relationship when you go to other people to get your sexual needs met.†

If your partner will not give you what you want, particularly sexually but in other ways, too, that's the stark choice. Go without or go elsewhere.

My warning isn't relevant just to one side of the equation. That is, I'm not just talking about opening yourself up to the stuff that revs your

---

\* I feel compelled to point out my personal belief that the openness (for lack of a better term) I'm encouraging extends to activities that are relatively benign in their lack of appeal for you. I'm talking about engagements that are, at best, simply not a turn-on for you or, at worst, mildly unpleasant. If something is physically or emotionally painful for you and/or disrespectful to your authentic feelings and values, then don't do it: You'll cause a whole bunch of other problems in your relationship by trying to fix this one. I'm saying bend where flexible, not to break yourself.

† If you're considering "open marriage" or "flexible arrangements," and you've read articles about how people in France and Finland do this all the time, and you're thinking about moving in that direction . . . good luck. And if you're in the greater New York area, my office number is (212) 627-5095. Feel free to set up a consult sooner rather than later.

partner's engine but does nothing much for you. For many people, in fact, that's the easy part. Most people in a functional romantic relationship who don't feel like getting into frequent arguments know how to feign interest in something their partner enjoys and they don't particularly care about.

It's harder, often, to be the partner with the itch that needs scratching. It takes insight to know what you like, and courage to share that knowledge with your partner.

Take Randy, who liked to wear women's panties.

He wasn't transgender. He wasn't gay. He just enjoyed putting on women's panties and, if he was being honest, the fantasy of putting on a wig and speaking in a high voice while his female partner put her fingers or a strap-on into his butt was a big deal for him. Not the easiest thing to bring up on a first date.

The problem was, Randy was in a monogamous relationship with Kristen and hadn't mentioned any of this to her during their three years of dating and six years of marriage.

And now, after nine years together, Randy had started to grow tired of his sex life with Kristen, which, in the grand scheme, was probably a relatively "normal" one for a married couple with two young sons. (Once or twice a week; after the kids go to bed; in the marital bedroom; for about twenty minutes; in relatively quiet voices so as not to wake the children or get the dog riled up.) He enjoyed their partnership as co-parents and companions. He respected her perspective on the world and found her to be a supportive, caring person with whom to share this life journey.

But he really liked wearing women's panties.

Randy had been raised, like me (and like many of you, perhaps), to believe that a "red-blooded straight guy" who (in his case) owns a tree removal business and watches football isn't supposed to admit, to anyone, that he likes wearing women's panties.

Randy started cheating on Kristen.

I'll spare you the details of how Kristen found out, and the drama of the custody battle that ensued. A decade has passed since the dissolution, and the last I heard, they (and their children) were thankfully doing well, getting along as co-parents, both in new marriages, both apparently enjoying their lives.*

Instead, I'll share with you the part where Randy cried in my conference room.

"I fucked up really badly," he said, then put his head in his hands.

We had just finished a productive but emotionally draining meeting with Kristen and her lawyer in the conference room of my firm's Manhattan office, and now he and I were alone in my private office.

"You mean just now? In the meeting?" I replied, somewhat confused. "You did fine. I didn't expect you to say much of anything. You pay me to do the talking."

"No," he replied, "I mean, I fucked up. With the marriage. Kris is a good woman."

I listened.

"I just started feeling more and more restless," he continued. "There were so many times I was going to tell her about how I was feeling unsatisfied with our sex, but I didn't want to hurt her feelings or upset her."

The painful truth, of which we were both acutely aware, was how much more he had hurt Kristen by cheating on her and lying to her.

"I almost said something a few times," said Randy. "On a few romantic nights where the kids were at her parents' and we both had a bunch of drinks and were feeling loose, I almost said to her, during the sex or just before, 'Hey! Why don't I put on your panties and we can fool around?' . . . but I chickened out. I was afraid she would be disgusted by it or freaked out and I would ruin the evening."

"If you don't mind me asking, was she conservative in bed? For lack of a better term?"

"That's what's so fucked up," he said. "She was actually really fun and open. It was just something I never expressed to her, and after being together for so long it felt like sharing it with her now would be admitting to keeping something from her and would feel really out of

---

* I say "apparently" because, of course, I don't really know. People don't come to me when their marriages are technically intact.

the blue, and I just didn't want to make her feel either of those things during an intimate moment."

"Did you ever think about telling her when you *weren't* in the heat of the moment?" I asked. "Like sending her an email or something? Dipping your toe in by putting the idea out there, and letting her reflect on it, to discuss some time later?"

"Of course," he said. "I even started an email where I wrote a bunch of other stuff and then a few sentences in, I wrote, 'You know what might be fun sometime?' But I never pulled the trigger. I felt embarrassed. Why should she have to indulge my silly sex fetish? I don't even know why I like it. It's just something that turns me on. It's so stupid. It wasn't worth blowing my marriage over."

Randy was wrong on multiple levels.

He was wrong to cheat on his wife and lie to her. I'm confident you'll agree with me on that one.

But his primary mistake—the thing he was most wrong about— was forcing himself into an unpleasant and possibly unnecessary choice: Go without or go elsewhere for something that gave him pleasure.

As with any couple that marries, when Randy and Kristen agreed to be monogamous and "forsake all others," they entered, at the core, a traditional contract: a quid pro quo. But if you're agreeing to a relationship in which you want to be the exclusive outlet for your partner's sexuality and want them to be yours, it's critical to be brave enough, and to have respect enough for the relationship, to share with your companion what you're hungry for in your sexual mate. *Even if* they might not understand it. *Even if* you don't completely understand it. Why not share it? And why not create a safe space for your partner to share theirs with you? Perhaps your own sharing might, unexpectedly, open up a dialogue where your partner feels comfortable describing their unmentioned desires—yes, even after years of sleeping together.

Whether your thing is women's panties, feet, pegging, or role-playing some obscure scenario, it might be very, very worthwhile to speak up. And if it's your partner who's the first one to speak up, you could hear it not as an expression of dissatisfaction with the routine of your sex life but, instead, as a commitment to keeping your sexual relationship fully satisfying, free from unfulfilled cravings that might lead either or both of you to the grass on the other side of the fence.

Maybe it will recharge your relationship. Maybe it will be a thrilling secret only the two of you will share, increasing the intimacy between you. Maybe it will get you to your fiftieth wedding anniversary. Maybe you will open your partner's eyes to something that they come to enjoy as much as or even more than you do.

Who knows? It's certainly worth a shot.


As hard as that is to read, maybe you're thinking it's easy for me to write. After all: divorce lawyer, spewing brutal truths, talking about the incredibly difficult task of saying incredibly intimate things, never mind that the person to whom you should communicate these things is the one with whom you've pledged mutual intimacy. It's easy (you might be thinking) for me to critique what happens when things *don't* work out, but he has no clue about how I should actually initiate that difficult conversation with my partner, or how I should respond to the difficult sexual demands that they would like to make on me. After all, Jim Sexton is not who you call to make your marriage better. He's no marriage counselor or sex therapist or faith healer. He's a gravedigger for dead marriages.

Actually, I *do* have ideas about ways to proceed with that vital, difficult conversation, ideas that are informed precisely by my clients and the horror stories and often tragic mistakes they've shared with me on this very topic.

- *Start slow.* Rather than getting drunk and just blurting out that for the past three years you've been secretly thinking about having them put their finger in your butt during sex, perhaps you might give more subtle signs of what you're looking for. Louder moaning when they hit that area of your personal geography might be a good start. Or ask them to touch you in a particular spot or way. If you've been craving some dirty talk, perhaps don't launch into full-on porn dialogue, but test the waters with a few choice comments, and appropriate pauses to assess reactions.

- *Do not wait until the heat of the moment.* It might seem as if mid-coitus is the best time to throw a new sexual idea into the repertoire, but if you've been in a sexual relationship for at least a few months, chances are you've already got your partner's sexual rhythms down and that you know, generally, what's on the menu, and whether it's appetizer, entrée, or dessert. Don't make an unexpected move in the midst. Give your partner a heads-up that the restaurant is offering (or you're hoping to order) some specials that evening—or, as I suggested to Randy after the fact, put it in an email or some other form of writing. I'm not into licking ears (to pick a random example) but if my partner sent me an email saying that it would turn her on tremendously to have me lick her ears, you can bet I would be all over it at the next opportunity. If she brought up the same thing, mid-sex? It might throw me off my game. Humans tend to be deliberate creatures—we like to know the weather a day before so we can plan accordingly how to dress, travel, when to get going. If what your partner is about to learn is radical, give them the space to let it sink in.

- *Realize that there are worse things than going without.* Suppose you show the courage to share your secret need—and your partner is simply not willing? Your partner hears you, is happy you feel safe enough to share this part of yourself, remains just as committed to you—but gives a loving no to your sexual suggestion . . . What then? Now you have to assess how important that particular flavor of sexual expression is to your overall happiness. Is it fundamental and undeniable, or whimsical? Is it possible that the appeal of this unfulfilled need is simply born of curiosity or absence? Don't we humans often fixate on the things we don't have? What if the itch that feels as if it will go on forever if you don't get it scratched would, in fact, be no big deal once you got it, and you could then stop fixating on it?

Randy sought to indulge a sexual desire and in the process lost an otherwise successful partnership with a loving spouse. From our conversations, I understood that he regretted his choice, that he could truly have lived without having that desire met, even had he shared it with Kristen (and been denied by her). No, the sex they'd been having was clearly not everything he needed—but it was good enough. It was okay enough. The rest of his life was more than okay, probably good. Sometimes "good enough" is absolutely worth keeping.

Remember the cardinal rule of Vegas: Don't put anything on the table you aren't willing to lose.

## Chapter 12

# DID YOU SPEND MORE TIME SHOPPING FOR YOUR CAR OR FOR YOUR SPOUSE?

Some jobs are simply cool—cool in theory, anyway: travel photographer, hedge fund titan, chef, brain surgeon, circus clown, assassin. Being and doing something like that must be exotic and fun and satisfying and stimulating—and often *is* that, as far as you can tell if you happen to be lucky enough to date someone with an exciting gig. Wow, right? To have achieved that position, your special someone must possess a great and rare combination of skill and talent, passion and dedication.

Will you feel the same way about that career if now it's your wife or husband doing it? Could it be that what's fun when you're dating is a pain in the ass when you're married?

My client Jeannie's husband, Ross, was a cartoonist and animator, a profession Jeannie found fascinating back when Ross was her boyfriend. (He found it fascinating, too.) But the reality of the animation life, after twelve years of marriage, was not nearly so cool—and not because Jeannie suddenly found animation uninteresting. Ross went from being the boyfriend who scrawled adorable little caricatures of her on napkins at restaurants or on Post-its he would leave in her apartment, to being the husband who, during the last several weeks of film production, would spend sixteen hours a day in the animation computer studio downtown. It's hard to have a stressed spouse, and all this for a career that, though sporadically rewarding as art, was not all that lucrative.

I've had dozens of clients who were, or whose spouses were, master-of-the-universe types: single-minded, dominant, Type A personalities.* That which reeked of excitement and/or creeping success in a boyfriend did not necessarily hold up well several years into marriage. Now, that "success" was of a more limited kind: Often the master of the universe was a shitty husband and/or father, as those roles became collateral damage of the prestigious breadwinner.

Steve had been married to Isabella for less than three years when he came to my Manhattan office for a consultation. "Marrying a chef seemed like a really good idea," he confessed after we finished the usual getting-to-know-you stuff. "She was an amazing cook and super confident. She had this passionate 'pinch of this, throw some of that in, and see how it goes' attitude in both the kitchen and the bedroom. She would meet me at the bar when she finished her shift and we would sip Negronis and tell each other about the chaos of our days. And the chefs, they're like a little Mafia in Manhattan: They all know each other and can get into each other's places and order off secret menus. It was a blast."

Like most stories told in my office, this one took a turn. "After a few months of marriage, the whole chef lifestyle lost its luster pretty quickly," Steve continued. "She worked such insane hours and would come home exhausted and wired from the adrenaline dump when service ended. She was always getting hit on by attractive aspiring model/actor waiters. She drank nearly every night, and the days when other couples would enjoy time together or with family, like Valentine's Day, Mother's Day, most holidays, and virtually every Friday or Saturday night, were all big work nights for her. Unless you want to see your spouse exclusively on Monday nights or after two a.m., do not marry a chef."

And it doesn't even have to be a spouse's livelihood that warps into a problem: how about a hobby or style or pursuit that you knew from the start was your partner's very cool, semiconsuming passion—but that is now competing for space in the marital bed? They say that every

---

* For this particular career niche, it's always a guy, at least in my experience. And given that they also tend to think of themselves as Big Swinging Dicks, maybe that's for the best.

guy wants a "good girl" who's bad only for him, and every girl wants a "bad boy" who's good only for her. I've had countless female clients describe how the amazingly charming, flirtatious bad boy they dated successfully was a nightmare to be married to; the same charms that made him so appealing as a boyfriend and conquest were magically transformed into the characteristics of a husband they had to keep an eye on. They felt as if they were often babysitting their young kids *and* their husband. ("Where is my bad boy of a husband? Oh, by the bar being a bad boy. Shit—hey! Stop talking to that woman!")

I'm not suggesting that you be wary of settling down with anyone who has a demanding, unusual job; I'm not suggesting you will come to hate it, and them, because of the job's demands and uniqueness. (Let's face it: Less uncommon careers, like teaching and the law and nursing, come with their own challenges—indeed, every job does—though the difficulties may be more apparent and manageable while you're dating.) Nor am I suggesting that the person with whom you first hook up be made to answer a questionnaire about hobbies or sleep schedule.

What I *am* encouraging: Look at the person you're marrying, at what they do with the majority of their time, and maybe at how they do it, and unwind from it. Are the characteristics that make a good boyfriend or girlfriend translatable to being a good husband or wife?

*Oh, come on, Jim. That's not very constructive at all. If we love who we love—and it appears that we do—where does this leave us?*

I'm not sure. So let's talk about cars.

I apologize in advance: A car-buying metaphor for assessing potential marital partners is rife with hypermasculine oversimplification. But I do think the comparison is apt in this instance. (Or maybe it's just an excuse for me to write about cars.)

Do we give more thought to the car we buy than the person we marry? Of course not. How can that be? Marriage is dramatically different from car-shopping, in this important respect: You don't expect to go "spouse-shopping" many times in your life (or even twice). Problem is, how do you shop for something right now that's supposed to still work for you half a century from now . . . and be both reliable and enjoyable each and every year in between?

Imagine: The car you buy in your twenties is the same car you'll be driving in your sixties. If I told you you'd have to go pick out such a car, you'd tell me I was insane! It makes no sense! It can't be done! If I advised you, in your twenties, "You should really buy a Lincoln Town Car," you'd laugh. "Why would I do that?" you'd justifiably ask. "A Lincoln Town Car is a car for a seventy-year-old!"

But if I told you, "I hear you—but I'm sorry: *You're allowed only one car,*" you would think again, and hard, about the choice. You might even say, "Okay, a boxy Town Car it is, because I'm going to be an old man a lot longer than I'm going to be young." Indeed, the phrase "Cadillac marriage" signifies a solid marriage of long standing.

A convertible is amazing in warm, sunny weather, but in the dead of winter the droptop is useless and you find yourself asking why you gave up all that trunk space for a feature you get to use just a few months of the year. There's a reason that sales of convertible cars rise in the spring. A second marriage to a hot, much younger woman is sometimes called a "Ferrari marriage." It often doesn't last that long. (Go ahead, sue me, Ferrari.)

Now turn the comparison. Is the dude you were attracted to when he was twenty—the one you met in a bar when you had a pierced navel—Is he the guy you want to spend your fifties through eighties with? Is he the one you want to be in a nursing home with?

Which may well get you to thinking: Why *did* you pick this particular partner, out of our planet's 7.4 billion residents? Can you do a realistic inventory?

Before you answer that question about a person, let's apply the same question to your car.

Why did you buy your car? Here are some typical reasons people give:

*I like the reliability.*

*I like the body on it.*

*I had a domestic model before and wanted to upgrade to an import now that I can afford one.*

With only slight word changes, those three reasons might apply pretty accurately to why you married your spouse or why you're with your current partner.

When buying a car, a person might actually sit down and write out comparisons: *This one is cool and sexy but do I really want to be cool and sexy in twenty-five years?*

*This one would be fun to drive for a while, if it's really only a couple of years.*

If someone said that the next car you buy will be the one car you drive for the rest of your life, I guarantee two things:

One, you would select that car very, very, *very* carefully. You would make that list, and weigh many traits.

Two, you would take very, very, *very* good care of that car. You would do everything to keep other cars from bumping into yours. You'd get fender guards. You might even become one of those assholes who parks his car in spaces far away from everyone else or takes up two spaces and parks kind of diagonally.

In short, you'd be willing to make sacrifices and changes to your life to take care of that car. And if someone asked, even a little critically, "Why do you take such good care of your car?" you'd say, "This is the only one I get for the rest of my life."

As daunting and even depressing (but fortunately hypothetical) as it sounds to consider spending the rest of your life driving one car, it's far more daunting (and not remotely hypothetical) to consider your choice of spouse.

Yet for all that, this is where my ridiculous car comparison exercise becomes, potentially, incredibly positive.

Why do I say that?

For one, there's a reason that we take care of the things we take care of: We have deep feelings for them. The thing we take care of is one we don't want to lose or see diminished. It's something we want to keep. It's something we want with us.

It's true that American culture is obsessed with the new and the next. If there's a major distinction between the iPhone 7 and the iPhone 8,

I've yet to notice it, yet the lines outside Apple stores when a new model is released suggest otherwise. That love of the new and the next is why we're such a disposable culture. We throw things away. We don't always fix what is fixable—yet, for all that, we know the difference between a cell phone, or a car, and a person, particularly our partner. (I mean, we do . . . right?) We are richer for those people who are worth holding on to.

For another: The previous answer may sound all sociological and abstract, but the more primal answer is that we fix things and hold on to things *because we ourselves don't want to be thrown away.* You don't want to feel as if you are disposable to your partner, your children, your coworkers. You want to be as relevant and vital as you can, for as long as you can.

When you yourself are showroom quality, it may be tempting to assume that you will always hold universal appeal to prospective romantic partners. Ultimately, though, I think most of us can agree: We're not looking for as many dance partners as possible, but for the partner with whom we can have the best and longest dance. We don't want to be thrown away when the newest shiny model with the latest options shows up at the dealership. We want to retain our value even if that value shifts from sexy traits like rapid acceleration and a dent-free exterior to less sexy traits like dependability and good handling in bad weather.

There's a reason people lease cars. They want to drive the latest model. Status and flash have become, in many ways, far more impressive than responsible choices and consistency of performance. You don't see people posting on Facebook a photo of the car they've been driving for ten years; you *do* see lots of "Picking up my new baby at the showroom!" posts.

For what it's worth, car leasing is on the rise. Vehicle maintenance (a.k.a. auto repair) is in massive decline. Five years ago, I represented Lonnie, a car mechanic. I had to review twenty years' worth of financials for his auto shop, and got to see, firsthand, how things in the business had changed. "People don't fix cars anymore," he told me, sadly, but not at all metaphorically (I don't think). "They get new ones."

I was trying to formulate a defense to his wife's request for long-term spousal support and an explanation to the judge for why the massive drop in my client's income over the past fifteen years was not just another case of SIDS—sudden income deficiency syndrome, the phenomenon in which one's income drops inexplicably just before a divorce action is commenced.* This disorder, by my estimation, strikes 99 percent of divorcing men who own their own business.

"I used to do brake jobs, transmissions; I'd replace parts when they wore down," Lonnie told me. "Lots of labor-intensive jobs that provided a solid profit rather than just the markup on parts. Now, people don't keep cars long enough to have those kinds of problems. And if they happen in the first few years, they're covered by warranty and fixed by the dealership."

"So where do you make your money?" I asked.

"I make a lot less. For the last few years we've been making ends meet with inspections and oil changes, but honestly, people aren't even doing basic preventive maintenance like oil changes anymore. If you don't change the oil frequently, it won't impact the car the first few years. It will just destroy the long-term value and create problems in the later years of ownership from slow deterioration. But nobody owns the cars long enough to care anymore."

I assume the parallels are clear.

At the risk of seeming nostalgic or engaging in what my favorite college professor called "golden-age thinking"—the tendency to believe, often with wild inaccuracy, that things "used to be better" and that humans weren't so awful to each other back in the day—I think it's fair to say that we don't look at cars, or marriage, the way we did twenty years ago. Our grandparents didn't lease cars. They bought a car and drove it as long as they could. They took care of it and they appreciated the fact that their car was reliable. They did what they needed to keep the car healthy in the long term.

You do the math.

---

* I know the usage is offensive. That's what lawyer colleagues of mine and I actually call it, for short. Sorry.

## Chapter 13

# ACTUALLY, PAST PERFORMANCE *IS* INDICATIVE OF FUTURE RESULTS

Three years ago, at age forty-two, Tim—a happily married dad, a gifted professional jazz musician, an accomplished triathlete—was driving to Wildwood, New Jersey, on a Friday afternoon to meet his family for a weekend of barbecues and relaxation. At 4:25 p.m., a truck driver with a blood alcohol level nearly three times the legal limit smashed his eighteen-wheeler into Tim's Subaru Outback and severed Tim's spine. He was paralyzed from the neck down, a quadriplegic for life.

Two and a half years later, he was in my office for the first time, telling me his story as he sat in his wheelchair. His wife, Barb, and he were divorcing. According to Tim, she had really been the one pushing for it: She claimed that she still loved him but that he had become psychologically abusive and she couldn't handle it anymore. He didn't appear to resent her very much for leaving him.

"She didn't sign on for this," Tim told me, initially without much apparent emotion. "I don't need a wife, I need a nurse. I'm not a partner anymore, really. I'm a full-time responsibility."

Never mind that Tim's soon-to-be ex was being dishonest with herself: The more I heard from him and countless friends and siblings who had a ringside seat to their years together both before the terrible accident and after, the more it was apparent that Tim's "psychological abuse" was convenient cover for the fact that, as Tim said, Barb hadn't signed on for this new life, which included changing diapers. From the beginning, she had signed on for a life with an active, physical spouse, a guy who had helped build their house, had completed multiple Ironmans, and played music festivals all over the United States. To couch the deterioration of their marriage in other terms made it more palatable for all concerned. And somehow Tim wasn't particularly bitter about the marriage's demise or the alleged reasons for it—sad, yes, terribly sad, but not bitter.

I want to focus not on the particulars of Tim and Barb's situation, but on the dramatic example it supplies of one simple, irrefutable fact:

Lives change.

Everyone knows this. Or should know this. If you don't? Spoiler alert: They do.

Yet we rarely prepare ourselves for this certainty. I'm not blaming people for that; it's important and good and perfectly human to embrace the now and to believe that it will persist. I won't go all Buddhist on you and talk about how the future is an illusion, though if you're so inclined, Thich Nhat Hanh's *Being Peace* is one of the best books on the topic.

Sure, we imagine and hope that the marriage we're about to embark on, the life journey we're about to take with this person, will be filled with positive changes—becoming parents (maybe), having a home (maybe even owning it), fixing it up the way we want, advancing professionally, traveling, enjoying leisure, celebrating mutual successes and anniversaries and birthdays and other family milestones.

Intellectually, we understand that there will be other changes, too, unhappy ones—the deaths of parents and other loved ones, occasionally professional failures, financial struggles, and the general physical and cognitive diminution of those around us, our partner, ourselves.

And yet.

There's an unspoken assumption about marriage, one I hear from people on the verge of getting married (amazingly, I've yet to be barred from the weddings of friends, colleagues, and family—*yet*), and then hear about, later, on the other end, when people are in my conference room, giving the play-by-play of what went wrong. The assumption? *"My partner is/was supposed to stay roughly the same as they were at the start of the marriage until the day they die, decades from now."*\*

That's not a marriage. That's a science experiment involving cryo-preservation.

My experience with divorcing couples is that sometimes the partner does stay the same, and sometimes they don't. Yes, that's a spectacularly unhelpful observation—but here's the part that matters: I advise my client to figure out whether we're dealing with the first condition (not much change) or the second (lots of change), because how we navigate the dissolution of the marriage is often determined by that answer. If my client first met her husband thirteen years ago, and if she can honestly say that he's pretty much the same person now as he was then, we might take one approach during divorce proceedings: e.g., relying on his tendency to do what he's always done, and structuring a settlement that roughly resembles the long-standing patterns he's demonstrated comfort with over the years. If my client compares her present-day spouse with the person she met years ago and feels as if it's hard to recognize one from the other, then we might take another approach: e.g., playing into his new self-image; using his desire for change against him; playing up, to the court, the switcheroo that he's pulled on my poor, sweet, stable, reliable client.

Karen met Brian during a fire drill at their undergraduate college dorm. He was tall, skinny, and eighteen. She looked cute in bunny slippers. (Then again, who doesn't?) They married and remained happily so for ten years. Eleven years into the union, Brian decided that he was tired of being Brian.† To that point, he had been a relentlessly driven Type A: had graduated from college and passed his CPA exam soon after, started a small accounting firm, trained for Spartan Races and Tough Mudders on the weekends. He had decided he was exhausted and could

---

\* Actually, the old saw goes: "Women marry men, expecting (and hoping) they can be changed—and they don't; men marry women, expecting (and hoping) they won't change—and they do."

† I don't mean that in the transgender sense, though I've had my share of cases involving Kevins realizing they were Kirstens, Jennys realizing they were Jeffs.

no longer keep the pace he had set for himself, the pace at which he'd been living when he met Karen and which he'd kept up during their entire relationship.

I represented Karen; whenever I conveyed to her the tactics that Brian and his counsel were using, or the demands they were making in negotiation, she was baffled. "His lawyer must be completely controlling things," she said to me. "No *way* Brian is saying we should sell the house. Brian loves our house."

It took me a few weeks to help Karen understand that although the Brian she'd married loved their house (let's call that guy Brian 1.0), the guy she was divorcing, Brian 2.0, saw it as an anchor to a past that he wanted to burn to the ground.

"We don't have to put anything in the agreement about Brian paying for the kids' cell phones," Karen told me. "He would never cancel their phones or insist I pay for them."

A couple weeks later, an email from opposing counsel made it clear that Brian 2.0 didn't see it that way.

You don't get to divorce anyone but the person you are married to (see also Chapter 27). The key: Who is that currently? What did I say in the car chapter about always looking for newer models of things? Sometimes they turn out to be unreliable. Or assholes.


Now, that's for divorcing couples, for strategic purposes.

What's the relevance if you're in a relationship you want to keep, to make better? What about couples who are not at their endpoint but rather are moving on indefinitely, perhaps until death does them part?

Think of your timeline up to now, and then extrapolate. If your partner is profoundly different now (in terms of looks, lifestyle, interests, hobbies, demeanor, other defining characteristics) from how she was ten years ago, it's fair to say that she may continue to change quite considerably over the next decade—even as we acknowledge that people don't always change at a steady rate, and that certain life stages are more typically filled with fundamental change than are others. But changeability is in her DNA; it's as essential as saying she's left-handed or green-eyed or that she can't carry a tune.

But even if your spouse doesn't "change" that often, the possibility is lurking.* The midlife crisis is a well-weathered cliché for a reason. Men and women both have them, quite often. My office is funded, in large part, by the fallout from midlife crises and the recoil of one spouse from the new version of their partner.

If your partner is a person who changes greatly, maybe it's time to look closely and honestly at who's sitting on the other side of the kitchen table. As much as you can, block from your memory the person you fell in love with and take a good hard look at the person in front of you. Would you sign up for that person? What motivates them? Do you have the power to motivate them? Where do you land on their list of priorities? (Did you make the top ten? Phew! Good work!)

Don't frame this in broad generalizations. Don't rely on intuition. Look closely at what this person has done and said in the recent past and see if you recognize them the way you once did. Presuming you decide to stay together, it will have been useful to see your partner with new eyes and a focus on things you might otherwise have missed while you were working with an outdated perception.

(And if you decide to end the relationship? It will be useful for you—and for me—to know who this new person is and how best to motivate him or her to reach an amicable settlement or to implode on the witness stand.)

Now turn the question on yourself: How much have *you* really changed during the years you've been together? If the honest answer is "Not much," then maybe pair that information about yourself with the information you've analyzed about your spouse (and where they currently are), and figure out whether this is a couple you might consider setting up on a blind date if both were single friends of yours.

It's entirely possible you've morphed, individually and collectively, into a new dynamic without even realizing it.

---

* To define "change" would be a whole book in itself.

Change is inevitable. It is also, in quite a few permutations, toxic to a romantic connection. We fall in love as a particular version of ourselves, with a particular version of another person, and we sign on to be a specific someone who loves that other specific someone for a very substantial period of time—during which events may fundamentally change the core components of our day-to-day lives and even our personalities.

When change comes to the marriage—either to your spouse, or to you, or via something outside both of you (a child with a significant health problem; the death of a parent; illness that requires a parent to move in; a car accident that creates impairments; a work scandal that brings public scorn)—are you the kind who's able to handle it? Are you willing to change his diapers? See her through Alzheimer's? Am I asking questions that you can't possibly answer in the moment? Or are these questions that, deep down, you probably *could* answer right now, only you don't want to (who does?), and hope never to have to? If things work out in your favor, maybe you won't ever have to.

Then again, you may.

That's what I believe happened to Barb, Tim's wife. She knew the answer, but had never had to consider it, especially not as she lived day to day with the vital man who was her husband, this gifted triathlete and professional musician and pretty great father to their young kids . . . until the awful day of his accident. And instead of truly answering the question, she instead came up with a lame-ass explanation for leaving the new Tim.

People tend to look closely and honestly at the changes in their marriage only once the marriage ends. And they often do it, at that point, mainly to reinvent the history of their marriage so the divorce isn't quite so devastating. I understand why they do it once the marriage is over. It's painful to see a marriage thrown away, even if you're the one doing the throwing away, or engaging in the behavior that caused it to be thrown away. It's easier to say "We were unhappy for a really long time," or "It was all her fault since she lost all that weight and became a different person."

But are you being honest?

You don't have to say it out loud. I won't be judging you. But be honest with yourself, right now, about how far you really think you would be willing to go for your partner.

The past may be prologue; and it may not be. What's less uncertain, and perhaps even somewhat in your control, is figuring out whether you're able to handle big changes. If yes, you might approach your life one way. If no, another.

(And yes: We all know there are people who are convinced that they will rise to some unnamed occasion or shrink from it, and then do the exact opposite when confronted by the actual reality.)

That's why I believe it's good to do a somewhat regular assessment of who you think your partner is, and who you think you are, and what you expect from this union, even as there are no guarantees.

"I still love you, but I didn't sign on for this."

"I'm not going anywhere. This is what life gave us, and we'll handle it best together."

Which of the above is your true bumper sticker?

As a divorce lawyer, I sometimes say, "If you want permanence, don't stand in front of people and recite marriage vows. Go to a tattoo parlor."

## Chapter 14

# THE FIVE KINDS OF INFIDELITY

Five. Not four, not six. Five.

Okay, that's not exactly true. There's really only one kind of infidelity. The kind that happens for a real reason, then proceeds (if uncovered, and often if not) to tear at and usually destroy the original relationship.

Yet, as I have observed, affairs really do have important nuances, and they tend to fall into five general storylines, none of which, I'm afraid, have particularly happy endings for everyone involved.

## 1. THE FRESHLY DISCOVERED SOULMATE

"I met someone, I'm in love with them, I'm leaving you."

We'll start with the most painful variety. Unfortunately, it's also the most common. I blame Facebook, romantic comedies, and television shows. Although Newfound Soulmate is occasionally the result of a lightning-bolt, love-at-first-sight moment, more typically it emerges from a friendship or acquaintanceship gone wrong (or right, depending on whom you ask). It culminates in the belief that you were "meant to be" with a specific person who is not your spouse. This creates obvious and enormous acrimony between the married couple since one of them is now convinced that they want to live happily ever after with the very person who is seen, by the non–newly soulmated party, as the singular cause of the demise of the wedded relationship. (Multiply what I just wrote by two if both freshly minted soulmates are already married.)

More often than not, the lovestruck parties will turn out to be wrong, or at least one of them will.

## 2. THE WAKE-UP CALL

"I fucked someone. I shouldn't have, but you know what it taught me? I'm not happy because I need more than what I've been getting in this marriage. Otherwise, I wouldn't have cheated."

It's unfortunate that people need to go through this kind of painful event, with all its fallout (jilted spouse; jilted lover; the kids who, ideally, have no idea what's going on, but whose lives are going to be forever changed). Then again, it's unfortunate that people need to have heart attacks to learn that bacon double cheeseburgers should be enjoyed only in moderation, if at all, but often a wake-up call is what it takes. In my practice, this is the second most common form of adultery. Some people start out thinking their infidelity is the soulmate kind (#1) but they figure out pretty quickly that it's #2 instead. (Hopefully, they don't figure that out after they've introduced the kids and relinquished the 401(k) in exchange for the freedom to promptly get remarried.)

## 3. THE BIG MISTAKE

"I fucked someone. I'm so sorry I did, because I really didn't mean to and I love you and I really, truly want to keep our marriage intact."

This one is the least common, and it legitimately makes my heart ache. A man or woman, who by their very nature is an imperfect being, genuinely fucks up (for lack of a more eloquent term). It really *was* a mistake. The mistake is typically discovered or revealed, and the cheating spouse is confronted. The cheater admits the affair (or the proof is undeniable) and throws him or herself at the spouse's mercy. Trust is broken. The wound runs too deep to allow the couple to find their way back to a place where the relationship is functional. (If the wound doesn't run too deep, then I don't meet them: They work it out, either by themselves or with the help of a marriage counselor.)

## 4. THE PUSH OUT OF THE CLOSET

"I'm gay or lesbian. I was pretending to be (or trying to be) straight. I can't pretend anymore." Or "I've been caught with someone of the same sex and I don't want to try to be someone I'm not anymore."

I'd like to think that this variety of infidelity is on the decline. Given our generally more tolerant society (though there's obvious work still to be done), we're hopefully reaching a time where far fewer individuals feel pressure to hide their sexual orientation and to marry someone of the opposite sex as cover for their true sexual identity. The cases I've seen often appear less acrimonious and less painful than the other varieties of infidelity. Why? Perhaps the explanation is as simple as (thinking here like the man I am): *"My spouse left me for a woman, someone with features and equipment I simply don't possess and can't try to imitate."* Which seems somehow better than *"My wife left me for another man, someone like me—just not me."* That feels a lot harder to swallow.

## 5. THE REVENGE

"You had an affair. We supposedly worked it out and moved on, but I was secretly (or not-so-secretly) still incredibly angry with you and now I've had an affair, too."

This one is typically a response to #3 or #2 but merits its own category because the motivation is transparent to even the most dimwitted observer. If the endgame is "You fucked someone, now I fucked someone, now we're even and can move on," it might make more sense— but that's not usually how it goes. This species of infidelity happens when the couple should have called it quits after the initial affair was discovered but decided, for various reasons, to keep it together. For those who like math: Two Wrongs ≠ Clean Slate.

Whatever the type of affair, it's always the beginning of the end of the marriage—either literally/legally, or figuratively: the end of the marriage *in that form,* because something's clearly got to change.

Affairs are scandalous and interesting. They also give unhappily married people something or someone convenient to blame their divorce on. I find blaming the affair is usually an oversimplification, though I understand why people embrace it. Life would be easier and less frightening if there were simply bad people out there doing bad things, and all we needed to do, to prevent harm from coming to us or those we love, was sequester ourselves from those bad people as much as possible.

Affairs are also banal and boring. They're incredibly predictable and, to the outsider, look completely ridiculous. They're the sexual equivalent of eating an entire Carvel ice cream cake. You knew from the start it was bad for you, you didn't plan on doing it, but somehow you ended up doing it, and you're not proud of what you've done, even if the cake was delicious at the time.

## Chapter 15

# INFIDELITY TYPE #3: THE MISTAKE

The old joke goes, "Speeches are like affairs: Anyone can start one, but it takes a genius to end one well."

I've lost count of the marriages that have died, and probably didn't need to die, because the cheating spouse did not know how to end the affair. Sometimes a random affair happens, and if only it could be ended "well" (that is, go undetected, and without the specter of blackmail or unacknowledged children hanging over the now-former cheater), the marriage could potentially be fine from there on in, maybe even better than that.

That's a gigantic if. It usually doesn't happen like that.

I'd like to focus on Infidelity Type #3, where there's still love and a modicum of marital functionality, because in the others, let's be honest: Stick a fork in it, am I right?

With #3, when the Mistaker or the Mistakee shows up at my office, they're really shook up. They just found out, or have just been found out. If my client is the "victim," they want to know their rights and options, in light of the behavior of someone who earlier in the week appeared worthy of trust, and now seems alien.

I think it would be preferable for these people to be in the office of a therapist who might help them navigate the maze of emotions they are feeling at that moment, but I understand why they're in my office instead. They feel afraid. Raw and exposed. They feel they need protection.

I tell them very simply: "No matter what, your marriage has to end."

Not—to be clear—"The two of you being married has to end." No. But *that* marriage, the one that led to the supposedly out-of-the-blue affair, has to end.

Now, whether the result will be divorce, or whether the marriage can and will be replaced by a better marriage, Marriage 2.0 . . . *that's* the question.

The marriage you had effectively ended with the revelation of the infidelity. You have to end that marriage. You've got to fully break the bone before you can reset it.

But can you two create a new marriage, one that takes the same ingredients to create something different? *It is absolutely possible.* After all, if you're a cook, you do it all the time. Same ingredients, different recipe. A cook does it by using the ingredients in different ratios. Or by blending them together using a different process. Or by adding a few new ingredients to the old ones and so changing the flavor of the resulting dish. You can't tell me, "I can't make a new meal with the same ingredients." It just takes an attentive cook—or two, in this case—willing to pay attention and do the work.

In the "new" marriage, you aim to handle things differently. Maybe to parent differently. The first recipe wasn't working, so maybe you need to add a date night or therapy or listen better or talk more. People can't hear what you don't say. Maybe you weren't telling each other what you needed (that's almost a certainty).

I've got some good news: If you're in a divorce lawyer's office, your relationship is all fucked up. You don't have much to lose anymore. You can try radical methods to fix it. You don't have to be afraid of breaking something that's already broken. There's nothing more dangerous—or liberating—than someone with nothing to lose. I hope you and your partner both feel that way.

But, really: Why does this third kind of infidelity happen, when you really still love your partner and it would devastate you to lose your relationship or wound your partner?

There's a restlessness that people feel in marriages. Not all people feel it, but many do. It's normal. I compare the situation to my job. I love my job—adore it, in fact. That doesn't mean that I can't occasionally wonder what it would be like to do something besides law. That doesn't mean that, at the end of a long week at this amazing job, I don't feel incredibly tired of it. You may love sex, but if you did it twelve hours a day for six days in a row, you'd get a little tired of it!

You can love something, or someone, and still tire of them at times. Feel restless. That's when things sometimes happen.

In many cases, my client will say that the affair (and there's infidelity in close to 90 percent of the divorces I handle) had "nothing to do" with their spouse. I think this is mostly inaccurate. In Type #3 cases, though, there's something to it.

Maureen—a high school Spanish teacher with two master's degrees, the mother of a five-year-old and a seven-year-old, the wife of a successful lawyer—started sleeping with her Argentinian landscaper. He didn't speak English but, hey, she was a Spanish teacher.

She didn't want the affair to be discovered. (Dumb statement. I've yet to meet a person who did.) But when David, unbeknownst to Maureen, logged on to their Nest Cam in the middle of the day from his office with the intention of seeing what their beloved dog might be up to, he got to overhear Maureen's phone conversation with her lover, which, even with only a rudimentary knowledge of Spanish, he could tell was explicit. When he confronted Maureen, she was mortified (of course), didn't try to hide it, and said (according to him) that she loved him, did not want to end the marriage, and didn't know why the affair happened. She also assured him that it had nothing to do with him or with her love for him.

Deeply hurt and confused by the affair, David had come to my office to talk about his rights and obligations, and what steps, if any, he should be taking to protect himself from having an "ugly" divorce. If the marriage was going to end, he wanted it to be "fair" and he didn't want the children to see their parents "at war" with each other.

As I wrote early on, when someone steps through the door of my office, the marriage, in virtually every case, is over; they're not there to have me talk them out of it. Every now and then, though, there's a glimmer of hope that divorce doesn't *have* to be the inexorable step (even as avoiding that path costs me money).

After I dispensed with some basic legalities—child support percentages, how Maureen's teaching pension was marital property and could be traded against the value of his 401(k)—David and I ended up having a discussion that was less logistical and more philosophical and psychological, about why people cheat. Who better to talk infidelity than a divorce lawyer?

I gave him my personal, honest opinion: that to judge by his story, and by all I knew about people from my job, what his wife had told him really could be true. (If I'd thought otherwise, I'd have told him that, too.) Maureen had said she had no feelings for the guy. She had explained the horrible bad decision as the result of a need for some excitement, and the opportunity was right there in front of her, and she shouldn't have done it, and she never thought she would hurt David because she wouldn't be found out. (This last part of her mea culpa is its own brand of self-delusion, sparking a deeper discussion, but I chose to focus on the other parts of what she had said.)

David listened. He didn't smile at any of it. But he listened.

"Look, if you need me, I'm here," I told him. "If you end up wanting or needing to go to war, my team and I will be one hundred percent ready at a moment's notice." I knew he needed to hear that, to feel safe. "But let's see if you do actually end up needing me. Maybe you'll take a gentler path like mediation. Or maybe you two can work it out on the back of a napkin and I can just write it up for you." I paused. "And maybe what Maureen is saying is legit. Maybe you can move past this. Don't let ego get in the way. Follow your heart and your head. Maybe you can use this as a lesson or a stepping-stone that leads you to a better and more connected marriage to each other, where something like this wouldn't happen."

When one online reviewer at my law firm's website described me as "the ruthless sociopath you want on your side in a divorce," I don't think he imagined me dispensing the advice I gave David. But it wasn't the first or last time I've had that conversation.

That was five years ago. Through the mutual acquaintance who referred David to my office, I heard that he and Maureen had gone to counseling. They're still married.

## Chapter 16

# IT'S SO MUCH EASIER TO CHANGE THE OTHER PERSON

How do you change a not-great situation in your relationship? By my count, there are a number of techniques, perspectives, and therapeutic modalities that, all bells and whistles aside, boil down to three specific choices:

1. Change yourself (more to the point, change the way you are in the relationship).
2. Change your partner (change the way they are in the relationship).
3. End the relationship.

That's it. The whole menu.*

---

\* Did I overlook Option #4, couples therapy? No. In my profession, couples therapy is affectionately referred to as "delaying the inevitable." It's a bizarre hybrid of the least effective aspects of combat and counseling: On one hand, confrontation without the authentic "no holds barred" catharsis; on the other hand, an attempt to gain insight but without the focus of looking solely at yourself or solely at the other person. It's like trying to learn to juggle with five balls all at once, right from the first lesson.

Now, it's entirely possible that there's some highly effective form of couples counseling out there that I've never encountered, perhaps one that keeps people out of a divorce lawyer's office entirely. But something tells me that if it existed, there would be at least some percentage of my clients who had found it during the divorce process, quit their divorce, and lived happily ever after. In nearly twenty years of practicing divorce law, I've encountered only two couples who started out in my office and, years later, remained happily married. In contrast, I've had at least fifty couples that "quit" the divorce to "go to counseling" and "reconcile," only to return to my office a week, a month, or a year later, ready

This is where I'm supposed to advocate for Option #1. In our age of self-expression, self-empowerment, and self-actualization, that's really the only possible solution, right?

Nah.

Can we agree that changing ourselves is not much fun? And a hell of a lot of work?

Changing your partner might actually be easier and more effective.

If that sounds coercive and puppet-master-y, let me explain. Because I believe we can change our partners lovingly, and make the new her or new him work for the benefit of both of you. (True, I manipulate people for a living—the other side, my client, the judge . . . )

Therapy-speak and corporate PR–speak have indoctrinated us to believe that there's a right way to communicate when trying to shift someone's behavior. We've been told that the best way for you to manipulate a person (usually a man, but that's another story) is to praise behavior you want to see, and to praise the opposite of unwelcome behavior. Now, there's a good way to do this (we'll get to it in a moment) and a bad way. The bad way is often known as "constructive criticism," which I personally believe should be referred to merely as "criticism."

For instance, say your partner is rarely spontaneous; he does the same thing over and over and you're dying for some variety. You could sit your partner down and say, "I feel we're in a rut and blah blah blah . . ." That "blah blah blah" isn't a placeholder but a fairly accurate representation of what your partner hears after the first few denigrating words. That's "constructive criticism," which tends to be useless because it's essentially saying, "There's this way you behave that I don't like—and here's how I propose we fix it."

Let's not sugar-coat: "constructive criticism" is rejection, pure and simple. Saying "constructive criticism" is like saying "a friendly smack" or "a positive punch in the face." *I wanted to help you learn how to defend yourself by hitting you.*

Lately, there's been an "empowering" new twist to this approach.

---

to continue the divorce, often from a far more disadvantaged position, having given their spouse advance notice of the battle ahead.

Human resource managers the world over are training other management staff to review employee performance by opening with praise, then leveling criticism, then closing with praise—a "praise sandwich."

It's offensive. It's bullshit. Whoever came up with these ideas is an idiot who knows nothing about people.

I've had countless clients who were unsatisfied in their sex life with their partner—yes, female as well as male.* Some of them (the more invested and/or communicative ones) decided to share that dissatisfaction with their spouse.

If they're smart, they phrase this admission in loving, cautious terms, something like: "You know, I've been feeling like we haven't been connecting on a physical level as intensely as we used to, which I know is normal and understandable. . . . I would really love to get back to that passionate connection we had when we were first dating and we couldn't keep our hands off each other."

If they're stupid, they phrase it less artfully: "What's going on with us and sex? It's been once a week for I don't know how long and it's been robotic and predictable and utterly devoid of oral. You're killing me. Learn how to do sex better."

I know: On the "Let's talk about sex" spectrum, there's a lot in between those two possibilities. Yet I'd suggest that both poles—the first, more empathetic, gentle, and mutual approach; and the second, more selfish, accusatory, just plain dumb approach—are both essentially the same statement: *"You're doing something wrong and I want you to change and do it better because you're not making me happy."*

This is criticism. Which is, in many ways, the opposite of why we fall in love to begin with. We fall in love not only because we feel affection for our partner, but because of the way their affection makes us feel.

---

* Recently, a female client and I were chatting during a break in testimony. We got onto the topic of "The Moment"—the moment when she realized, for the first time, that the marriage was over. (It's a topic that interests me greatly; I tend to ask about it, to enlighten me for helping future clients.) Her response surprised me. "It was about two years ago, on a Saturday night, we were having sex— actually in the middle of having sex—and I remember a specific thought popped into my head, and I realized my marriage was probably over." What, I asked, was the thought? "'One of these days I really need to get laid.'"

The ways our partners accept us make it easier to accept ourselves. The ways our partners embrace and enjoy us make us embrace and enjoy ourselves more fully. Perhaps that's why it stings so much more when your romantic partner criticizes you. You didn't just gain a critic. You lost a cheerleader.

After a couple of decades watching how these various attempts at modifying the behavior of the other person don't work, I'm convinced there's a better way to change your romantic partner. Find some nugget in their behavior that you want to see more of, even if it's a truly little, ridiculous thing that you're going to have to blow out of proportion to get your point across. "The other night, when we went to that new diner that opened up rather than our usual Italian place? I loved that you did that. It was so spontaneous. It's so sexy when you do stuff like that. It reminds me of when we were first dating." Give them the credit for the idea. Double down on that behavior and give it way more praise than it's due. Make it seem like an inspiring moment. Praise the potential until the potential becomes the reality. You think they're not going to want to do that again, soon, when this is the glowing response they got?

Is this dishonest? I don't think so. Is wearing a sharp suit dishonest? What about a Wonderbra? It's changing the focus, massively accentuating the positive and distracting the eye from the negative. That's not the same as misrepresentation. At worst, it's misdirection which, as any magician will tell you, is a key ingredient of any kind of magic. But honestly, it's just a nice way to get what you need.

Or use sex—yes—as a way to get more of the behavior that you want. That's right. I said it. If behavior you like seeing from him— say, taking care of the kids while you go out with friends—leads to the reward of you becoming very affectionate or sexual, you will very, very likely see more of that behavior. What's true for lab rats is true for men.*

Clients share with me the intimate details of their sex lives, often as

---

* This is not intended to disparage lab rats. Some things you can't get a lab rat to do. With many men, if the reward is really good sex, there's almost nothing you can't get us to do.

a way to justify their infidelity. Frankly, I don't care who they were sleeping with, or why. But since they view me as a representative of the justice system and therefore as an authority figure, I listen. It seems to make them feel better.

Nathan had been cheating on his wife, Jennifer, for two years. It was not with anyone in particular: The first time was a backseat romp with an old college girlfriend, also married, whom he reconnected with on (where else?) Facebook. Next was a part-time secretary in his office who worked late with him one evening. Jennifer never found out about her, either. The one that got him caught was Marla, a divorced single mother whose son was in his eight-year-old son's class. They met on a class trip, for which they were both volunteer chaperones, to see *The Lion King* on Broadway; their later meetings were typically held at small motels on Route 17 (sexiest highway in the state) in Paramus, New Jersey (sexiest state in the union), where they would slip off and have adventurous sex on breaks from work.

Six months into the ugly custody litigation that ensued, Nathan and I had a short lunch break during the trial. Although I try to get some client-free calm during those recesses, Nathan walked into the Chipotle where I was eating a fajita bowl, and it would have seemed unfriendly not to invite him to join me.*

"I don't know why Jen was so shocked I was sleeping with Marla," Nathan told me. The affair had been the subject of the morning's testimony, so the wound was fresh. "She had slept with me hardly at all for five, six years."

"How frequently is 'hardly at all,' if you don't mind me asking?" I said. I'm a sucker for details. Occupational hazard.

"Twice per month?" Nathan guessed. "And really routine, predictable sex. Like you're both checking a box and having the sex so you don't have to have a conversation about why you haven't had sex."

---

* During a trial, you only really get to interact with clients during lunch breaks or just outside the courtroom. Otherwise I'm returning calls or emails or doing literally anything other than talking to this client that I've spent the last day or five days with. Lunch breaks are the only time I really talk personally with them, since we're often forced to sit together, but I usually don't feel like talking about their case, and they usually don't either.

Nathan paused over his burrito. "Is that typical? It's hard to know how much sex anyone else is having. But I guess you would know better than most."

"I don't see an accurate cross-section of people," I said. I'm fully aware that not one client or potential client of mine is what you would call happily married, or even adequately contentedly married. (The couples I see for prenups almost all look very happy, but they're not married yet.) "I see people who are in a divorce lawyer's office," I told Nathan. "It's kind of like asking an oncologist, 'Do a lot of people have cancer?' Pretty much everyone who walks into his office has cancer. It's not a representative sample."

Nathan paused for a moment. "We had a ton of sex on vacation."

It was the most interesting thing he had said to me thus far. "Really? Did you vacation often?"

"Once I realized how good and frequent the sex was on vacation . . . we sure did."

"Did you vacation much before that?"

"Not really. I'm not a big travel guy. I don't like flying. I like sleeping in my own bed. But Jen was super into travel. She loved it. Wanted to see everything. Go everywhere."

"So you started vacationing more for the sex?"

Nathan paused, as if he hadn't reflected on this until that very instant. (One might argue that the degree to which Nathan's life was unexamined may have contributed to the demise of his marriage.) "I guess I did. After a few trips, I used to joke that there was Jen, and then there was Vacation Jen, and how Vacation Jen was super-permissive in bed, slept in, and ate and drank without restriction or rules. We used to laugh that Vacation Jen liked putting things in her mouth. . . . We were talking about food, but also . . . you know . . . because—"

"I get it."

Granted: Jen and Nathan got divorced. But when they were still together, Jen's experiment, whether deliberate or unconscious, worked like a charm, on two levels.

First, it helped shape her husband's associations. It was no longer

"Travel=long lines, airports, and not sleeping in my own bed," but "Travel=more sex, dirtier sex, good food and alcohol."

Second, the shift in Nathan's attitude helped to shape Jen's own reality: Rather than having a husband who needed to be convinced to vacation with her, she had one who actively helped plan trips, so he could spend more time with Vacation Jen.

I hear the counterargument: This isn't an example of Jen changing Nathan more than she's changing herself. I disagree. I strongly believe that Vacation Jen was very much a part of who Jen already was, not some creation to make Nathan more engaged and adventurous. She got to be who she liked to be, and Nathan had to change to be with that person.*

Ideally, you never let your partner know you're engaged in extensive experiments in behavior modification. Ideally, after one or two or three occasions (though one often does the trick because remember: lab rats), they'll come to the change organically.

Then again, maybe it doesn't even have to be so secretive, as long as it's rooted in the positive. For example: Rather than telling him you don't like his beard, tickle his chin when he's clean-shaven, or kiss it and comment on how sexy his smooth face looks. It doesn't take much for us men. A woman in my life once commented that I looked "good, a little like Don Draper" when I was freshly shaved. It happens that I tend to grow some scruff if I don't have a trial going on. But for the rest of that relationship, I shaved every day, including weekends. If she had told me "I don't like scruff," I probably would have resented it.

As to changing yourself? It's possible, sure—but it can also build resentment in you, if you feel you have to change some piece of yourself to be appreciated. Who wants to choke down medicine?

Is it cynical and distasteful and just plain wrong to suggest that a

---

* I can't one hundred percent confirm that last point about Vacation Jen: As the adversarial party, Jen was not about to answer my queries about her innermost thoughts, ex parte, especially after I spent two days cross-examining her.

good, healthy relationship might feature a fairly steady diet of both partners manipulating each other? Not at all. We manipulate our children all the time—promising them rewards if they win the "quiet game" by going the whole car ride home without talking; telling them that maybe Santa will bring whatever stupid piece of plastic crap they're clamoring for in the store so we can get out of there without having to debate the matter—and it would be ridiculous to suggest that in doing so, we somehow don't love them with all our heart.

And you're not manipulating merely to serve *your* needs. You do it to serve the greater union of the two of you. If you do it right, you make yourself happier, your partner happier (or at least no less happy) . . . and the marriage incontestably better.

How is that not a great thing?

## Chapter 17

# GRATUITOUS TIME-OUT:
# LIE TO ME;
# EVERYBODY ELSE DOES

(This is another in a series of gratuitous, yet memorable, anecdotes. If you are looking only for advice, not stories, please skip to the next chapter, where I will return you to your regularly scheduled program.)

Just because I encourage, even demand, full disclosure from my clients doesn't mean I always get it. In fact, I very often don't. People lie to me all the time. I'm not sure why. Doctor, lawyer, therapist: Why would you lie to any of those three professions? They exist for one reason: to help you. Why lie?

This happened in 2011. My client Roy, who claimed he was broke, owed his ex a shitload of money. When Roy and Donna had divorced, five years earlier, they divided their assets. Roy kept the house, which was valued then at $700,000. After calculating what they paid for it and what they'd put into it, it was decided that he would buy out Donna's interest in the house for $260,000, in two payments of $130,000 each. One payment was to come right after they divorced (2006), the second within three years.

Roy held on to the house, hoping and expecting that its value would continue to rise. Then the real estate bubble burst, followed by the recession. The home's value plummeted, and Roy was now "underwater"—the house was worth less than the balance on the mortgage. Selling it would not bring in the money Roy needed to pay off his obligation to Donna.

When I told Roy he needed to find the money, one way or another, he shrugged, a gesture reminiscent of my son when I tell him to clean his room.

"I don't know what to tell you, counselor," he told me. "I don't got it."

Was he really broke? If he was lying, then he was a great liar. Or he had convinced himself he was telling the truth; most people I deal with are deluded when it comes to their finances. When people say, "I don't have the money," they generally mean, "I don't want to put my money toward *that*." They'll say they have no money, yet they really have a bunch socked away in savings—and, hey, who doesn't want to leave his or her nest egg untouched? Or put it toward a Mercedes, or a trip to Paris with the new girlfriend?*

The problem—and I was certain that when we convened before the judge, she would zero in on this, to the exclusion of all other considerations—was that Roy was supposed to have finished paying his ex in 2009. It was now 2011.

When I don't have all the information I need, I can't do my job the way I want to. This means I'll proceed to talk even faster than usual, as cover. When Roy and I went before the judge, I resorted, for maybe thirty seconds, to some lame-ass argument about the sour state of the American economy being the true culprit here. "Your Honor, my client's inability to pay his ex-wife," I said, overflowing with moral indignation, "is due to market forces beyond his control, and if this court were to hold him in contempt, the only thing it would accomplish is his losing his home, providing this woman with no satisfaction. Whether you believe my client or not, Your Honor, there's no benefit to be had here, except for my client's ex-wife getting to jab her ex-husband with a fork—"

The judge I was arguing before, Judge Goodman, was having none of it. Nor should she have. She demanded a conference in chambers.

---

* I once had a client "explain" to me that the reason he couldn't pay his bill to my firm in full and on time was that his money was "in accounts and I don't want to take it out of there right now"—as if that were a perfectly valid reason not to pay. My money is in accounts, too. Can I use that argument when my rent is due?

Opposing counsel and I followed her in, where I was one hundred percent sure I would get my ass kicked.

I got my ass kicked. Judge Goodman said flatly that there was a contract; that she, the judge, was enforcing it; that maybe the enforcement of the contract would motivate my client to find money he claimed he didn't have. Or maybe it wouldn't: "It's not for me to decide," said the judge, and inside I agreed with her completely. "Your client entered into a contract. If the real estate market had boomed instead of busted, he would have benefited from that. I'm sorry he chose to roll the dice, counselor. He lost on this one."

Ten minutes later, I was out in the grand hall of the Kings County Courthouse, explaining to Roy that if he couldn't find $130,000 within thirty days, he would be found in contempt of court and could well go to jail. Roy barked at me for a while, as if I were the problem. "I don't have the money, Jim," he said. "I'm just hangin' on."

I felt genuinely bad for him.

Here was my client: a hardworking man, a man who worked with his hands, a man who, unlike me, built things and knew a craft. A man who tried to keep his home after a divorce and give his ex a fair buyout and was now, through no fault of his own, the victim of big bankers and a global lending crisis. I had done the best I could for Roy. But I couldn't fix his problem.

I patted him on the shoulder, and we parted at the lip of the courthouse parking lot. As I reached my car, I looked back to see, a few rows over, Roy, climbing into a vehicle—a monster black Escalade, all shiny and with new-car temporary tags in the window rather than official license plates. I eyed it with suspicion and admiration both. He caught me watching him. As if he read my mind, he volunteered loudly, "It's not what you think, Jim. This is for my business! I need it for my business!"

He yelled out a few choice things about his ex-wife, as if she, not dubious lending practices or banker greed or lax regulation, were the primary cause of the global recession. He pulled his cab door closed with a slam, then roared away.

A few weeks later, he appeared at my office with a certified check for $130,000 payable to his ex-wife. I didn't ask him where he got the money. Months afterwards, however, I learned from opposing counsel (we had found ourselves working against each other on another case) that Roy owned a half-dozen properties in Florida as well as commercial real estate in New York, all of which he inherited from his father, none of which had mortgages against them. And none of which he had ever told me about.

A couple of years ago, I ran into Roy in a Starbucks in Tribeca, where his company was doing a big plumbing job. I asked how he was doing. "Business is good," he said. He told me he had referred one of his buddies to me for a prenup. I thanked him and wished him the best.

A few minutes later, when I started to pay for my espresso, the barista said, "The construction guy took care of it."

## Chapter 18

# THE YOU, THE ME, AND THE WE

There's you. There's your partner.

And then there's the relationship.

A marriage or long-term relationship is, in a strange and subtle way, something more than just 1 + 1. It's an organism unto itself. It needs to be appreciated, if not actually treated, as something separate from the two individuals. Sure, you or your spouse can change a habit, thus making you happier, or your partner happier, or, ideally, both of you happier. But you ought to assess how even a positive change in the balance of things changes the health of the *marriage*. They're not always the same thing.

I'm not suggesting that the marriage is more important than either of the two people who entered into it. I'm saying: You guys decided to do this thing, so you ought to really, really consider what it is and what it needs to stay vital.

I often think getting married is like getting a puppy at Christmas.

You get a puppy. It goes perfectly with everything. It's fun. It's adorable. It's new.

Now, you may find at some point that you've had a change of heart. Or that you had no idea how much work was involved. Or you realized that the puppy does not stay a puppy for very long. And maybe your solution—no judgments here—is to part with the puppy.

But here's the thing: *No one told you you had to get a puppy.* And since you did get the puppy, you need to take care of it as long as it's living in your home.

You got married. You went to all this trouble to do it, and then to be married. You should periodically assess: Am I doing my part to take care of the marriage so that it thrives? How important is the marriage itself? There are dozens of monthly wedding-planning magazines and thousands of wedding-planning websites. Are you putting as much effort into the marriage as you did into planning the wedding?

What are you willing to do to maintain it? How willing are you to make compromises? Do you have a my-way-or-the-highway attitude? American culture, as I wrote earlier, is a distressingly disposable one; we've grown so used to simply getting rid of things as soon as they present a problem or seem outdated (whatever that means). Do we look at marriage in such a binary way—all or nothing?

It doesn't have to be that way. You can adjust a marriage and in so doing strengthen it. Our needs and those of our partners do not stay in exactly the same proportion all the time; our need for (say) companionship or stability or support or spontaneous sex will wax and wane over time, often abruptly and significantly, so of course there has to be adjustment. What's Option B—starting over again with someone else?

My clients are those who have decided it makes more sense, difficult and sad as it is, to end the marriage. I appreciate that. But far too often the person sitting in my office is someone who may have forgotten to think about the marriage itself—not just their needs, or their spouse's, but the marriage's.

Some suggestions:

1. *Remind yourself from time to time that the only rules defining marriage, as an institution, are those that we as a culture have made.* And the only rules your particular marriage has are the ones that you and your spouse agree to. You get to pick which side of the bed you each sleep on. Or whether you sleep in the same bed. Or whether you sleep in the same room or even in the same house or time zone. Marriage is a tool, and as with any other tool, you

don't have to use it the same way that everybody else does. Your marriage is a unique union of two unique individuals. Embrace that. Make it work for you.

2. *Think about divorce.* I'm not saying that to drum up business. I mean think about the reality that you don't have to stay married. Marriage is a contract; every day, you wake up and decide to continue the contract. You can terminate the contract anytime you like. Sometimes contemplating what it would really look like to be separate from your spouse can help to bring things sharply into focus, either giving you a renewed appreciation for your spouse or bringing home some hard truths about the state of your union. People are resistant to talking or even thinking about divorce, but keep in mind that all marriages end. They end either in death or in divorce. As to the former: You (hopefully) see doctors regularly to postpone it; still, you (again, hopefully) should have had occasional discussions about things like funerals, cremation, life insurance, and other difficult but inevitable stuff. As to the latter: Why not engage in a discussion, with your spouse, about the other way your marriage *could* end—a discussion that would probably strengthen all but the most fragile unions?

3. *Know that a marriage can end without the marriage itself ending.* Huh? What I mean is this: If a marriage is a series of chapters in a book, it might help you to realize that each chapter can be viewed as its own mini-marriage. What worked to feed the marriage you had pre-children might not work after the children leave home. It might be missing an ingredient or two, or it might have new limitations that make the old ingredients ineffective at producing the same result. To look at your marriage not as a singular event or contract but as a series of contracts might remind you that you have more control over its shape than you often feel (and passively lament) that you do.

If I may put it another way: I don't think there are any hacks to a good marriage.

From the way the majority of my clients talk to me, they regard marriage as an end. And that, I believe, is a big reason why they're in my office. Because *marriage is not an end. It is a means to an end.* It's about getting you to the destination; the destination is connection and companionship, comfort and trust. Getting you to the destination is an ongoing process that requires alertness, energy, and consistency.

Yes, as I implied in the first point above, you don't have to use marriage the same way everybody else does. And in our individual-centered, consumer culture, where everything from the ads that Amazon and Facebook serve us to the endless variety of breakfast cereals in the supermarket aisles responds to our particular needs and wants, we increasingly demand that the world, and its institutions and traditions, form-fit to us, not the other way around.

But that works only up to a point. Traditions, and many of the benefits that come from adhering to them, cannot survive if everyone comes up with their own completely personal take. You can attempt some disruptive innovation, sure—open marriage, say, or agreeing to pay attention to each other only on Tuesdays, Thursdays, and Saturdays—but I believe that, generally, there *isn't* a better way to do marriage. If there were a shortcut to gaining a deep, lasting connection to another person, we'd have found it by now. Someone would have made a ton of money publicizing that shortcut.

I just don't think we can Uber marriage. Sorry.

## Chapter 19

# IF WE WERE DESIGNING AN INFIDELITY-GENERATING MACHINE, IT WOULD BE FACEBOOK

From time to time, in moments of transient loneliness, do you long for some temporary distraction or brief mental escape from your day-to-day life? Do you ever think about people you slept with when you were single, or people you wanted to sleep with? Wonder what they're doing now? Would you like to peek in, perhaps anonymously, on what those people are doing from time to time? Is it pretty innocent and kinda silly to satisfy these whims, killing time just as you do with Angry Birds or Candy Crush?

Except you don't scroll through Angry Birds looking for pictures of the birds in their bathing suits.

Don't kid yourself. You're an idiot if you use Facebook. If you're vaguely unhappy with your relationship or marriage, and especially if you're *more* than vaguely unhappy with it: Stay away from Facebook. The vast majority of what you'll find there is unhappiness masked as happiness. It will fuck with your head, your heart, and your relationship.*

Facebook is the single greatest breeding ground ever for infidelity. Nothing that has come before—not swingers' clubs and key parties, not chat rooms, not workplace temptations, not Ashley Madison, Tinder, or

---

* If I had a dollar for every divorce caused by infidelity that started on Facebook, I would have ... well, just about the same amount of money I have. Bless you, Mark Zuckerberg.

Grindr; no, not even porn—comes within a thousand miles. I don't keep detailed statistics on these things, but if I had to estimate, I would say I get two or three new cases per week that feature infidelity that started or was made easier to perpetuate by Facebook. Who knew one platform could cause so much chaos?

Seriously: If we were given the assignment to create an adultery service, isn't the following how we would design it, step by step?

1. Okay, on this platform, let's include every person each user has ever slept with, or once fantasized about sleeping with.
2. Let's give you, the user, the ability to communicate with each and every one of them, both publicly and privately.
3. There will be other people on the service, too, people you know (family, friends, close coworkers), sort-of strangers (not-so-close coworkers or people you met briefly at a party but might find interesting to learn more about), and total strangers, so that when you *do* communicate with people you once had or have long maintained a sexual interest in, you have plausible deniability. ("Why did I 'like' the picture of her in a bikini? Fifty other people liked that picture! And I was mostly 'liking' the Hawaiian setting!") As a bonus, businesses will advertise on this service, so when your spouse asks why you're using it so much, you can say, "I'm reading reviews for pool cleaning services!" You can say you're checking on your 401(k) while actually checking out your prom date from twenty years ago and seeing how her boobs appear to be holding up.
4. You have the ability to post photos of yourself, showing this other person (or persons) what you've been up to . . .
5. . . . but not in a candid, unfiltered way that captures your bad side, your blemishes, spinach between your teeth, etc. No, you'll get to curate which pictures you display, and of course you'll post only those in which you look good, where you're doing interesting things, and which show as much or little of your outside life (spouse, kids) as you wish to share. Want to show you're a family

person? You can do that! Want to keep this intriguing person (or persons) from knowing for sure that you're married? You can do that! You're the curator. Obscuring the fact of a so-called, alleged spouse is easy-peasy.

What's just outside the frame? Your real life!

Yeah, no one has to see that.

6. You can flirt with this person (ex-girlfriend, ex-boyfriend, potentially-fun-to-sleep-with person) in so many ways—micro-interactions known as "commenting on her status," "commenting on his photo," or simply "liking" his witty posts or posting items on your own page that comport with his or her interests and/or political perspective, etc. Again, there's plausible deniability up the wazoo because it's not just a bald-faced one-on-one encounter (we'll add that feature in a minute). It's as if you're in a crowded bar, and you have absolute freedom to stare at this person, or whisper something to him, or compliment her—and it's totally cool because there are other people in the bar. What could possibly go wrong?

7. Okay, maybe you *do* want a one-on-one encounter after all. No problem: You can privately message him or her, and discuss all kinds of subjects.

    (Hold on: *Why are you even talking to this person in the first place?* Because you can! The mere existence of this cool technology justifies its use. And if that doesn't sound like a credible claim to you—that a new technology in itself facilitates new sorts of behavior—just glance at every individual around you, in public or private, at work or at play, young or old, in constant thrall to their smartphone.)

8. You can access this service from the office, or while sitting on the couch at home, three feet away from your spouse. You can get it on your mobile phone or your tablet. Wherever and however. And it's so easy, even a baby boomer can use it. If you're at the store with your wife, you can't stare at a woman but you *can* pass the time scrolling through every picture she ever

posted. And, as mentioned, she's probably only posting the best ones.

Now get this: What if within a few years of creation, this app got so popular and ubiquitous that if you *didn't* use it people would look at you as if you were trying to hide something? And regard you with a mix of scorn and skepticism? *You don't use Facebook? Why? Are you trying to hide where you ate from us? Are you some kind of sociopath or something? Why don't you want to see photos of my children's dance recital?!* And if you respond with "Because I don't want to see photos of my ex-girlfriend in a bikini and get messages from people I slept with in college," people will think you're a jerk.

One more thing: The service is free—at least, it's free to acquire and use. The repercussions can be a little more expensive.

We wanted to create an infidelity machine? Check, check, check, check.

For a lawyer looking for evidence of said infidelity, Facebook often means checkmate.

Facebook is foreplay. Facebook facilitates adultery and infidelity generally. Facebook gives you the means, the excuse, and the cover to communicate with people you have no reason, no business, to talk to. Their day-to-day life has nothing to do with yours—not anymore, anyway. In many cases, perhaps the majority of cases, you follow and chat with this individual because you remember him or her fondly, as he or she might remember you; the memories are from a simpler time in your lives, when you were in college, or high school, when maybe you had a lot more sex, and when nervous possibility was in the air. (You're probably remembering it with more fondness than it merits.) Your life was about going to class, and smoking weed, and working a crappy part-time job with no real responsibilities so that you'd have enough money to afford frivolous, enjoyable garbage.

Look at enough bullshit, highly curated vacation photos on Facebook and you're bound to find the truth of your life gradually, then suddenly, more depressing than it probably is.

I am confronted by infidelity every day of my work life. I have heard about so many mountains and oceans of it that I even came up with an infidelity taxonomy (see Chapter 14). In my own practice, and I would wager in the practice of almost every other divorce attorney in the era of social media, infidelity that begins online, usually through Facebook, is the single most common seed for the mighty oak that eventually becomes a full-blown affair.

Oh, and in case you're interested: Every status you post on Facebook may be used against you in a court of law. In addition to those terms of service that everybody agrees to and nobody reads (not even lawyers), there should be some Facebook *Miranda* rights that are read to you when you sign up:

> You have the right to refrain from using this service to document where you are, what you are doing, what you are spending money on, and whom you are spending time with. If you give up that right, anything you post (or anywhere you check in or any photos you get tagged in) can and will be used against you* in a court of law. You have the right to try to delete things from your page once your divorce has started, but I can assure you that my staff captured screen shots of everything before you were even served with the divorce papers. You have the right to unfriend your spouse but, trust me, some of your "friends" like your spouse more than they like you, and they're more than willing to grant us continued access even if you block your spouse. You have the right to choose what you post, but remember: Other people can tag you in photos, mention you in their comments, and give access to anyone who might be looking for a solid trail to follow if we want to track your movements and/or spending. Oh: And Facebook complies with properly issued subpoenas from divorce courts.

---

\* By me.

I was going to write a sentence or two here about how it isn't my intention to single out Facebook among the numerous social media platforms, but let's be honest: Facebook is in a class by itself. Instagram has some of the same features (and the beautiful filters make your life look even better!) but not so much of the business stuff that gives the plausible deniability needed for efficient infidelity. Married people aren't really using Snapchat for that reason. You can't really claim you're using Snapchat to "check what time the tire store opens this weekend" or "read reviews of the new dim sum place down the street."

There's a popular saying in Alcoholics Anonymous, meant to discourage people in recovery from hanging around bars: "If you sit in a barbershop long enough, eventually you're going to get a haircut."

Quit Facebook. You don't need the temptation and you don't need to create the temptation for someone else. Let the past be the past. Don't put the future in jeopardy just to indulge in some frivolous nostalgia. The negatives far outweigh the positives. I quit Facebook a year ago, and when people ask me why, I tell them candidly: I don't want to look in people's windows anymore to see what they're doing. Even if they want me to. Especially if they want me to.

Don't waste your life crafting an advertisement for how great your life is. Get out there and live a great life.

## Chapter 20

# ONE OF THE PILLARS OF MARRIAGE IS SEX

"Blowjobs are like eggs Benedict," a male client told me, while recounting the story of his marriage that ultimately led him to me. "You're not getting them at home."

If you've been married longer than ten years and still want to fuck your spouse, and they still want to fuck you, you're clearly doing something right. I know there are many, many of those marriages out there. Professionally, I just don't get to interact with the individuals fortunate enough to be in such unions.

There are marriages in which neither party is all that into the sex anymore. Maybe they never were. It's just not much of a priority. Maybe they both have hobbies. Maybe they both got so out of shape that sex seems like too much cardio to be fun. And then there are many marriages, as I've learned in my life as a divorce lawyer, in which one person can't keep their hands off the other person—which the recipient would ideally take as a huge compliment, but which in fact is not reciprocated to anywhere near that degree of enthusiasm.

That's what I want to talk about here: Scenarios in which an imbalance exists. In which sexual desire is no longer a two-way street. In which one person is still feeling highly sexually attracted to their partner (or has a tremendous libido that needs to be satisfied with someone, and the person they married is, legally, supposed to be that someone), while the other partner feels sex is little more than a chore that needs to be performed with a certain regularity to prevent discord.

I'm not saying anything shocking or revolutionary—or that your average marriage therapist wouldn't say—when I note that, of all the many things that marriage is about, *sex is one of its core values.* Sex is a pillar of marriage. It's right there in the traditional vows—"to have and to hold." (That's just the PG-13 version for all the old people at the wedding. It also sounds better than "to do unspeakable things to you after the kids go to sleep.")

When I say that sex—semi-regular, "good" sex—is one of the pillars of marriage, I don't mean it in the biblical sense, or anything.[*] Every couple has a different idea of what good sex is; it's probably whatever you were doing when you settled into dating seriously. So let's use that as our working definition here.

It can feel almost transgressive and provocative to acknowledge that marriage is fundamentally about sex. It's about other things, too, of course, but it's basically about sex. A friend once told me that her mother's advice, on the eve of her wedding, was simply "Sex is the glue to a good marriage."

So, okay, fine. Sex is part of marriage. An important part of marriage. What am I going to suggest next—that the steering wheel is a part of driving? Am I basing this chapter on research conducted by the Center for the Obvious? Sex is part of marriage. No shit. That's what separates a marriage from a long-term committed friendship.

In Chapter 11: Go Without or Go Elsewhere, I discussed the cruel choice, when your sexual needs aren't being met in a monogamous relationship, between having those needs remain unfulfilled (go without) or having them fulfilled by someone other than your partner (go elsewhere).

---

[*] When my recently married former college roommate was in town for dinner for the first time in years, he asked me—not as an old pal but as a divorce lawyer, an "expert" in all matters marital— "The first year of marriage is the toughest, right? And sometimes sex isn't always the greatest, right?" Much as I believe in brutal honesty for all, including friends, I didn't have the heart to tell him that no, in *my* experience (and I don't believe it was novel), the first year of marriage was mostly about putting together IKEA furniture, paying off student loans, and having insane amounts of great sex.

But this isn't about feet or women's panties or bondage. This is about sex, at a basic level. I want to share some stories of how a disparity in sexual need and fulfillment, while never the lone reason for the demise of the client's relationship, played at least some role.

Seth, a construction worker with a self-described big libido (I have no reason to believe he was boasting as he recounted the frank details of his marital downfall), told me that, for years, he had wanted to have sex every day, ideally twice a day. When he first met Pauline, she knew he had a big libido, and they had lots of sex when they were dating. They had lots of sex when they first married. But eventually, both the frequency and the intensity of the sex changed dramatically, and after ten years of marriage Seth had reached the point where he had to come to Pauline like a beggar with a cup. "She would sleep with me most of the time," he said, "but I didn't want to just have sex with her. I wanted to be with someone who *wanted* to have sex with me. It gets exhausting and kind of humiliating always to be, like, 'I *need* you to do this for me. . . .'"

I've heard some variation of Seth's story from hundreds of clients. It's sometimes offered in justification of an affair by the person who had the affair. It's sometimes offered as a possible explanation for a spouse's affair in the painful "How could this have happened?" reflection common to those who've been cheated on.

Let's be candid: When relationships begin, there's usually a lot of sex (let's call that variable frequency) and the sex is fun and exciting and, to varying degrees, adventurous (let's call that variable intensity). So Early Relationship = High Frequency × High Intensity.

As a monogamous relationship progresses, there are a host of reasons for frequency to drop. A selection from clients:

"I'm exhausted at the end of the day with the kids."

"I'm so busy at work we're rarely in the same room awake to chat, much less fuck."

"I'm just not as into it anymore. I like skiing/scuba diving/fusion cooking, but if I did it every day for six years, I wouldn't find it as exciting anymore."

The reasons for the decline in intensity are in some ways similar and in some ways a bit more complicated:

"After watching her wipe the butts of our children all evening and listening to her talk on the phone to her sister for half an hour before bed, I don't really view my wife as an object of lust as much as I did when we were dating and still a mystery to each other."

"My husband has really let himself go in the past five years. He put on twenty pounds and isn't as sexy or energetic and fit as he was when we were dating, and I just don't find him as sexually exciting as I used to."

These examples might seem harsh, but they're honest. There's little reason to lie to your divorce lawyer about why your marriage fell apart or why you and your spouse stopped sleeping together.

Sometimes even the best-intentioned couple, while trying to have great sex with each other, can inadvertently screw up their sex life by throwing off the intensity variable (often by trying to maintain the frequency variable). I've seen this happen many times, and it always makes me a little sad. Having lots of bad sex does not equal a good sex life.

John and Mary were two people who found a way to make sex boring without intending to, and their example is not unique. They had been married for five years. Each still found the other attractive. Neither had any particular hangups about sex; both were committed to a marriage that featured, among other attributes, a mutually satisfying sex life.

Like any two people who have had sex with each other a few hundred times, John and Mary had each figured out (through communication, observing reactions, and noting what was requested or selected) what the other liked best. John liked, among other things, intermittent eye contact during blowjobs, and when Mary bit his ear during sex. Mary liked, among other things, sex from behind while lying on her side, when John pulled her hair a little (but not too much), and when John said her name just before she climaxed. Each aimed to work the other's "highlights" into their sexual experiences, both to maximize their partner's enjoyment and to increase the efficiency of sex (to get and give the most pleasure in the shortest time). This approach is why, for some people who like sex, monogamy can be ideal: Sure, you give up the novelty of frequent new partners, but you trade it for a partner who knows your sexual highlight reel, who knows what buttons you like pushed and how best to push them.

As their day-to-day life together progressed in the ways that lives do, with careers and/or children and/or social obligations taking up more and more time, John and Mary, mindful of their desire to maintain a healthy sex life and keep each other satisfied, tried to remember to "fit" sex into their life together. Their lives had taken on a structure, whether intended or not: Mary practiced yoga on Saturdays, John went to the gym Monday and Friday mornings. As a result, they (without conscious deliberation and with only good intentions) began having sex on somewhat predictable days, at predictable times, when the four most important conditions were met: They were together, they were alone, they were awake, Colbert wasn't on.

Can we agree that John and Mary had expressed, thus far, only the best of intentions?

Here's where the perfect storm arrived, culminating in one of them showing up at my office. John and Mary, after a few years of marriage, and with the specific goal of having relatively frequent and mutually satisfying sex, had inadvertently created conditions under which sex became unsatisfying and, eventually, infrequent.

Sex happened on the same days and at the same times, under generally very similar scenarios (say, Tuesday evenings after they finished dinner but before bed, and in the master bedroom, where they preferred to watch TV after they'd gone upstairs for the evening). They had created the conditions for predictable sex. "Predictable" is not an adjective people use to describe an ideal sex life.*

And sex, when it happened, featured the same specific sexual acts,

---

* Though it would no doubt be considered a great virtue by one demographic—blue-balled teenage boys.

acts that, as mentioned earlier, John and Mary knew from experience were the ones their partner liked best.

So now we had two people mostly doing the same things to each other, in the same place, at the same time. In short, the sex was routine—another adjective never employed to describe a superior sex life, or a sex life (for those who really like and need sex) that motivates one to remain monogamous.

Many, many of the couples I've worked with have distinctly differing perceptions of their sex lives. I'm reminded of the split-screen scene in the movie *Annie Hall,* where Alvy Singer (Woody Allen's character) is in a session with his shrink, while his girlfriend, Annie (Diane Keaton), is in a session with hers.

"How often do you sleep together?" Alvy's shrink asks him.

"Do you have sex often?" Annie's shrink asks her.

"Hardly ever," reports a frustrated Alvy. "Maybe three times a week."

"Constantly," says a tired Annie. "I'd say three times a week."

Many women clients have told me some version of "I really thought we had a satisfying sex life"; many men have said to me, usually defensively, "Yeah, we didn't have a lot of sex."

I am not here to set forth an idea of how many sessions of what duration constitute too much sex, enough sex, not enough sex, great sex, good sex, okay sex, or rotten sex. No one size or shape fits all. There are points in any relationship where more-than-usual sex happens, and those where less does. There are points where the sex is satisfying, and points where it's routine. There are times when routine sex is good enough to keep both people happy, and times when it leaves one (or both) longing for something more or different.

The problem is, it's hard to tell when there's a problem. Or, more specifically: It's hard to tell when exactly the problem starts.

Indeed, I have found that, for all the candor I'm exposed to behind closed doors with divorcing parties, when I'm out and about with married people, perhaps even happily married people, they pretty much never volunteer how much sex they're having, not even in unguarded (or somewhat inebriated) moments, or how amazing or terrible it is. It remains, along with why people tend to leave their socks on, one of the great sexual mysteries of the universe.

Even I, a divorce attorney who has gotten more than his fill of messy human revelation, admit to sometimes wondering about my married friends, or really about any married couple I run into: *Are they having more sex than I am? A lot more? Is it enough? Which one of them initiates? How does the "negotiation" unfold? What positions do they do? How long do they do it for? Is it usually volcanic? What do they say to each other before and after?*

Or is that just me?

Doing what I do for a living, I see how important sex is to people. We all know how important it is. It's so important, in fact, that an entire massive industry is based on us all watching or reading about *other* people having sex. (Hell, the Internet should be called "Strangers Fucking and Other Things.") People sign up for the contract of marriage in large part because of sex. They also, pretty frequently, screw that contract up because of sex, especially when they have it with people other than their spouse. Advertising is saturated with sex. Our favorite movies and TV are filled with sex. None of us would be here if our parents hadn't had sex. And yet married people are silent when it comes to providing any of us—including other married couples—any quantifiable standard by which to gauge how much sex (and what kind of sex) is "typical."

And this coy but understandably self-protective reticence leaves many married people feeling like they are getting too little or asking for too much.

In my professional experience, for many men, "married sex" is akin to—simply put—not enough sex. Men cheat more often than women, or at least cheat in ways that more often lead to revelation and divorce, and they more often cite the inadequacy of their sex lives as a prime cause of their willingness to be unfaithful. It's a universal stereotype viewable on any of a dozen shitty weeknight sitcoms: the married guy who doesn't get laid as often as he would like.

And it's actually not all that funny. (Then again, nothing about those shows really is.)

The secret to staying out of my office for these reasons is—once again—simply to talk to each other. Ideally, that conversation happens before the wedding, with a realistic eye toward the kind of predictable life progressions I've outlined. Sure, you don't know precisely what's going to happen when you marry someone, but you should try to account for change in your projection for your married sex life. You would have a business plan if you were opening up a cupcake shop. You don't just leave things like this up to chance.

If a man with a significant libido knows he won't be satisfied by sex with his wife once per week or once per month, he owes it to his wife (or future wife) to have a frank discussion about that. At the risk of being terribly unromantic, maybe it's as plain as this: "I like to have sex at least three times per week. Minimum. There's no maximum. That's what I'd like. That's what would satisfy me. I would prefer for all of that sex to be with you. Nobody else. But if we get into a routine for any reason that ends up with me having sex less than three times per week, I'm going to get unsatisfied pretty quickly and I'm only human and humans are prone to doing stupid things when they're unsatisfied . . ."

(If that doesn't work, you could say, "What are you doing Monday through Thursday at eight p.m.? No plans? Great! See you there!")

Of course, such a conversation is best conducted very early in the relationship, and maybe it would seem premature and presumptuous and odd then. Or maybe dynamics are evolving too quickly to lay down such a seemingly strict regimen. Still, expressing at the outset what you want is helpful. You're not always going to get what you want. There will be times when you want more, times when you want less. But by expressing your wants early and honestly, at least you've established a basis for an ongoing conversation and a point of reference in the event that you feel the sexual part of your relationship is getting off track.

It's a whole lot easier to start practicing such candor from the start. Remember that person you've been introduced to a bunch of times and didn't quite catch their name but didn't want to admit that you didn't get their name the very first time so you just faked your way the next few times? Now, here you are: You've met this person a dozen times and you're way past the point where you can ask their name without seeming like an asshole. Somebody comes up and asks for an introduction and your only plan is to jump out the nearest window and hope there's something soft down below. It's better to plead ignorance early, when you've still got an excuse. Wait too long, and ignorance becomes evidence of something far more nefarious.

No conversation = far less understanding. And in my experience as a divorce lawyer, a reluctance or fear or ickiness about having such a conversation makes consideration of an affair easier, because

1. an affair makes the straying spouse feel sexually desired; plus, if you're now having "affair sex" along with semi-infrequent married sex, you're much closer to getting your desired quota of sex (so where's the physiological incentive to stop?).
2. you can avoid having that difficult conversation with your spouse about sexual needs for . . . well, as long as the affair is going on.

Of course, as I said, it's not just the frequency of the sex that matters but also its nature or quality.* We might call this the Cuddling vs. Fucking Theorem.

I don't like watching a movie with someone who isn't into it. Without even looking over, you can feel them rolling their eyes. Nobody wants that to be their sex life, either.

You want one kind of outcome from your episodes of intimacy. Your partner wants another. Sex does not have to feature just one outcome, of course; ideally there will be enough outcomes to make everybody happy. So it's important to say, "I'd like it this way."

When you don't (and even sometimes when you do), you get the eggs Benedict lament. Many men feel as if they get what they want sexually only on special occasions—a birthday, an anniversary, Arbor Day—and the buildup of frustration is toxic to their satisfaction with their spouse.

---

* And please don't put "frequency of sex" in a lesser category than "quality of sex." It deserves a place alongside.

There are relationships in which one partner is into things such as BDSM, while the other partner is not. There is no easy fix for this, but—at least for those who are early in their relationship or currently uncoupled—I recommend your being upfront about your needs as soon as possible. (See also Chapter 11.)

Even if you are upfront, things may not work out the way you hope. My client Jess, a relatively mild-mannered accountant, liked to get tied up and spanked during sex. When he started dating Gwen, Jess incorporated that proclivity into their sex life, and Gwen seemed okay with it. It wasn't really her "thing" necessarily, but it seemed to make him happy, so she went along with it. When they got married, Gwen got less into Jess's kink. When they became parents, Gwen pretty much stopped Jess from doing it. ("What if the kids walked in?") Jess tried to change his ways. But to be tied up and spanked was something he still wanted. He suggested to Gwen that they take more regular weekends away and "it'll be part of that." She was not agreeable (she was fine with more weekends away, but not with the light bondage). "Why is this so important to you?" she asked him—though, clearly, it was less a question than a condemnation.

Now, after twelve years of marriage, Jess was in my office. "Hey, I was *as advertised*," he told me. "I told her I liked it from the beginning. She knew that. It's not like I pretended to be some choirboy who was satisfied with once-per-week missionary-style sex. And it's not like I'm asking her, every time we have sex, to tie me up as a precondition. I told her, early on, that this was something I was into. This was something important to my feeling sexually satisfied. And she was okay with it. We enjoyed it together. Or at least I thought we did. There was spanking in the previews! And all of a sudden I'm two hours into the movie and the spanking isn't in the movie! I know I shouldn't have cheated on her—but what she did isn't fair."

Can you get upset at your partner for having unusual sexual desires and needs? Well, sure; but if you married a man who you knew liked to wear women's panties, or a woman who liked to tie you up or be tied up, or someone whose sexual arsenal is similarly kinky, is it fair, years into the marriage, to tell him or her, "I find that really unattractive"? Or "I want to stop because I don't find that sexy anymore"?

Granted, couples who early in their dating or married life are into threesomes or sex clubs may well decide to manage their desires differently once they have kids. A client named Rachel complained to me of her husband's continued sexual adventure-seeking—which had been their shared habit years before—putting it this way: "I'm more of a mom now, so when Arthur asked, 'Can we go to the [sex] club?' I kept telling him, 'No, we're going to the petting zoo with the kids.' How can he be disappointed?"

I've seen this conundrum quite a bit with gay men. In my experience representing gay clients who are decoupling (and, soon enough, divorcing), frequency and variety of sexual activity don't emerge as core divisive issues: The how-much-I-want-it-versus-how-much-he/she-wants-it and the how-I-would-like-to-get-it difficulties are much more rooted in fundamental differences between men and women (from my experience). That's not to say such a tussle can't happen in a same-sex relationship—not *all* men have huge libidos; not *all* women have more modest libidos. Still, from what I have observed, men with men have lots more sex, and are more capable than women are of separating the act of sex from intimacy. Because of the great need for sex, and for variety, gay men may have relationship rules that aren't as common among heterosexual pairings. In multiple cases I've handled, committed male partners created a hack of the go without/go elsewhere conundrum with what might be best deemed "flexible monogamy." There's the "We can get blowjobs from other people but we can't have anal sex with them" rule; the "We always use condoms when having sex with others but not with each other" rule; and the "We can have sex with other people, but both of us have to be having sex with other people at the time" rule (apparently popular during the summer months in Fire Island).*

---

\* All this admirable clarity and openness did not help the durability of the relationships I've seen, or they wouldn't have ended up in my office.

I can't tell you much about the issue of sex in lesbian marriages. I now have a busy same-sex practice, but I've done only about a dozen lesbian divorces. And since same-sex marriage is still relatively new to our culture, there aren't adequate statistics regarding the rate and reasons for same-sex divorces. One might argue that many American same-sex couples, having had the right to marry granted to them across the board only in 2015, are (irrespective of the duration of the underlying relationship) still in the honeymoon phase of their marriages. That might carry a bit of a collective emotional burden. I might feel bad getting a divorce if the nation fought and marched for my right to get married! Maybe lesbian women are better at staying married than gay men and heterosexual couples. Maybe they just don't hire male attorneys. Maybe their relationships take longer to fall apart and will all, in a few years, explode simultaneously. You'll have to check back with me on that one.

Someone reading this chapter might be offended. It's loaded with stereotypes about men and women, gay men and lesbians, married people and newly coupled people. It's unfair to put people into such broad categories and to say "Men are this way" and "Women are that way." But my goal is to offer observations of specific trends from a very specific demographic: the people who sit in a chair across from me because they made a legal (and arguably spiritual, emotional, and social) commitment, and now need my help to break it or to clean up the mess left from the breaking.

Sex is important. It probably shouldn't be so important. When you think about it, it's ridiculous, really: how rubbing our parts against each other in a way that feels good can cause such profound animosity and upset. It's stunning how the very act that creates life and amazing pleasure also creates so much chaos and brutality between us.

Marriage should ideally be rooted in something deeper than our desire for sex, and it should be held together by something stronger than the "glue" of sex.

Yet here we are. Still, as a culture, insisting on keeping marriage and sex tied together until death (or divorce) do them part.*

How to correct this? Be honest—even if retroactively.

The Johns and Marys never mean to end up in my office. But they do, more than half the time. I'm not saying Mary has to skip yoga every now and then on a Saturday morning to roll around in bed with John for a few hours. I'm not saying John should skip the gym and be late for work some Monday morning and see if he can still do that thing that, back when they were dating, made Mary hit a high note. Sex, and departing from a sexual routine, are unlikely to be the cure-all for any marriage.

I'm just saying: It certainly won't do anything to *hurt* the marriage, will it?

---

* I meet lots and lots of people who, in a last-ditch effort to stave off the emptiness and discontent they're experiencing in an obviously bad married life, have attempted an open marriage. In virtually every case (again, I see a very particular, self-selected segment of the population), it only delayed the inevitable, giving the one party who really wanted to sleep with other people cover for doing so, while the other party got the chance to risk contracting chlamydia. Good stuff!

## Chapter 21

# WE KNOW WHAT WE KNOW
# UNTIL WE MAY NOT WANT
# TO KNOW IT

We deny realities all the time—about ourselves, about our partners. Denial is a protective measure. It's a deeply human instinct. It's often heartbreaking, occasionally noble.

And it's almost never helpful, at all.

One client, Theo, literally walked in on this scene (as he described it to me): He came home early to find his wife sitting at the kitchen counter; the normally made bed was unmade (he could see into the bedroom from the living room of their small apartment); and the shower was occupied. By Terry, a friend of Theo's.

Theo's wife said that Terry had come over to help her fix the garbage disposal in the kitchen sink, which had jammed and broken. He got dirty doing it, of course, so he took a shower.

Theo chose to believe this.

Three months later, when he walked in on his wife giving Terry a blowjob in the kitchen, he assumed, correctly, that Terry hadn't been fixing the disposal. He had just used it that morning and it seemed to be working fine. To his credit, Theo didn't go nuclear, didn't go Lorena Bobbitt on Terry. He just turned around, walked out the front door, called my office, and came in for a consultation a few hours later.

It's amazing the lengths to which people will go to believe what they want to believe. Sometimes, it takes seeing a text between their spouse and a third party that reads "Thanks so much for the sex! Glad my husband will never read this" before they'll accept what's going on. (That's not a hypothetical. That, verbatim, is the godawful pedestrian message one client happened to see.) Once, I had a man come into my office and say about his wife, "I don't know, she's been really distant lately."

"Okay. Tell me what's going on," I said.

"She's saying she wants to separate."

"Have you been having problems?"

"No."

"Have there been any dramatic changes in your life circumstances or her behavior?"

"She's lost a lot of weight. But that's because she's been going to the gym lately. She has this trainer she's good friends with, and she talks to him a lot."

"How often?"

"They talk every day, maybe two times a day."

(Later, when I got hold of a copy of the phone bill, I saw that over the previous two months, his wife and the trainer had texted each other 877 times.)

This is where I felt entitled to say, "You think she might be having a relationship?"

"Nah, I don't think so. She says they're just friends. She's not the type to have an affair. She's not really that interested in sex. We've only had sex once a month for the last few years, even less in the last year. . . ."

I often wonder: Do these people hear the stuff coming out of their own mouths?

Of course, the opposite happens, too, and this is where I start feeling more like a private eye with a paranoid client rather than a legally bound truth-teller. Not infrequently, clients or potential clients come to my office and provide me with highly circumstantial evidence that their spouse is cheating. "You see this?" said Roger, showing me the printout of an innocuous email between his wife and a male colleague of hers.

"He addresses the email to 'J,' not Jane, and not Mrs. Parker, like a professional businessperson should."

"Roger," I interrupted, "do you seriously call your coworkers Mr. Smith or Mrs. Jones?"

"No, but that's not the point. They're super chummy here. The way he writes to her. She's fucking him, for sure."

I did not know if Roger was right. In my experience, if you think your spouse is fucking someone, they probably are.* And, all too often, people your spouse is fucking are like cockroaches: For every one you see, there are ten in the walls.

But what do I know?

---

* Divorce lawyer joke: What do you call a woman who always knows where her husband is? A widow.

## Chapter 22

# GRATUITOUS TIME-OUT:
# I LOVE MY JOB,
# EXCEPT FOR WHEN I HATE IT

I told you I like telling stories. And while this is an advice book, it's my advice book, so you can get over yourself for a minute and listen to my story, or you can go to Chapter 23. You bought the book already, though, so you might as well stick around. The punch line is worth it and may make you rethink the next time you say something like "The world is unfair."

'Cause it sure as shit is.

Last year I won a custody battle for my client Louie, a creep who absolutely, positively did not deserve custody. He's a pimp—an actual pimp—and that's not even close to the worst thing about him. He's violent and abusive to women. He's a multiple felon who's served time for drug and gun convictions. And he's a rampaging narcissist with anger issues. He has five children, each with a different mother, and for the past ten years I've represented him in countless child support–related matters.

So you don't think I'm a sociopathic mercenary: I should make it clear that when Louie first hired me, so many years ago, I had no idea who or, more candidly, what he was. He told me he owned a liquor store in the Bronx, which was true. What he failed to mention, however, was that ownership of the store was not his primary vocation but a way to launder money from other, less-than-legal ventures. By the time I learned of Louie's nefarious activities and reprehensible behaviors, we'd established an attorney-client relationship. Under the Code of Professional Responsibility, my duty to "zealously advocate" for Louie and preserve his confidences had already commenced. Louie could fire me at any time; I, unfortunately, could not quit being his lawyer unless one of the following conditions applied: One, I had "affirmative knowledge that he was actively making false statements under oath" (hunches and gut feelings don't count, nor does someone winking at you; essentially, they have to tell you explicitly that they plan to lie under oath—a degree of premeditation that no client, in my experience, has ever actually acknowledged). Or, two, there was an "irretrievable breakdown in the attorney-client relationship" (such as his attacking me physically). Or, three, I retired from the practice of law (a possibility that cases like Louie's make me whimsically ponder; alas, my sons' college tuition bills make it unrealistic for another couple of decades).

Bottom line: I was with Louie for the ride. I had, for many years, helped him shirk his moral and legal obligations, primarily with respect to child support.

But this was my first time simultaneously defending a domestic violence charge and pursuing a custody case for him. It felt far more repugnant than helping him minimize his child support payments, but it was a "legitimate legal objective," thus my duty as his attorney.

Louie was trying to take custody of his daughter Ferrari (he picked the name; he named all five of his kids after luxury car brands) from Candy (he picked that nickname, too; her given name is Patricia). Candy had been for many years one of his "girls." She had a drug problem, along with other problems that come with being one of Louie's girls.

I rarely admit what I'm about to, and before I admit it, let me state for the record that I have never "thrown" a case or refrained from doing all I could to win. But secretly I hoped we would lose.

The problem was, I wasn't going to lose. Not that I couldn't; just that I wasn't. As is too often the case in the American legal system, people get only as much justice as they can afford, and Louie could afford more justice than Candy could. Candy's lawyer was fucking up one very simple question, with profound and horrible consequences.

Candy's attorney was an assigned lawyer, what we around the courthouse call an 18B lawyer after the provision in local law that created the "assigned counsel plan" for persons unable to afford an attorney. These lawyers generally fall into one of three categories: They're fresh out of law school, with no courtroom experience and looking to gain some; they lack the business and marketing skills to build a practice and the courtroom talent that would develop their reputation; they're old, looking to get out of the house and into court a few hours a week before admitting to themselves that it's long past time to hang it up. (See? Lawyers suffer from self-delusion, too.)

My adversary on Louie's case, Gabe Lawson, was in the first category. In some ways, he reminded me of myself when I was a young lawyer taking 18B cases so I could learn to swim by being thrown into the pool. Gabe was nice, and he was eager, but the things he didn't yet know as a lawyer could fill a book.

During Candy's testimony, Gabe was asking her a seemingly simple question: "Do you recognize this photo?" And things were about to go very badly for him and, unfortunately, very favorably for Louie, my scumbag client.

"Do you recognize this photo?"

Gabe was attempting to build a foundation to put the photograph into evidence. The photo was of Candy, and it had been taken after my client, Louie, had brutally beaten her, leaving her face almost unrecognizable.

Except Gabe was doing it wrong.

If you're thinking of one day becoming a lawyer and want to get a photo into evidence, let me point out the simple, right way to go about it. A second-year law student could do it in her sleep. I coach high school students who participate in a statewide moot court competition each year; it takes me five minutes to teach them how, and the same five minutes for them to learn.

Have a clear copy of the photo you want to put into evidence. Blow it up if you like—to poster size, if that helps. Or shrink it down. Print it in color. Print it in black and white. Whatever.

Have it marked for identification purposes by the stenographer or court clerk.

Have the court officer show it to the witness.

Ask the witness what it is a photo of.

Ask the witness if the photograph "accurately depicts" what the witness just said it was a photo of.

Ask the judge to move the photo into evidence.

As they say, not rocket science.

Except for Gabe Lawson, apparently. First, his copy of the photo was printed on regular copy paper, not photo paper, which made the image harder to see; it didn't bring out any of the colors to highlight the bruises and lacerations from the beating. That was Mistake #1. But it was hardly a fatal one.

"Do you recognize this photo?" he now asked Candy. And this, Mistake #2, *would* prove to be fatal.

I wasn't sure why he phrased the question that way, but I didn't object. I knew this subject was coming up. I knew the photo would get into evidence. I had served opposing counsel with a written demand that required him to provide me, twenty days prior to trial, with copies of any photos he intended to attempt to introduce into evidence.

"That's a photo of me," Candy replied.

"Okay. And who took this photo?" asked Gabe.

"I don't know," said Candy.

Gabe looked confused and a little surprised by the answer.

*Does this guy seriously not know how to get a photo into evidence?*

"Umm . . . well, when was this photo taken?"

"On the night he beat me up," Candy replied.

"Right, but do you know the date?" Gabe was now visibly shaken.

"No, I don't."

Gabe paused. I could tell he wanted to remind his client of the answer. There are about twenty ways he could have done it—five or so of which are actually legal and ethical—but he appeared to not know any of them.

*Gabe, man, what are you doing? This is the easy part! Get the photo into evidence. This case is insanely easy. My client is dead-to-rights guilty and you've got photographic proof of it! Just get the photo into evidence.*

"Well . . . did you take this photo?"

"No, I didn't," Candy replied. I wondered at what point she would realize that her life, and her child's life, were taking profound turns here, almost entirely due to her lawyer's inexperience.

"Your Honor," Gabe said to the court, "I would like to enter this photo into evidence."

I stood. "Objection! Counsel has not laid the proper foundation for this proposed exhibit to be entered into evidence at this time, Your Honor."

Judge Webster, a long-sitting (thirty-plus years) family court judge, looked deeply unamused that this attorney, who was licensed to practice, was not following the simple, required rules for getting the photograph into evidence. He looked pissed and, more crucially, uninterested in offering counsel a free clinic on basic evidence (which sometimes happens).

"Sustained," grumbled the judge.

Gabe looked as if he had been punched. He went back to his trial table and started shuffling papers, the go-to move for any lawyer to buy some time to think.

*Get your shit together, Gabe. This woman is counting on you. Just say the words: "Does this photo accurately depict your face on the night the respondent beat the living shit out of you?" or anything resembling that, as long as the words, "Does this photo accurately depict" are in there somewhere.*

"Okay," Gabe said, addressing Candy, "what is that exhibit that you're holding?"

I hated to do it—but I had to. "Objection, Your Honor!" I interrupted. "It's improper for the witness to refer to the contents of a document that hasn't been entered into evidence."

"Sustained."

Gabe tried again. "Okay, that photo you're holding. That's a photo of you from the night where—"

"Objection!" This time I used my incredulous tone. "Counsel is both attempting to reference the contents of a document not in evidence *and* leading the witness."

"Sustained." The judge practically sneered at poor Gabe. "Counselor, watch yourself."

"I'm sorry, Your Honor," Gabe replied. He looked ready to cry. We all did.

*Come on, Gabe, you know this! I know you do! Don't let me rattle you. Don't let the judge rattle you. Just take a breath and ask Candy the question. You need to use the phrase "accurately depict," that's all. But you can't not use it. Any permutation that includes the phrase will do the trick. Even if you missed that day of law school, you had to have read Mauet's* Trial Techniques. *This would have been on at least one test. Go ahead. Do it.*

Gabe stopped. He looked broken.

"I don't know how to proceed, Your Honor."

At this point, the court could have done a number of things, including throwing Gabe a life vest and simply walking him through it and telling him what question to ask. But it was a Tuesday and it was just before lunch. The judge didn't seem in the mood to help anyone to anything.

"If you're trying to get the photo into evidence, counselor, which I assume you are, you need to ask the appropriate foundational questions," he said, condescendingly, as if speaking to a child.

*This is wrong, so absolutely wrong. I usually want to win—but in this case we don't deserve to win, and we certainly don't deserve to win this way. My client doesn't deserve to get away with beating this woman mercilessly because she's poor and her lawyer didn't pay attention in trial advocacy class.*

"Is this a photo of you that you took?" Gabe asked, in a frustrated, exhausted tone.

"Objection." I no longer even feigned real energy; I didn't spring up, sounding almost stricken by the preposterousness of it all, the way I usually do. I was just going through the motions. This thing was already over.

"Sustained."

*Jesus, Gabe! This shouldn't have happened. I genuinely should have lost today. Instead, we all lost. The world lost. Everyone but the domestic abuser pimp.*

"I don't have anything further, Judge."

Gabe sat down. The petitioner's counsel rested his case. I moved to dismiss the action for failure to establish, by a preponderance of the evidence, the basic allegations in the underlying petition—in short, asking the judge to toss the case out without my having to even put on a defense, because Candy didn't prove, during her testimony, the basic charges in the petition: that my client beat her up.

The court dismissed the petition. Louie left the courtroom a free man, getting primary physical custody of their child.[*]

As we walked down the hall, I was aware of the echo of our footsteps against the floor.

Louie smiled, then outright laughed. "I swear, man," he said, shaking his head, looking like he'd just gotten away with the perfect crime, because he had. "One good lawyer is better than five stickup men."

I fear he's right.


What's the point of this story?

I think there are two.

First, my work is full of nuance and contradiction. Very rarely am I representing some vicious, clawed monster. A client might start out seeming like that, but soon enough things come more into focus. Or maybe it's the other way around: Clients who describe the emotional abuse they've suffered for years soon turn out to have been giving as good as they were getting. I sit in a room with a guy who's an accused— or proven—wife beater. I listen to him long enough, though, hear the

---

[*] Had he lost, Candy would likely have retained custody, with some services in place for her.

awful things he's been through—the dozens of foster homes he clocked into and out of as a boy; the absence of a father, of education, of opportunity, of a kind word; watching the men around him beat their women and just figuring that that's how adult men are supposed to relate to women—and suddenly I understand him, at least parts of him. Remember: I spend my days believing no one. It's as Solzhenitsyn wrote:

> If only there were evil people somewhere insidiously committing evil deeds and it were necessary only to separate them from the rest of us and destroy them. But the line dividing good and evil cuts through the heart of every human being. And who is willing to destroy a piece of his own heart?

The line of good and evil runs through the human heart—yours, mine, Candy's, Louie's, Judge Webster's—the heart of every single one of us beautifully fucked-up people. And, hey, who wants to cut out a piece of their heart?

The second point: I don't need to give you an incentive not to get divorced. We all know divorce is, at best, a difficult life transition; at worst, a brutal battle with a formerly trusted intimate partner. Even in our disposable society and the age of "no-fault" divorce, it's not something that people go off and do without compelling reasons.

We have a legal system in which, unfortunately, people often get only as much justice as they can afford. All divorce lawyers aren't created equal. Just as I can't tell, at the initial consultation, which clients are abusive, angry, and awful, so it's difficult for a client to tell which attorneys know what they're doing in a courtroom. I'm frequently astounded by the incompetence of some of my most successful colleagues who are, apparently, better salespeople than they are trial lawyers. Just because someone drives a nice car and wears an expensive suit doesn't mean he knows what he's doing at divorce law. Just because a lawyer drives a Volkswagen doesn't mean she isn't an amazing attorney. Lawyers aren't all created equal.

I can't imagine anyone reading this would enter into a divorce lightly. But if you needed any further incentive to try to improve your marriage, let the threat of a terrible outcome in the courtroom give it to you.

Sometimes the bad guys win. The only thing more expensive than a good divorce lawyer is a bad one.

## Chapter 23

# YOU NEVER GO TO BED WITH
# JUST ONE PERSON

It might be nice to think that all marital and relationship problems are solvable, if only the two parties could tackle them alone and unbothered. I find it's rather rare, though, for such a vacuum to exist. You are not just you. I am not just me. When you marry someone, you marry their circle, and they yours. Circles, plural, actually. So many of my clients will at some point say something like, "I had no idea how awful her best friend was" or "I did not realize how much he would rely on his brother for even his small decisions."

A friend of mine says, "We become the average of the five people we interact with the most." If that's true, then, before getting married, you might want to get to know the five people your boyfriend or girlfriend interacts with the most.

My client Tracy was divorcing her husband, Lenny, after a pretty consistently tension-filled five years of marriage. The tension had been stoked by the two sets of very involved parents-in-law—but, as far as I could tell, Tracy's father, Dean, was the main culprit. For one thing, he was loaded (with money, I mean). For another, he was deeply involved in her day-to-day life, sharing his opinions, his financial advice, and, of course, the ever-present threat that he might (though so far never had) withhold money, in the short term or down the road.

At first, Lenny was deferential to Dean. Lenny wasn't the most enlightened fellow, but he was savvy enough to understand that the boy-friend is always something of a challenger to the father and to his long reign as patriarch, so he didn't mind when his future father-in-law would pick the restaurant for a family dinner, and he certainly didn't mind when Tracy's dad picked up the check. When the happy couple went house hunting, Lenny felt slightly put off by the weight his new bride gave her father's opinions on everything from driveway design to faucets and door handles. (Lenny was in construction and knew a thing or two about houses; Dean sold cosmetic dental supplies, hardly a field that gives one special insight into customized plumbing fixtures.)

When Tracy and Lenny's second child was born, fifteen months after their first, Lenny was surprised to find his father-in-law insisting that the family of four "needed a bigger house," and that for Lenny to build an addition onto their existing house was "out of the question."

It wasn't so much that Lenny felt that moving was unnecessary; he didn't feel terribly strongly either way. What worried him was that Tracy's father presented moving as a foregone conclusion, and that Tracy nodded in immediate agreement, without casting even a glance in Lenny's direction to see where he stood.

Nothing is more expensive, goes the old saying, than that which is given for free. Lenny learned that lesson repeatedly as tensions in his marriage escalated. When Tracy's father insisted that Lenny expand his construction business so he could "provide for Tracy and the children," Lenny reluctantly agreed to the interest-free loan from his father-in-law that would enable him to buy more equipment. The loan then became the trump card Tracy and her father used anytime Lenny dared to question her dad's intrusiveness into the couple's lives: "Dad is only looking out for our best interests! I mean, he loaned you all that money and didn't even ask for interest. You should at least give him the respect of honoring his perspective on this."

Eventually Lenny said to Tracy, "Look, I'm the husband here, I'm not trying to be antagonistic, but which of us are you more interested in? Whose opinion is more important to you?"

Tracy picked her father.

\* \* \*

While I wouldn't say that involvement (or overinvolvement) of in-laws is more prevalent now than it was a century ago, I wonder if it's *perceived* as more of a problem because of the way marriage has changed. Until not that long ago, and for centuries previous, marriage was not about the union of two individuals; it was primarily regarded as the union of families, of clans. You weren't marrying a person but a family. Royal families married other royal families to expand their holdings; marriage was an institution for the preservation of wealth and land ownership.

As economic and technological developments altered so many conventions in our culture, that notion of marriage was replaced by the idea of romantic love—that two souls, rather than two clans, were uniting. No more daughter-for-sheep swaps!

Yet, for bad or good, you can't get away from that underlying truth: When you marry, you're marrying your partner's whole family dysfunction. You're marrying her drug addict brother, and his crazy-ass sister who's forever getting into trouble and needing to get bailed out. You're marrying the mother who's constantly having nervous breakdowns on the phone that her son has to tend to, invariably interrupting a quiet evening he could have spent with you.

When I do mediation, I sometimes tell the two parties, "When your child was being born, you were the only two in the room." I say this to make them feel unlike the strangers they've become, to drag them back to their commonality. It helps the mediation a lot. But I also say it because I want the parties to acknowledge that once upon a time they were this *force,* just these two folks, and that it was possible to figure things out without the background noise of everything else. I know, I know: Kids are not background noise . . . but actually they are. They're the greatest, but they're also totally antagonistic to a marriage in so many ways. And it's okay to admit that. You can admit that and still love your children.

Marriage turns a lover into a relative. There's no getting around that.

Children turn a lover into a co-parent. It's easy to lose sight of the lover, friend, and confidant under all that obligation and all those roles.

What you think and feel about your marriage, and what your spouse thinks and feels about it, should compose about 98 percent of what matters.* It's the two of you who live with the success or failure of your decisions, and everyone else (aside from your children) is a stunningly distant second or last place—yes, even deep-pocketed daddies. The two of you are partners in crime.

What your cousin thinks of your marriage is just not that important. Period. Many of my women clients, in particular, want to keep the house after the divorce, at all costs—even when they don't like the house, it's not that nice a house, and they can't afford the house. But their cousin told them that "it's really important to keep the kids in the house," in part because that's what *she* did in *her* divorce.

I'm not saying you should take zero advice about your relationship. That would be rich coming from a guy who, for a living, gives a specific form of relationship (or relationship-dissolving) advice, and who appears to prize that advice enough to get it down in the book you're reading. I'm simply saying: There comes a time to shut off the advice-gathering valves in your brain, pick your path, and make your move, whatever that entails.

Own your marital decisions.†

It ended badly for Tracy and Lenny. He started sleeping with a Slovenian waitress who worked at the local bar where he would sit for a few hours every night to delay coming home. I won't give him a pass and blame his infidelity on the emasculation he felt from both his wife and father-in-law: The waitress was beautiful and young and probably impressed with the early-thirties guy who "owned his own business" and

---

* Kidding. It's 99.8 percent.

† And know this going in: No matter what you choose, someone will say you chose wrong.

"worked with his hands"; Lenny was starved for the attention of some-one who didn't think he was, at best, second-best.

Tracy went ballistic when she found out about Lenny's infidelity. She—and, naturally, her dad—deployed all of the father's resources to make Lenny's life a living hell. My team and I spent hours tracking every penny that went into his business, every dime of unreported cash income, and every dollar spent on the girlfriend. ("A shockingly brazen example of the wasteful dissipation of marital assets, Your Honor, that must be restored to the marital estate with credits provided to my client!")

Lenny hired a local solo attorney who agreed to barter legal services in exchange for a kitchen renovation. I hope the kitchen turned out well, because it was the most expensive kitchen in history: Lenny lost every-thing. His business, the new Ford F-150 truck his former father-in-law had encouraged him to buy ("I can't have my grandchildren riding around in a jalopy!"), even the small nest egg of his own earnings he had managed to set aside just in case they ever needed it.

Not the waitress, though. He didn't lose her. She stuck with him through the whole thing, and the last I heard they were living together in a small rented apartment with their young son. The two kids Lenny has with Tracy visit on alternate weekends, and Lenny does his best, even with limited means, to make it fun for them.

Seven years later, Tracy remains single. She continues to attend family dinner with her parents and siblings every Sunday and Wednesday. Her father still picks the restaurant.

*Chapter 24*

# DIVIDE AND CONQUER

Single-handedly managing the marital finances is like anal sex: Most people don't really enjoy it. A few people pretend they like it (so they can impress their partner, often while secretly resenting them for it). A very few people genuinely enjoy it (but they understand it's complicated and should be approached with some mix of respect and caution).

Clients are constantly coming in and telling me how their spouse "doesn't do anything" about this or that particular issue (usually multiple issues): handling money, maintaining the home, dealing with taxes, feeding the kids, planning for family togetherness (vacation, camp, a bar mitzvah . . . ).

When your partner is good at something (for example, managing money), it's tempting to let them handle that aspect of your collective lives. They're good at it (and, yes, may even enjoy it). You're not good at it (or maybe you don't enjoy it). And since other, equally important responsibilities fall largely, if not almost exclusively, to you—"He does the financial stuff, I handle the kids' medical stuff"—it may appear efficient and sensible to abdicate nearly all responsibility for certain crucial tasks, secure in the belief that as long as there's a solid overall balance of tasks you each handle, all will be well.

Step back and look at this from the perspective of a divorce lawyer.

If the marriage falls apart, that sharp division of labor can leave one party (or both) entirely ignorant of important aspects of the union. I once had to eviscerate a father on the stand when he couldn't tell me the names of his children's dentist or math teacher, or the name of the street or even the neighborhood where any of his kids' best friends lived. I've seen women who didn't realize their husband had cleaned out entire bank accounts, because the women didn't know the accounts existed. That virtually every marriage has at least some task imbalance has provided me with the leverage to inflict damage on the opposing spouse who, in all honesty, was genuinely trying to help by handling an area in which they were particularly adept.* On cross-examination, I once turned a mother's active daily involvement in her children's lives into the appearance of obsessive control over the kids and refusal to allow her spouse to participate in their care. In another case, when asking for a massive alimony award for my client, I turned a husband's gratification at balancing the family checkbook and writing out the checks for utilities into "The defendant fiercely controlled our family finances and refused to allow me access to even our most basic account information." (You'll hate me, or hate what I often do, even more when you get to Chapter 26: The Myth of the Perfect Parent. Promise.)

On the one hand, no matter how competent and energetic you may think you are, a reality check: The chance that you are excellent at all the shared jobs or roles expected in a marriage—partner in finances and life planning, co-parent, cook, housecleaner, social planner—is almost zero. (Similarly, there's no way that either party will be extraordinary at each and every one of the more intimate roles you're committed to doing or being for each other—best friend, ideal sexual partner, conversationalist, champion encourager, healer). Give yourself a break. It's fine to acknowledge that while you might be great at three or four of your big shared duties, you're mediocre at (or simply loathe) a couple of them. Fortunately—hopefully—those are duties that your partner happens to be good at, or loves. (And vice versa for your partner.)

Still.

---

* This is not my attempt to get husbands to cook more in case they're someday asked on the stand, "How does your child prefer his salmon to be seasoned?" But wives, feel free to scare them into it.

No one wants to be the "responsible" or stricter parent (more often than not, Mom) while the other (usually Dad) gets to be the "fun" parent.

No one should be completely clueless about the family's finances.

And heaven knows, no one wants to do three quarters or more of the housework (almost always the woman).*

How do you create strategies within a marriage that acknowledge that each party has individual strengths and affinities, without building resentment that you or your partner is pulling significantly more weight? How do you prevent either party from being utterly useless in one or more important areas?

So many of my clients would have benefited from either a more balanced sharing of responsibilities or, at a minimum, a periodic update on the information relevant to their life that the other was "in charge of." This update could be as simple as providing an abbreviated list of accounts and balances, to keep the other informed of the location and value of marital assets and expenses. It could be as extensive as switching off who handles household responsibilities (such as cleaning or laundry) for a week or two. Think of the reality show *Wife Swap,* only without some stranger being injected into the relationship.

There's a pleasant side effect of this kind of switch-off: Not only does it keep the person who wasn't doing that task informed and empathetic (they appreciate the effort required to manage that big, regular task), but also a fresh approach may turn out to be more effective and less time-consuming, or may bring a splash of joy to what had become drudgery. After all, when household responsibilities are delegated, by design or by default, to one party or the other for an extended period of time, the household falls into a pattern about "how we do this thing" that may or may not be the most efficient. If you switch up responsibilities, even on a temporary basis, that fresh set of eyes may spot new ways—hacks—that the primary chore-doer can't see anymore, or never saw in the first place. Something like this happened with a divorcing couple I worked

---

* Marriage, for so many women, is "Snow White" in reverse. It starts with her in a beautiful gown and ends with her cleaning up after little people.

with. Shelly had never been very involved in the marital finances. She was the homemaker of the marriage, focusing most of her energies on raising the parties' two children, who, at the time of the divorce action, were already off at college. Phil, the husband, was a recognized expert in antique clock repair, his services in demand worldwide. They enjoyed a comfortable middle-class lifestyle for most of their twenty-four-year marriage.

The divorce wasn't acrimonious—in fact, it was almost friendly. The two had simply grown apart. Phil was deeply involved in his cycling club and loved traveling all over the United States for charity riding events. Shelly was a homebody and didn't share Phil's wanderlust. They had little to talk about anymore. The children were grown. They decided to move on separately, but they maintained a friendly relationship and wanted to keep things civil. Shelly hired me with the clear understanding that I was not to inflame or exacerbate any conflicts. Phil hired Amy Eisenberg, a New York attorney who, like me, is ready to punch it out when needed but equally happy to have a rational and civilized discussion. I've had many cases with Amy over the years and we enjoy a healthy balance of respect for and fear of each other.

Phil handled the couple's financial affairs during the marriage. His skills in the detail-oriented art of clock repair served them well: He was precise and organized. He kept handwritten ledgers of various account balances and expenditures and made sure that the bills were paid in full and on time and monthly statements reconciled.

As part of the divorce action, I requested that Shelly, like any client, provide me with as much information as possible regarding the marital finances. It's important that I know the size of the pie before I can advise how we might cut it up. Shelly told me that Phil was in charge of the financial records and that she believed he could be trusted to provide me with the detailed accounting I was looking for. I called Amy, who agreed to share with me the asset information she too had requested of Phil.

"See that, Amy! We just saved these people a few thousand dollars and they don't even know it."

"I'm not sure if that's evidence to support the fact we're ethical attorneys or just stupid," replied Amy.

A few weeks later, we were getting ready for a finalization meeting at Amy's office. After a brief negotiation, we had agreed on who would keep what (Shelly, the house and the 401(k); Phil, the business and the Roth IRAs), I had written the agreement up, Amy had made some changes, and now Shelly and Phil were ready to sit down in a conference room and finish up the paperwork. As we were reviewing the documents, Shelly said, "Oh, by the way, Phil, I found us sixty-five thousand dollars."

This caught Phil's attention immediately. "What?"

"Sixty-five thousand, seven hundred and sixty-nine dollars and forty-seven cents, to be exact," Shelly replied.

"Are you serious?"

Amy and I looked at each other, also puzzled.

"Yep," Shelly said, smiling. "Remember we got that life insurance policy for you when Chris was born and they took the premiums out of my account every month until we sold our first house, and we paid it off so I wouldn't have that deduction every month?"

Phil chuckled in recollection. "Oh yeah! I remember that. Oh, wow. That's so funny. That policy has cash value?"

"Apparently so! When I got all the paperwork from your lawyer, I thought it would be smart to put it all on the computer so I can keep track of it better, now that you're not going to be balancing my checkbook for me. Turns out the insurance policy is tied to the bank account still, even though it doesn't make withdrawals anymore for premiums, and when I created the online account it showed me the cash value. So we each get an extra thirty-two thousand dollars we weren't expecting."

Phil was impressed. So were Amy and I.

"Well, look at you!" Phil laughed. "I guess I'm getting a new bike."

"What you do with it is your business now, Phil," Shelly teased. "I probably should have kept my mouth shut and kept the extra cash."

We all laughed at that last bit—but Amy and I were acutely aware that 99.9 percent of clients would have done exactly that.

Phil and Shelly signed their documents and, with a few swipes of a pen, ended the legal aspects of their twenty-four-year union. As Amy and I left (to get off the clock as fast as possible), they were both huddled over Shelly's computer screen at the conference table. Shelly was showing Phil how the online interface of their longtime bank could be used to reconcile with QuickBooks and, in a good-natured tone, teasing him about how his ledger system was "way more confusing" than it needed to be.

Shelly turned out to be very good at bookkeeping, though it wasn't a skill she'd exercised during the marriage. I wasn't surprised: The skills needed to manage the lives of two active children and a household—attention to detail, an ability to identify shortcuts—are many of the same skills that make for a good bookkeeper (or ninja, for that matter). Phil, even with the best of intentions, had fallen into routines that ignored technological advances. When Shelly's fresh eyes were forced to look at the marital finances, she could see things Phil had been staring at but had ignored over the years.

I don't believe, not for a second, that Shelly and Phil's marriage would have survived had she assumed the role of financial manager of their shared home before the divorce required her to become adept. They were ultimately incompatible as spouses, though comparatively well-suited as friends and co-parents.

But theirs is a good example of how a couple can fall into roles that evolve into habits. Those roles may, at the time they are formed, make sense based on available data. They also may, as the marriage continues, make less sense or even become nonsensical.

Occasionally shifting roles in the marriage is a potential win-win for even the happiest couple. At best, it gives each partner insight into what the other is doing, potentially creating new approaches to tasks. At worst, it reinforces why each spouse has fallen into the existing roles and routines (because the other one sucks at that task), and ensures that neither party knows nothing about anything and both parties know something about everything. Everybody should do something about everything, and neither of you should do everything about anything.

That last sentence is a mouthful—but you get the point.

## Chapter 25

# WHAT YOU'RE GETTING AND WHAT YOU'RE GIVING

My client Emily's soon-to-be ex, a high-end carpenter named Walter who makes beautiful bookshelves and coat racks out of reclaimed lumber, was a complete idiot—or maybe just horribly unlucky. You decide: After more than a year of denials to an increasingly suspicious Emily that he was cheating on her, and leaving no concrete evidence to the contrary, Walter, in an improbable collection of circumstances, finally got caught with another woman, at a Toby Keith concert, on the jumbotron screen that was, unbeknownst to Walter, nationally broadcast live on Country Music Television.

Within half an hour, three of Emily's friends had called to tell her.

The lesson? No one should ever go to a Toby Keith concert.

Okay, seriously: Is there another lesson?

How does that incident provide a grain of insight into relationships? (Aside from the seemingly obvious, "Never conduct an affair in full view of television cameras.")

Foremost, it's yet another example of the endless knuckleheadedness that all people are capable of in their search for connection, love, desire. But I also included it so I could talk about Emily's misplaced sense of entitlement during the divorce proceeding, and the lesson it might provide others.

For all his failings as a husband (not just infidelity but also bad choices in facial hair* and two terribly disrespectful teenage daughters from a prior marriage), Walter had considerable skills and talents as a carpenter and handyman; as a result, the house he and Emily shared was well-maintained, and he was always creating and refining cool little fixes to household glitches. Emily might remark that "it would be nice" to have a little hook by the bathroom sink where she could hang a hand towel and, *poof!,* a day later there would appear a perfectly positioned, well-secured hook made from wood that matched the sink cabinet.

During the divorce, Emily, who had obtained exclusive possession and occupancy of the house while the action was pending, accidentally dropped a fork down the garbage disposal while it was running, and she was ill-prepared, solo, to address the resulting flameout under the sink.

After almost two decades of marriage, she expected that some things should stay the same: She actually believed that her estranged husband would—*should*—come over to fix the sink. No matter how great her anger at him, and how broken their current level of communication, she felt entitled to this.

"He always fixed everything that broke at the house," Emily rationalized to me, "and technically we still co-own the place until the divorce is finalized." She was indignant when Walter told her plainly that no, he was not coming over to fix the sink in the house she had kicked him out of three weeks earlier. (Walter was living in a motel and wearing mismatched clothing from Walmart after Emily had burned all his favorite T-shirts with various country-western singers on them. The Toby Keiths had been the first aflame.)

No, Emily was not entitled to this aspect of her husband anymore. Yet it took her a few minutes to believe me when I pointed out this fairly obvious fact.

(If he *wanted* to fix things, of course he could; if he was still in love

---

* I've lost count of the number of female clients who have shared with me how much they secretly detested their ex- or soon-to-be ex-husband's facial hair. This does not merit its own chapter, but here's a freebie: If she dated and married you when you were clean-shaven, don't grow a mustache or beard afterward. And it doesn't matter what facial hair you had when you got married, under no circumstances should you ever grow a goatee. Just telling you what I hear.

with her, he might. In the movie *Crazy, Stupid, Love,* Steve Carrell's character, who has always done the gardening in the marriage, slips onto the grounds at night to prune and water the plants surrounding the family home, now occupied by his estranged wife and their kids.)

Emily's response got me thinking about an entitlement mind-set. How many things, both little and big, do we rely on our spouse or partner for in our day-to-day life? From making your morning tea so it's waiting, fully steeped, when you wake up, to bringing *The New York Times* in from the doorstep—do you realize how inconvenient or off-putting it would be to suddenly have to do for yourself the things your spouse or partner does for you? Can you imagine, after a divorce, calling to complain that they didn't come over to make the tea and fetch the paper?

"Um, it's seven thirty a.m. and I'm drinking out of an empty cup like an idiot, Harold . . . Harold?"

When you're married, especially if you've been married for a long time, you take for granted what you get from your spouse. Often, you stop being sufficiently grateful for it, or even thinking about it. (Meanwhile, divorcing couples are very clear on what it is they *don't* get, or get only insufficiently, from their partner.) For partners who've been together a while, how do you guard against slipping into the entitlement mind-set?

Sit down and write a list of all the things your spouse does for you.

Is it hard to do? Did you ever stop and think about it?

You can go big or small. You can start with the big ones, such as companionship, conversation, sex, or you can get more logistical—"picks up the kids," "takes out the trash."

Hopefully, the list isn't limited to "takes out the trash." I bet you'll be surprised at how much your spouse does. What would you miss if they were suddenly gone from your life or from the home you share together? If we humans, as Joni Mitchell suggested, "don't know what you've got / Till it's gone," perhaps some imagining of that loss, while we still have what we have, is in order.

## Chapter 26

# THE MYTH OF THE
# PERFECT PARENT

Why am I so sure that there's no one out there even close to a perfect parent? Is it because my clients are such consistently imperfect parents? No. Is it because I'm no perfect parent, and I'm projecting? No. (I mean, I'm not close to a perfect parent, but . . . no.)

I'm sure there are no perfect parents because it's my professional responsibility, like it or not, to sometimes make good parenting seem like less-than-good parenting.

If by this point in the book you're feeling slightly less natural antipathy toward divorce lawyers, I fear all that good feeling is about to go out the window. Because this is the part where cultural hatred for divorce lawyers comes out in full bloom, even if we're just doing the job we were hired to do.

Some background is important. The best attorneys, on cross-examination, don't wait for people to break down and admit their wrongdoing, as when Tom Cruise's character takes apart Jack Nicholson's in *A Few Good Men.* I've had a moment like that happen only twice in my career. (And as amazing as it was to see, my strategy had been only to get the witness to the breaking *point,* not see them actually break.) In the best cross-examinations, the lawyer sets up questions to ensure that whatever answer the witness gives is the "wrong" answer. When I do it, I aim to get the witness to commit to a set of principles that they could not possibly disagree with (to do so would make them look like a horrible parent and an outlier), then ask them to confirm a variety of facts that run contrary to the principles they just committed to.

For example: I was on the second day of Michael Swanson's cross-examination. Michael was married to Gretchen, my client, with whom he had a nine-year-old son. Both parents were seeking primary legal custody (essentially, veto power in the event of disagreements on any major issues related to the child's educational, medical, and religious development).

"Mr. Swanson, your child's education is important to you, isn't it?"

"Yes."

*Of course he says yes. He has to say yes. What's he going to say—"Not really?" "It's only recently important to me since I've been in custody litigation? Before that it was just above my wife's general happiness and just below my bracket picks during NCAA March Madness?"*

"Vitally important, yes?"

"Yes."

*It's always good to get the emphasis.*

"And of course you would do everything in your power to make sure they get that education, correct?"

"Yes."

*Of course you would. Why wouldn't you? I try to ask these questions in an almost indignant tone, as if to anticipate he will answer in the affirmative as only a total scumbag wouldn't.*

"And you have concerns about my client's commitment to ensuring that the children get that education, is that right?"

"Yes."

*Sometimes, for effect, I look over at my client or gesture toward her when I ask that one. And I deliberately phrase the question mildly, so that the concern sounds entirely reasonable. Again, this is the part where the witness is supposed to be comfortable and committing. At this point, if I'm doing it right, he's thinking I'm a bad lawyer and he's super-excited that he's getting to reiterate his concerns. This man does not watch* Law and Order.

"And, in sum and substance, without disparaging her parenting, you think you can handle overseeing educational responsibilities for your son better than she can. Is that right?"

"Yes. That's right."

"And, sir, you aren't new to this whole parenting thing, are you? I mean, you've been involved in your son's education his whole life, isn't that right?"

"Absolutely."

*If Michael says no, he's hurting his argument that he's not a Johnny-come-lately father. So he has to say yes. Everyone wants to brag about what a good parent they are!*

"So you aren't just speculating when you say you could handle overseeing your son's education. This isn't just a theory. You've been actively involved in his education for years. Isn't that right?"

*Again, what's he going to say? "No, I just got involved once I was served with divorce papers and realized I would be subject to scrutiny."*

"So, for example, sir, your son had difficulties in math last year. Isn't that correct?"

"Yes."

*I know, I gave him that one. Trust me on this. I watch* Law and Order.

"And when you realized he was having these issues, you and your wife took steps to address it. Is that correct?"

"That's right. He got a tutor."

*I know Michael knew about the math tutor. He complained to my client about the expense a few times by email. That's why I'm giving him these softball questions. He's loving this.*

"And what's his tutor's name?"

"Ben Kippler," Michael replied immediately, with a smile.

*Oh no! He remembered the tutor's name! I must have been hoping he wouldn't. I even try to look surprised that he remembered it. " 'Come into my parlor,' said the spider to the fly . . ."*

I deliberately paused and look at my notes, as if I was expecting him not to know that one and am a little thrown off.

"And his math grades have improved since he got that tutor, haven't they?"

"Yes. They have. I mean . . . he's not going to be a mathematician anytime soon. I fear he inherited my math skills."

*Go ahead, Michael. Try to charm the judge. It's going to make what's coming stand out all the more in contrast.*

"Now, when he had difficulties in science last year, did you get him a tutor also?"

Michael was on a roll now and feeling confident. "No. We didn't think that was necessary."

"I see. So what did you do, personally, to address his science performance?"

"I helped him with his homework, talked to the teacher, just kept an eye on things and made sure he was doing his best."

*Here we go.*

"And you said you spoke to Mr. Ryerson, his science teacher?"

"Yes."

"And what did you discuss, if you recall?"

"I don't really remember. It was quite a few months ago. Just his overall performance."

"Did you have those discussions in person or on the phone?"

"Both."

"Did you meet Mr. Ryerson at parent-teacher night?"

*I know he didn't attend.*

"No. I had a work obligation that night. But I met him on other occasions, and we emailed and spoke on the phone, as I do with all my son's teachers."

"Thank you, sir, but right now I'd like to focus on Mr. Ryerson. You spoke to him on the phone?"

"Yes."

"More than once?"

"Yes. I don't remember how many times, but at least a few times."

"What about Ms. Schlesinger, his history teacher this year? Have you spoken to her?"

"Yes."

"Have you met with her concerning your son's poor performance in history this year?"

"Yes."

*Pause for effect.*

"Now, sir, do you realize that Mr. Ryerson, the science teacher you claim to have met and spoken with several times, is actually Kathleen Ryerson, a woman?"

"I'm sorry?"

*Umm . . . I think you heard me.*

"I kept referring to Mr. Ryerson as a man—and you kept agreeing with me, and using male pronouns—but you never corrected me. The person I was calling Mr. Ryerson is, in fact, a woman, isn't she? Kathleen Ryerson, your son's math teacher."

*Okay. He's doing damage control in his brain right now.*

"Yes. I was a little confused when you were saying it, but I didn't want to correct you."

"Well, I appreciate that, sir, but in the future you can feel free to correct me if needed. Ideally, your testimony should be accurate, as it's under oath and all."

"Okay."

"Any other corrections you need to make?"

"No."

"What about Ms. Schlesinger, the history teacher you met and spoke with?"

"What about her?" Michael asked reluctantly.

"Did I get that one right?"

"What do you mean?"

"Is your son's history teacher a woman or a man?"

*He's done.*

"I'm not sure. I would need to look at the names."

"I'm sorry, Mr. Swanson, you would need to look at a list of names to determine if a teacher you've met with and spoken to several times is a man or a woman? You've got one child and he's got four teachers right now, one of whom we've already just discussed and confirmed, after some debate, is, in fact, female. Do you really not recall if his history teacher is a man or woman?"

"I don't really remember right now."

*I know it's one of the two. Does that help?*

"Okay. Let's move on. Now I'm sure you can agree, sir, that for your son to do well at school he must, at a minimum, be in school. Is that fair to say?"

"Obviously."

"And to that end, if you had primary physical custody of him as you are requesting, you would get him to school on time with his assignments completed. Is that correct?"

"Yes."

"And you have concerns that my client would be unwilling or unable to do so. Is that also correct?"

"Yes."

"Now in reviewing your son's attendance records for the past three months, your son has been marked tardy on nine occasions. Are you aware of that?"

"Yes. I'm worried about that. She's got him most of the time right now."

"I see, sir. So you're concerned that she's going to continue this pattern of lateness for your son and it's going to have a negative impact on his best interests. Is that right?"

"Yes."

*Pause for effect.*

"I would like to have this marked for identification as Plaintiff's Five, please."

I handed the court officer a piece of paper from the school records we'd subpoenaed. It was marked and shown to the witness.

"Now, Mr. Swanson, I show you what's been marked as Plaintiff's Five. That's your son's attendance record for the past three months, isn't it?"

He examined it carefully, trying to process it quickly and figure out where it fit into his testimony.

"Yes. That's what it looks like."

"And you see the key at the bottom right: That's where it has what stands for what?"

"Yes."

"And 'A' means absent, 'T' means tardy, and no marking means your son showed up on time and all good, right?"

"Correct."

"Now, sir, you testified a few moments ago that you have great concerns based on your son's tardiness on nine occasions in the past three months. You recall that testimony?"

*You should. It was, like, four minutes ago.*

"Yes. But those aren't my only concerns."

*Thanks, Michael. Do that. The more you try to get cute and answer something other than the questions I ask you, the guiltier you're going to look here.*

"Thank you, sir, but I didn't ask you that. I asked you, specifically, about your statement, a few minutes ago, under oath, that you had concerns that my client wasn't getting your son to school on time and that it was potentially having a negative impact on his best interests. Do you recall saying that?"

"Yes."

"Now, reviewing that document, sir, isn't it true that all the tardy markings for the past three months are on Tuesday mornings?"

He took a moment to look at the attendance record it and digest this.

"That's what it says."

I paused. "That's the official school record, isn't it?"

"Yes."

"So you don't have any reason to think they got it wrong, do you?"

"No."

"So in the past three months, how many Tuesday mornings have there been total?"

Michael didn't answer, so I continued.

"I know you said earlier that math isn't your strong suit—so I won't quiz you on it. There have been twelve Tuesday mornings in the past three months. Isn't that right?"

"Yes."

"And your son has been late to school on nine of those twelve, isn't that right?"

"Yes."

"And, sir"—I paused here for effect—"isn't it correct that you have your son for overnight parenting time on Monday nights every week?"

"Yes."

"And thus you're the one who gets him to school on Tuesday mornings. Isn't that right?"

"Yes."

"The one who gets him to school *late* on Tuesday mornings. Isn't that right?"

"Not every Tuesday morning."

"I'm sorry. You're right. I'll rephrase. You're the one who gets him to school late on seventy-five percent of Tuesday mornings, isn't *that* correct?"

*Game. Set. Match.*

There are a few lessons to be learned from all this (aside from, *"Shit, I'm 166 pages into this book and actually thought I could find a reason to like a divorce lawyer. Nope."*):

1.  *It's easy to express commitment to a principle; it's tougher, and more important, to ask yourself whether your actions demonstrate that commitment.* It's child's play to attack someone's parenting (or behavior as a spouse) on the witness stand, as I did—just get them to state (or agree with), in broad terms, a principle the individual claims to be committed to ("I want my wife to be happy"; "I want to be fair"; "I care about my child's safety"), then demonstrate, in painful detail, how their behavior undermines their credibility and belies that commitment ("So then why did you send her this insulting email?"; "So why did you remove money from this account?"; "So why did you post a selfie on Instagram while

driving with your child in the car?"). It's important to reflect, from time to time, on how your behaviors match up with your stated ideologies. This kind of reflection would ideally take place well before you end up in a situation where your behavior might be subject to scrutiny (for instance, on a witness stand, in a divorce or custody action).

2. *Don't lie. Or if you're going to lie, don't lie to yourself.* The most dangerous lies are the ones we tell ourselves. We don't want to look at the role our own behaviors play in our failings (in our successes, sure), so we tend, by my observation, to claim responsibility for our wins and blame the losses on conditions beyond our control or on the failings of others. I understand the desire. It feels good to create a worldview in which you have to own only the victories. But it's a dangerous way to approach the rocky terrain of marriage and parenting. It's far better, on and off any witness stand, to be painfully honest with yourself about what you've done, what you could be doing, and what you sometimes failed to do.

3. *There's no such thing as a perfect parent, so don't make yourself crazy.* Is this one of those moments where I contradict my own advice? I just said that you should worry more about what you're doing and how it matches up with your stated principles . . . and now I'm saying not to pay too much attention? I don't see the inconsistency. I've cross-examined hundreds of people about their parenting, and I can confirm that if you scrutinize them closely enough, *every parent screws something up.* Every parent could parent better. Not one could survive an hour on the witness stand with a good trial lawyer without looking as if they've got a few things to learn about how to parent.

I can take precisely the same behaviors and spin them to make someone look like the best or worst parent in the world. Let's take sleeping in the bed with your children:

"Your Honor, the subject child in this custody dispute is so closely bonded to my client that he sees him as a shelter in the storm. When he has nightmares, the child takes comfort in the simple presence of my client, sneaking into his daddy's bedroom and tucking into bed with him—to find safety and comfort. And my client, knowing full well that this lovely little boy kicks like a mule in his sleep, puts his own comfort and rest second to ensuring that this child grows up knowing the security of a loving parent who is there for him in times of fear and need."

Or, if his ex is paying me: "Your Honor, it's been brought to my client's attention that the defendant has been allowing the parties' young son to sleep in the former marital bed with him at night. I'm not sure if this is a way to sequester the child from my client at night, as she is now sleeping in the guest room, or if there's something more disquieting here, but I think we can all agree that it's inappropriate for a middle-aged man to be pressed up against a toddler, sleeping in his boxer shorts, in the former marital bed where the child was conceived. Further, Your Honor, it's irresponsible for the defendant to prevent the child from developing age-appropriate coping mechanisms and learning how to sleep independently by infantilizing the child with this kind of behavior."

Don't beat yourself up for your inevitable parenting deficits. Parenting is a tough gig. Yes, there are lots of ways you can screw up—but there are also lots and lots of ways to be okay as a parent, maybe more than you think.

If you do your best, then you can be sure that you've done your best, which already puts you way up there, as parents go.

Oh: And, if possible, stay off the witness stand.

## Chapter 27

# YOU DIVORCE WHO
# YOU MARRIED

"I'm not sure why I'm here."

I get that a lot during the initial consult. From women more often than men.

Other things I hear a lot, in the first moments of the first meeting:

"I'm not sure if I actually want to get divorced or if I just want to understand what my rights are. Things haven't been good and I'm not sure what direction we're going in at this point." (You may not know, but I do. We all do.)

"I cheated."

"She cheated."

"He secretly squandered all our savings."

"Her drinking is out of control."

"I can't stand his family."

"I'm just not happy."

"I just can't do this anymore."

But whatever the stated cause for their presence in that brown leather chair across from my desk, with the bowl of candy and box of tissues placed conveniently within reach, the troubled individual typically asks, at some point, "Should we go to counseling?"

That usually follows the "not sure why I'm here" declaration, though not always in the initial consultation. Sometimes it's said weeks later, after they've retained me but before I've fired the first shot over the bow. Sometimes it's said after the jarring reality of the first court appearance, and the first time my client hears a court bailiff say, "Number Four on the morning calendar: Johnson versus Johnson" (at least when your last name is Johnson).

"Should we go to counseling?"

That's like standing over your car after it's been totaled, and asking, "Should we get AAA in case we get into an accident?"

I'm sorry to tell you that, in my opinion, the answer is no (to both questions).

The traits you need to fix the marriage are, unfortunately, the traits that would have been required to prevent it from breaking in the first place.

I would ask you to read that sentence again. It's important.

When a marriage is broken to the point that you're in a divorce lawyer's office, there's a long list of things that may have brought you there: infidelity, money issues, substance abuse, dishonesty, discourtesy, impatience, narcissism, avarice, sloth, untreated mental health issues, aggressive stupidity—pick your poison.

But the list of things that have the potential to pull you back from the brink is, in my estimation, a whole lot shorter: patience, rational discourse, profound empathy, and, perhaps above all else, the ability to forgive and forget.*

I would argue that those are the traits that, if possessed by your partner and you in sufficient quantities, would have prevented you from ending up in the situation you're currently in. (Indeed, if I were bold enough to join all those cocksure people who write books about what makes a good, lasting union, as opposed to my book here about what I know makes a bad one, I'd probably say that those assets just named are always in healthy supply in both individuals.) You can try to bolster or build those traits in yourself with the specific goal of fixing what's broken in

---

\* My mother imparted a lot of commonsense wisdom to me. The two most profound thoughts: "The hard thing to do and the right thing to do are usually the same thing" and "The forgiveness is in the forgetting."

your marriage . . . but, to repeat: Had those traits been part of your core relationship with this person from the start, you wouldn't be where you are right now. Or: If your spouse was capable of the kind of empathy, forgiveness, and affection needed to turn a broken marriage into a fixed and functional one, they would probably have applied those traits to the marriage to begin with. Right? And it wouldn't be broken—right?

An example:

Colleen didn't mean to fuck the intern.

Okay, rewind the tape a little. Colleen had been working for nearly two decades as a middle manager in the risk management department of a major insurance company (the irony wasn't lost on me), about as secure as one can be in present-day America. Kevin was an editor at a financial publication. So the jobs weren't what you'd call glamorous, but they paid well, with matching 401(k)s. Colleen and Kevin had been married for fifteen years, with three kids: twins, aged twelve, and a little one, two. (His nickname might have been "Whoops!," though he went, more conventionally, by Ryan.)

The Intern was twenty. He had the body of a swimmer and though he wore neatly pressed khakis to the office every day, his haircut was that of a surfer from La Jolla. He was not old enough to drink. Colleen and her women colleagues joked about how adorable he was and how they all gave a little more attention to their posture when the Intern was coming around for Starbucks orders on Friday mornings.

Colleen was one of the first women in the office ever to actually speak to the Intern (beyond ordering a Frappuccino), and the only one to initiate a substantive conversation with him. It started with simple chat—the weather, where to park—but, within a few weeks, moved to comparing weekend plans and favorite movies.

Talking to the Intern reminded Colleen of something. She couldn't put her finger on precisely what, but she knew it was something familiar and something she liked. Perhaps it was how she felt when she was his age. Perhaps it was how she felt when she was younger and single and felt like a prize waiting to be won by a seemingly endless succession of charming young men, offering their best reasons as to why they should be considered a contender. Maybe it was just the swimmer's body.

Colleen didn't have any plans to cheat on her husband. If you had asked her, six months before, if she would ever cheat on Kevin, she would have told you no without hesitation. She was content with her life. She was happy with her family. Her relationship wasn't terribly exciting any-more, but she was comfortable with that and felt she had enjoyed her share of exciting relationships during her college and grad school years. Stable was the new sexy, and Kevin was nothing if not stable.

Then Betty from accounting announced her retirement. It was company tradition to take any departing employee out for drinks at O'Shanahan's, the local Irish pub. The Intern sat next to Colleen at a table for two dozen people. Nobody thought much of it, including the Intern and Colleen.

After several hours and several drinks the party broke up and the Intern, who had been raised properly, offered to walk Colleen back to her car. It's unclear to Colleen, even to this day, who initiated the kiss, but she admits that it was clear both of them were willing participants. Maybe he wasn't raised properly.

On the drive home, Colleen promised herself that the kiss was an isolated incident. She wasn't interested in hurting anyone (including, but not limited to, herself, Kevin, and the Intern). It just happened. It wasn't a big deal. It didn't mean anything. It was only a kiss.

Within two weeks they were fucking in her car in the parking lot. Twenty-year-olds are, apparently, very romantic.

It's unclear, in retrospect, which was more surprising to Colleen: the amount of legroom available for sex when you fold down the backseat of a Jeep Grand Cherokee Laredo, or how easy it is to inadvertently leave your phone face up on your husband's side of the sink when you're in the shower and get a text from the Intern commenting on "how good your body felt next to mine last night."

Colleen broke it off with the Intern immediately, but the damage was already, and profoundly, done. Kevin was furious, when he wasn't devastated. For the first few weeks, he was brutal in his grilling of Colleen, demanding details and scrutinizing every word of every admission. He replayed every moment of the past few months, trying to re-create a timeline of the infidelity. Colleen had hoped (naïvely, if you ask me) that this kind of honesty might lead to healing, particularly as it had come at Kevin's request; it seemed only to fuel his anger.

Six months later, life had returned to something like normal—but frequently, and with little discernible pattern, Kevin would suddenly seethe with hostility and throw the affair in Colleen's face whenever he needed a trump card to justify his own imperfections.

When Kevin stayed out much later than expected, or came home drunker than someone who was operating a car should? "At least I wasn't out fucking a girl at work." He forgot to get the twins the insurance forms they needed for baseball registration, so Colleen left him a note to bring them home from work. His response? "Sorry I'm not super focused right now. I've had some things on my mind ever since you've been fucking people at your office."

After about a year of doing weekly (sometimes daily) penance for her sin, Colleen had reached her limit. She didn't care anymore if the affair was her fault. She had said she was sorry every way she thought she knew how. She had tried to show Kevin that she was committed to the marriage and to their partnership and that her dalliance with the Intern was a mistake—nothing more, nothing less. She did all the right things: She apologized, she accepted the blame for her behavior, she was patient, she was empathetic. She was available to Kevin. She didn't know what else she could do, but she couldn't stay married if her marriage was going to be like this forever.

And now she was in my office. She had already told Kevin that she was seeing a lawyer to talk about "next steps," but now she was having second thoughts.

"Should we go to counseling?" she asked.

I told her to give it a try. Who am I to encourage the demise of a marriage? (Okay, I know.) Particularly one with children involved? I gave her the name of a good therapist who focuses much of his practice on work with couples. Within a month, Colleen was back at my teakwood table.

"We've been working with the therapist," she said, "but nothing is getting any better. Kevin is still as angry as he was the day he found out about the affair, and he's nastier to me than ever. Should we stay in counseling?"

"I don't know," I told her.

I wanted to say, "No. Just quit. It's over. It's dead, and I know it hurts to have to admit that and bury it. But you're only making it worse for both of you trying to pretend it isn't."

I wanted to say, "To get past this, you and Kevin would both need to be deeply committed to your partnership, willing to concede your respective roles and responsibilities in creating the conditions under which this affair happened, and your individual culpability in creating the disconnect between you that left room for the Intern to become even vaguely appealing.

"To get past this, you and Kevin would both need, in large part, to forget what had happened and put down the pain it caused you both—the pain you inflicted on Kevin, and the pain you inflicted on yourself. You'd have to address the way your affair changed Kevin's perception of your love for him and the way it changed your perception of yourself.

"To get past this, you and Kevin would both need to want your marriage to work, want it so badly that you would devote the time and attention required to deconstruct the way the distance between you was created, and to develop specific, quantifiable strategies to prevent it from happening in the future. You would need to be brutally honest with each other about how you were feeling about yourselves, each other, and the marriage (as three different entities) and what you thought, from time to time, you needed from each other to optimize the way all three were functioning.

"In other words, Colleen, you and Kevin would each need to possess the kind of traits and skills regarding this relationship (and each other) that, had they already existed between you, would have prevented this kind of thing from happening in the first place.

"And you didn't. Because you couldn't. Because that's not what you have together. Sorry."

Love can be brutal.

That's what I *wanted* to say.

## Chapter 28

# GRATUITOUS TIME-OUT: THE CASE OF THE SHRINKING PENIS

I'm pretty sure the following story provides zero relationship insight. Then again, you can't eat just broccoli. Every now and then we need a candy bar, right? And by "candy bar," I mean "penis story." If you believe a higher purpose is required, I'm sure I could come up with some underlying principle that justifies the telling. I just can't think of one at the moment. So. Here it is. The penis story.

Sana wanted her marriage annulled.

This is something divorce lawyers rarely encounter. In eighteen years of practice, I've done approximately twelve hundred divorces and three annulments. When I was starting out as an attorney, my mentor was an incredible divorce lawyer named Bill Frank; he managed to enjoy a thriving forty-year career without ever handling a single annulment.

Sana had met her husband, Fazal, through an online matchmaking service for religious Sunni Muslims. At the time, he lived in Pakistan. The matchmaking service's algorithm suggested that they were exceptionally well-suited, particularly astrologically. Sana and Fazal decided, through their online communication, that they should be together. She was thirty-six and had never been married. Fazal, thirty-three, arrived in the United States, they met for the very first time, and within forty-eight hours they were husband and wife.

Two weeks later, Fazal withdrew more than half the money from his new wife's bank account and moved out, apparently never to be heard from again.

Now Sana was in my office wanting an annulment.

"We can annul the marriage only if we can prove very specific and limited grounds, like fraud in the inducement," I told her. "That means we have to prove, not know, *prove* by a preponderance of the evidence, in court, that Fazal made a material misrepresentation of fact prior to the marriage. It has to be something big. Like he said he was a certain religion and he's actually not. Or he wants to have children but, in fact, he knew he's sterile. And fraud is, from an evidentiary standpoint, very hard to prove. Plus, an annulment can't be granted on default—that means we have to find Fazal, have him served with papers, and proceed with a hearing. If you don't know where he is, it's a logistical nightmare."

She looked at me like I was trying to sell her a used car.

"I'm giving you advice that's good for you and bad for me," I continued. "Getting you an annulment will be more labor-intensive and take longer, greatly increasing your legal fees—all with the goal of not having to be married to this guy. I can help you to reach that goal a lot faster with a divorce than an annulment. I don't have to find him; I can serve him with notice in a local newspaper, in that back section of legal notices that nobody ever reads. When he doesn't show up, we move for a default and then immediately to an inquest, basically a trial where the other side doesn't show and you get what you're asking for, unopposed. Bang. Done. Easy. Five grand instead of fifty grand."

Sana was quiet, but her expression remained skeptical. "I don't want a divorce," she said. "I want it that I was never married. That's very important to me." In her culture, as in many, the distinction is important. Then she said, "The marriage was never consummated."

While helpful, such a fact was almost certainly even harder to prove than fraud. How do you verify that you never had sex with someone? It's difficult to prove a negative. Particularly when the act in question takes place in private and leaves little evidence other than occasional STDs and pregnancy. And the absence of an STD or pregnancy doesn't prove the absence of sex.

Still, I promised Sana I would do all I could to get an annulment. We filed an "action for annulment." (The clerk commented that it was the first one she had seen in years.) I figured that, after what he'd done to Sana—coming to this country on a probably false pretense, largely emptying her bank account, and fleeing—Fazal wouldn't fight the case, if he had a shred of decency. Plus, an annulment, as I'd told her, also requires a finding of fraud, and if the marriage was proven fraudulent, then Fazal could be deported. Sana knew he wanted to stay in the United States. He wasn't going to want to be found, period.

So now I had an adversary with an incentive to fight. He was unlikely to go quietly. Normally I would enjoy the prospect, but I had a problem of proof, and not the kind I could remedy with fast talk and folksy metaphors.

It took two months for my private investigators to find Fazal. He was living in Wisconsin and working at a restaurant. George Colby, my favorite investigator, an ex-cop whom I'd represented in his own divorce a decade earlier, served Fazal with the papers himself. George was perfect for it: He's afraid of no one, he loves a challenging case, and his old-school-gentleman streak causes him to view himself a chivalrous knight in shining armor for the firm's female clients. A few days after he returned, he told me gleefully about how he "shocked the shit" out of Fazal, who appeared to believe he would never be found and kept saying over and over, in his heavy accent, "How you did find me? How you did find me? This isn't me! You have the wrong man!"

Three months later, we got our day in court. Fazal, wearing a suit, was present. He had chosen the always prudent legal strategy of representing himself.

Under oath, Fazal testified that his marriage to Sana had been legitimate. They'd just decided to split up shortly after it was consummated, is all. He brought "evidence" of the legitimacy of their marriage: photographs of them together in New York City just before the wedding (purportedly to prove their courtship), a few photos of the ceremony. None of this, mind you, was proof of a legitimate marriage, but, even as a non-lawyer, Fazal must have known that our "proof" regarding his intentions was entirely circumstantial, and he had the common sense to fight fire with fire.

Under my initial cross-examination, on the first day of the hearing, Fazal reiterated his claim that the marriage had been consummated. I asked him, specifically, if he meant that he and my client had had sexual relations. He confirmed that that was what he meant.

So this wasn't a matter of differing perspectives. They both couldn't be telling the truth. One of them was lying.

After we left the courtroom, with a two-week break in testimony to accommodate the judge's Acapulco vacation, I reiterated my concerns to Sana. "I still think you might consider going for the divorce. I don't know how we're going to prove, by a preponderance of the evidence, that the marriage was never consummated and you two never had sex. He's saying you did. It's your word against his."

"We never did," she insisted.

It's almost quaint when clients express shock that someone could lie on the witness stand. I want to tousle their hair when they say things like "But that's a lie!" People lie on the witness stand all the time. It's a wooden box. It's not Wonder Woman's Lasso of Truth.

"I believe you, Sana. But how do we prove it? I'm a lawyer. It doesn't matter what I know. It matters only what I can prove."

"I'm a virgin."

I tried to hide my surprise and just kept walking. "Okay, well," I started, regaining my footing, "it's a long shot, but if we're going to prove your virginity, you need to go to your gynecologist and see if your hymen is still intact. If it is, then it's game, set, match, because Fazal perjured himself. If it isn't, we have to roll up shop and think about going for the divorce."

I was not confident about what Sana would find out, and even less so after I called a friend who's an ob-gyn.

"What are the chances a thirty-six-year-old virgin has her hymen still intact?" I asked.

"Almost none," my friend said. She told me that the hymen can break during menstruation, during the insertion of a tampon, during exercise, or for a host of other reasons. Plus, my friend continued, as a woman ages, the hymen thins, becoming increasingly likely to break. There was almost no way it was still intact at thirty-six.

Two weeks later, my office manager buzzed me to say that Sana was in the conference room, crying hysterically.

"Okay, okay," I said when I got there, "I know this is hard to accept, but it isn't the end of things. It was a long shot. It was worth a try. But we both knew it was a real possibility that your hymen would be broken for a host of nonsexual reasons—"

"No, it's intact!" said Sana, through her tears. "*That's* why I'm crying."

They were tears of relief.

*Holy shit,* I thought. *Okay, then. Game on, motherfucker. This case just got fun.*

A little more than a week later, we found ourselves back in the courtroom, sitting next to a largely uninterested but decidedly tanner Judge Greyson. My excitement was hard to contain. I put Sana on the stand.

"Ms. Krinanan, you heard the defendant testify, on his direct examination, that you and he had sexual intercourse. Do you recall that testimony?"

"Yes."

"Was that true?"

"No."

"Now, ma'am, is it your testimony, under oath, that you never had sexual intercourse with the plaintiff?"

"Never."

"Are you certain?"

"Yes."

"Did you ever engage in any sexual activity with him?"

"No. We kissed before we got married, and the night after our wedding ceremony we slept in the same bed, next to each other, but we did not have sex. We did not even take our clothes off."

I paused for effect.

"I have nothing further, Your Honor."

The judge's body language made it clear that she was ready to wrap things up. While this was a novel proceeding, it was the usual "he said, she said" dynamic that judges in matrimonial cases deal with every day.*

"Any further witnesses, Mr. Sexton, or does the plaintiff rest?"

I smiled. This was part showmanship and part genuine amusement over what I knew was coming next.

"Your Honor, the plaintiff would like to recall the defendant to the stand." Fazal strolled casually into the box and raised his right hand once again to be sworn.

"Now, sir, you understand the oath you just took, don't you?"

"Yes."

"And you swore, under penalty of perjury, to tell the truth. You understand that?"

"Yes."

"And you understand what perjury is, right? It's taking an oath and then telling a lie. And it's a crime. You understand that?"

"Yes, I understand."

"Now sir, I want to ask you again, are you sure you had sex with my client?"

"Yes," he said.

"And when you say you had sex, you mean you had vaginal intercourse with her?"

"Yes."

"Meaning it's your testimony here today that you inserted your penis into her vagina. Is that correct?"

He looked at the judge. The judge and I both, I suspect, understood Fazal's look to be his non-lawyer version of standing up and stating, "Objection!"

Judge Greyson looked at me suspiciously. "That's what *I* took it to mean, Mr. Sexton—unless you're aware of a different definition of the term that I'm unfamiliar with."

"Your Honor, I appreciate the court's discretion but the specific

---

* After the judge retired, she told me this was the first and only annulment trial in her thirty-five-year tenure on the bench.

details of this alleged sexual experience are going to be more important than Your Honor may realize at the moment and I would respectfully request that you permit me to, with no pun intended, explore this area more fully," I said.

The judge looked unconvinced, but also slightly less bored. "Very little leeway, Mr. Sexton. This is not an adult film festival."

I turned back to Fazal. "When you had sex with my client, what position were you in?"

"I was on top."

"Any problems with the sex? You were fully able to insert your penis? You're certain of that?"

"I am certain."

"And your penis was erect when you were having sex."

"Yes."

"And about how long is your penis when erect?"

The judge shot me another look. "Mr. Sexton, where are you going?"

"Your Honor, I believe the size of the defendant's penis is directly relevant to contested issues of fact and would, again, ask that the court permit a limited inquiry on the topic."

The judge nodded unhappily. "You're on a short leash with this one, counsel. You're dangerously close to being told to move on to the next topic." She turned to Fazal. "That being said, you may answer the question, sir."

"I have an average-sized penis," said Fazal, somewhat incredulously.

"I would object as nonresponsive, Your Honor, and I'd like that answer stricken from the record," I said.

"It's normal. Why do I have to answer this?" Fazal was now looking directly at the judge, who seemed unamused and eager to move the case forward. Probably missing the beach very much by now.

"Please answer the question with a specific answer, sir."

"It's average. It's regular. Normal. Healthy."

Fazal was apparently attempting to throw as many nonspecific synonyms into the record as possible. I was not going to let him off that easy.

"Your Honor, I would ask that the witness be directed to provide a specific and accurate answer. I'm not asking that he show us, but I think we have a right to know what he means when he says things like 'normal' or 'average' in regard to the size of his penis."

"Mr. Sexton, I believe the court can understand the plain meaning of the term 'average-sized penis' without requiring the defendant to take out a measuring tape. And frankly, I'm still not sure why any of this is relevant to these proceedings."

"Again, Your Honor, I believe the relevance will be made abundantly clear to the court, but it is essential that a specific measurement, or at least an approximate range of measurement, be provided, under oath, by the defendant. I'm not aware of what an average-sized penis is. I'd like to believe I have one. But I don't think the answer the defendant gave is adequate or legitimate."

"As distasteful as this whole inquiry is to me, counselor, I'm going to direct the witness to answer the question."

I turned to Fazal. "Can you show the court, using your hands, how large your penis is, when erect?"

He placed his hands roughly five inches apart.

"Your Honor, may the record reflect that the witness has placed his hands approximately five inches apart?"

"You can put that representation on the record, counselor. I'm not getting involved in this more than I've already been forced to."

"Now, sir, when you allegedly had sex with my client, you were aware that she was a virgin?"

"Yes," he said.

"And you had no problem with the sex, is that correct?"

"That is correct."

"You had it to completion?"

"Yes."

"And you were fully able to insert your penis?"

"Yes."

"And you did it more than once?"

"Yes."

"And during the sex, you moved your penis in and out of her vagina for some duration of time, varying the depth of penetration?"

The judge jumped in. "Okay, Mr. Sexton, that's enough. If you skipped that day in sex education class, that's how it works. I'm not going to make the defendant walk you through it."

"Thank you, Your Honor. Nothing further of this witness."

I dismissed Fazal and called Sana's gynecologist to the stand.

"Dr. Castel, you're the plaintiff's gynecologist, is that correct?"

"Yes."

"And in that capacity you've conducted an internal examination of her vaginal area, is that correct?"

"Yes."

"When did you last perform an internal exam on her?"

"Approximately ten days ago."

"Now, Doctor, in your capacity as a gynecologist, you're familiar with the physical mechanics of heterosexual vaginal intercourse, aren't you?"

The judge interrupted. "I've never heard it referred to that way, counselor." She shook her head. "Very romantic of you. You may answer, Doctor."

"Yes, I'm personally and professionally familiar with the topic."

The judge laughed. (Oh, sure, when the *witness* makes a quip, it's funny.)

"Is it possible," I asked her, "for a hymen to remain intact if there has been sexual intercourse?"

"No," she said. "There are really only two scenarios. If there's penetration, the hymen would rupture. Or if the hymen was unnaturally thick or strong, then the penis would not be able to break through and would, for lack of a better term, bang into it, preventing penetration."

"Now, Doctor, you've examined my client's vagina and her intact hymen. Is it possible that a five-inch penis was inserted into her vagina at any time? Much less pushed in and out of her vagina repeatedly, as would occur during vaginal intercourse?"

"That's simply impossible."

"Nothing further. The plaintiff rests, Your Honor."

As the doctor exited the witness box, the judge turned to glare at Fazal, who looked down at the table and his purportedly five-inch penis.

Fazal asked the judge if he could retake the stand and "clarify" his earlier testimony.

"Sir, the plaintiff has rested her case. Which means you can call any witnesses you have now, including yourself, if you wish."

"I call myself."

Moments later, Fazal was back on the witness stand.

"I made an error," he said. "I was embarrassed when I was asked questions by the lawyer before. My penis is much smaller than I said. I was exaggerating. It's actually very small. Very, very small. I didn't want to say anything before."

"Thank you for that, sir," the judge said. "Did you have any further testimony, evidence, or witnesses you wanted to offer?"

"No. That's it. Just that it's not five inches. It's much smaller."

"Thank you, sir," the judge replied, "it's duly noted. The defendant appears to be resting, Mr. Sexton. Any rebuttal witnesses?"

"Yes, Your Honor. I would like to briefly recall my client's gynecologist, Dr. Castel."

"Please make it brief, Mr. Sexton. I don't know how much more of this I can handle today." She looked off into the distance, reminiscing undoubtedly about tropical drinks and sunsets.

I recalled the doctor to the stand. "Could a penis of small size—less than three inches—have entered the plaintiff's vagina without rupturing the hymen?"

"Absolutely not. It's just not possible. Even if the person claiming to have had sex with her had a microphallus, which is clinically defined as a penis less than two and three-quarters inches, it would penetrate her hymen."

I was about to make oral application for an independent medical examination of Fazal's penis when the judge waved me off.

"I've heard enough testimony," she said to Fazal. "Enough games. I'm going to make this simple for you. You're going to consent to the requested annulment or I'm going to deliberate for about thirty seconds, grant it anyway, hold you in contempt of court, and refer the transcript of these proceedings to the district attorney for perjury charges."

Sana got her annulment. Fazal was very fortunate: He got to stay in this country because Sana, a forgiving sort, was not interested in his being deported.

And I got to have one of those cross-examination moments that lawyers dream about: where you know you're leading a liar down a path of no return, and he doesn't realize it until it's too late. I also got to put a man in a position where his last, best hope was to argue, under oath, that he had a microphallus.

If I didn't have kids to put through college, I would have dropped the mic right there and retired.

As to the redeeming life lesson of this story . . . Don't lie under oath? (Too obvious.) Don't lie about the size of your penis? (Unrealistic.) Don't lie about the size of your penis if you're in court and the size of your penis is at issue in litigation? (Yes, but I concede that that seems a tad specific to be of much use.)

It was really just a story I felt like telling. It feels like the kind of story a divorce lawyer would tell at a cocktail party. I just don't get invited to cocktail parties. So I included it here. I hope you enjoyed it.

## Chapter 29

# KNOW YOURSELF

In the early months of the Trump administration, Mike Pence, the vice president and a born-again Christian, was slammed on social media when it was revealed that he refuses to dine alone with a woman not his wife.

I found some of the criticism legitimate: His stance seemed to demonize women; because of his power, he was depriving individual women of the opportunity to make professional connections or deals or be mentored in such a situation, whereas a man no more qualified would not be deprived.

And yet.

Leaving aside his politics, the idea that Pence's religious and marital worldview forbids him from even breaking bread, alone, with a woman not his wife is not such a bad concept—*for him*. (In the end, don't we all come up with behaviors that work best for ourselves?) Some reformed alcoholics can maintain their sobriety around those who are drinking, while others forbid themselves from even setting foot in a bar because they know if they do, they're seriously increasing their chance of caving.

Should we be critical of those people for knowing themselves and their weaknesses?

Look at dieters. The key to losing weight and healthy eating may be as simple as this: Don't keep anything in your home that's bad for you. Is that transgressive? Nutritionally incorrect? Maybe it's just acknowledging what most of us already know: It's easier to control your environment than your brain.

Such abnegation can seem severe, even un-American. We're all about constant, abundant options, and it should always be up to us to choose. McDonald's most memorable advertising campaign of the last few decades was "You deserve a break today," as if no one and nothing has the right to get in the way of your enjoying something, even if that something is bad for you. (I understand why they chose that campaign for their products.) It was intended as a catchy slogan, maybe not an overarching worldview, but let's unpack it a bit. Who's the "you" who deserves a break today? The entire audience hearing the advertisement? So, essentially, everyone in the United States? In the world? They all deserve a break today? *All* of them? I had a roommate in college who, having inherited money from his grandfather, several years later became a barely part-time stained-glass artist and full-time pot smoker. He needs—pardon, he *deserves*—a break from that? And (to stop picking just on Sebastian) in what sense do they mean "break"? And "today"? As in, every day? Like, after a long, tough week, do I deserve the break of sleeping with anyone I choose? Do I deserve a certain level of happiness, no matter what means I use to achieve it? Do I deserve to be happy all the time? Is marriage fun one hundred percent of the time? (No.) Is parenting? (No.)

Well, shit . . . why not?

The language of "deserving" and "entitlement" and its offshoots—such as the now ubiquitous term "self-care," used to validate virtually any self-indulgent behavior as some progress toward the greater good—sounds very much like the language used by so many of the people I speak with who've had ruinous affairs. They rationalize their behavior as something they "deserved," even as what they took for themselves destroyed the trust, peace, and sanctity of their marriage. (I've written a lot in this book about what every partner *should* feel entitled to, and I'll continue to write about it; this is not that.)

So, Pence. Maybe—like the ex-drinker who steers clear of bars because he knows if he hangs out long enough he'll have a drink—Mike Pence is saying, by default, "I can't handle being around women." Maybe he knows his limits. Maybe he knows he can't be trusted with women.

Many people understand themselves well enough to know that if they hang out long enough with attractive (and even unattractive) members of the opposite sex, eventually the temptation will make them take the bait. (Change "opposite" to "same," if you're gay. Just don't tell Mike Pence.) Obviously, this isn't true with everyone, or in every situation. (Lunch, Mike? Really, you can't keep your hands off of them *at lunch?*)

I don't have much in common with Vice President Pence, and don't feel my monogamy is threatened by my choice of lunch companions. But I'll be honest: I understand what he's saying. If you put me around a plate of nachos, I'm eventually going to eat them (nachos, unlike women, have no agency). I can't be trusted to control myself around the things I find delicious even when I've promised myself I'm going to stick to my diet. It's easier to control my environment than my brain. I'm not comparing women to nachos (though if you understood how much I enjoy good nachos, you would see such a comparison as a tremendous compliment). But one sort of desire is, to some degree, all desire.

I don't think I'm alone on this.

Maybe the Pence Rule sounds so distasteful because his obvious lack of self-control affects those around him. Lots and lots of women who are more than capable of having a perfectly platonic, nonsexual lunch with Mike Pence will never get that chance.

You may be turned off by our vice president saying, in essence, "I'm not going to hang out with other women because I may very well end up sleeping with one of them," but I've got to say: For him—*for him*—it's probably the smart move.

One of the most important traits that the strong possess, from what I see, is knowing their weaknesses. When I take on a new case, the first thing I focus on are my client's areas of potential vulnerability—not only to get a full, honest picture of the presenting situation, but also to begin shoring up their defenses.

Being able to do that for yourself is a virtue.

## Chapter 30

# INTIMACY WEAPONIZED, PART I

Jacob, a confident (some would say arrogant) client who owned half a dozen optometry stores, was quick to tell anyone what a success he was and how innovative his business and accounting methods were. (What he called "creative accounting," others might call "tax fraud.") After Jacob enlisted me to handle his divorce, he and his wife sparred over (among other things) the value of his business assets and the amount of income that should be imputed to him for support purposes.

He sold one of his stores to a cousin for a ridiculously reduced sum that made it clear that he was either taking a much larger payment in cash on the side or getting paid after the dust had settled in the divorce. He changed the business hours of one of his most profitable stores so that it opened late and closed early, essentially driving it into the ground in a way that might be easy to repair, post-divorce. He abruptly changed the computer program he used to track inventory to one that was far less detailed, and, for good measure, he deleted the data and then drilled holes in the hard drives of the computers with old inventory files on them.*

---

* In my attempt to explain that last bit, I briefly considered telling the judge that my client had recently read that "tidying up" book and decided the old hard drives didn't "spark joy." But I reconsidered. Thankfully, even after all these years, I'm still not "nose deaf" to my own bullshit and can tell when I've piled it too high.

I did for Jacob what any reasonable divorce lawyer does in situations of this kind: came up with innocent-sounding alternative explanations for his behaviors, doing my best to deflect attention from his transparent plan to minimize his income and thwart a fair outcome for his wife. The sale of the store? It was an "arm's-length transaction" with a family member, and the "discount in any hypothetical value" was "tied to the lack of marketability in businesses of this format" and included "adjustments in value for a variety of relevant economic factors." (Don't ask me what any of that means. It means he lowered the price because he sold it for a lower price. Exactly. Circular nonsense. With a change in tone of voice here and there, it can resemble an actual explanation. It's not.)

The problem with Jacob's case, as with so many cases I handle, was that my client was full of shit. I couldn't prove it, but I knew it. I knew it in my bones. He hadn't admitted to me that he was preparing to perjure himself and lie under oath (which would have freed me to quit the case and get away from him as an officer of the court), but my gut told me that I was helping a bad person do bad things, and there was nothing I could do about it without betraying the oaths I took when I was sworn in as an attorney.

The truth, however, has a way of coming out (sometimes in spite of my best efforts to the contrary). I didn't have to shirk my lawyerly duties to Jacob to see justice happen. *Jacob* would be Jacob's undoing.

You see, Jacob ignored a very basic, unavoidable dilemma in divorce: You've been talking to (and in the presence of) your spouse for years. This isn't the first time they have met you. While you don't get read your *Miranda* rights when you marry someone, anything you have ever said to your spouse can and will be used against you in divorce proceedings.

Like many divorcing couples, Jacob and his wife were still living together—and still on speaking terms. At one point, his wife said something about needing money. Jacob said he didn't have any.

"How is it that suddenly you don't have any money?" she asked, to which Jacob "explained" that his stores weren't making money. Yet only a few months earlier, he had been bragging to her about how much money they *were* bringing in. And in her testimony, in response to the eyebrow-raisingly low value Jacob had given for his business, his wife coolly recounted their conversation from a few months before.

We marry our lovers, but ultimately we spend more time talking with our spouses than having sex with them.* We talk to them. We talk at them. We talk over them. We overhear (intentionally or unintentionally) their conversations with other people. Sometimes we talk to ourselves, and our spouses happen to be in the room to hear us.

I'm astounded at how many people, even in the midst of an ugly divorce action, continue to debrief their spouse on what's happening in their life. I assume it's force of habit. Once, a client named Chloe, in the middle of a nasty divorce from her husband of fifteen years, Stuart, the chief financial officer of a firm that manufactures parts for satellites, told me, "Stuart told me his company's expanding to China."†

"Wait—why would he tell you that?" I found myself stammering. The expansion of Stuart's company to Asia would thoroughly undermine the credibility of his prior claims that the business was "experiencing a significant reduction in income that may, at best, create long-term revenue reduction and withholding of bonuses for senior management and, at worst, ultimately cause the demise of the company."

Yes, that's a quotation. He wrote that, under oath, in his papers opposing my client's motion for spousal support. Now this admission?

"I don't know," said Chloe. "I think he was excited about it or bragging or some combination of the two. It's good, though, right?"

Two weeks later, at his deposition, Stuart seemed surprised when I asked him about his company's expansion plans.

---

* Therein may lie the whole problem.

† A side effect of practicing matrimonial law is how much you learn about a whole bunch of bizarre topics, the result of having studied up on them in preparation for a trial. I now know a lot about how satellites are manufactured. I can tell you how auto dealerships build in profits when you buy a car. I know a ton about optometry, the currently prevailing professional consensus among rabbis regarding which parent should bless the children on the first day of the Jewish holiday of Shavuos, and how many nanograms per milliliter of 6-Monoacetylmorphine metabolize in the blood after the use of heroin versus after the consumption of a poppyseed bagel.

The case settled a few months later. Stuart's attorney told me, in a postcase moment of candor between counsel, that Stuart worried that I was having him followed, or else I was clairvoyant. How else could I have known so specifically about his company's expansion plans?

I wanted to tell Stuart: "No, I'm not psychic. It's just that your wife isn't deaf."

People never cease to amaze me.

## Chapter 31

# INTIMACY WEAPONIZED, PART II: CROSS-EXAMINATION

If I could offer all future clients only one piece of advice, it would be this:

*Keep in mind how your behavior would look if you were being cross-examined.*

Put another way: Suppose your spouse were helping opposing counsel write the cross-examination. What does she or he know? Does your spouse know where the bodies are buried? Do they know the skeletons in your closet? The answer, of course, is usually yes.

Spouses have a front-row seat to their partner's life—the good times and bad, the stressful or tragic events and the joyful, celebratory ones, the day-to-day minutiae and the extraordinary circumstances. Your spouse has watched you, this organism, evolve, just as you have watched them. To have any sort of functional marriage, even a short-term one, you have to reveal things to your spouse, and vice versa. One of the foundation stones of marriage is having someone with whom you can be candid, intimate, entirely yourself. Which—on the flip side—means that your spouse knows your weak spots, your "tells," your dislikes. In the event of a divorce, your spouse is probably going to share this with their attorney. *Yeah, she doesn't handle the pressure of having to gather documentation well. . . . If you request copies of all his credit card statements, it'll piss him off.*

It's one of the elements of divorce that most scares people: *Shit, they're gonna come at me—and they know all my dirty secrets.*

I can make the most benign behavior seem nefarious and the most atrocious conduct seem damn near benevolent. Unfortunately, so can a worthy opponent.

Remember Jacob, my client with the eyeglasses business that was, depending on who was asking, either thriving or about to shutter the windows?

He did a terrible job on the witness stand. That was partly because he refused to let me prep him ("I'm not paying you six hundred dollars per hour to practice asking me questions about things I already know about," he said. "I don't need to study. I know my business. I know the truth.") All of his sins, personal and professional, were laid bare by my smart and talented adversary.*

But there's a school of thought that would suggest Jacob's problems didn't start when he took the witness stand, or even when he decided that a lack of preparation was a good strategy. His problems started when he engaged in behavior that would be difficult to defend when subject to confrontation.

And that's the question that deserves to be asked: Should people, even happily married people, think about how what they say and do would sound if they were testifying about it on the witness stand?

Agreed: No one wants to live like that. A relationship is unlikely to improve if one or both partners judges everything that's said or done by how it might look under cross-examination someday. That would weaponize intimacy. It's like trying to live while a second self watches you live. Albert Einstein said, "You cannot simultaneously prevent and prepare for war." Not fun, not easy, not natural.

Still, for those in solid partnerships, it can be a worthwhile exercise to view the union through that lens now and then: How *would* your behavior toward your partner come off, if described on the witness stand? Or, perhaps more plausibly, imagine that any email or text you write could

---

* To see how truly lethal it can be when you're both arrogant *and* a lying son of a bitch, please read Chapter 36.

be forwarded to anyone, or posted publicly. What's the positive way to spin it? What's the negative spin?

Ask yourself: What's your relationship like? How would you describe your behavior in it?

The version we give the world tends to be highly curated (see Facebook). Even the version we give, in person, to a very dear friend probably goes only so far; it's limited by our inevitable denial (though we differ, person to person, in the depth of our denial).

When foibles and flaws and intimacy are weaponized, as they can be in a divorce claim, it's highly unpleasant, to say the least. But if you're in a good relationship, then to assess your strengths and weaknesses as objectively as possible, as if recounting them for a lawyer, can lead to a highly positive outcome.

Maybe reread an email or text you were going to send to your spouse. If you had to listen to a lawyer read the email or text out loud in a courtroom, would you change the tone?

When I was a teenager, my mom used to tell me not to put anything in writing that I would feel uncomfortable seeing published on the front page of *The New York Times*. I understood, even then, what she was suggesting: Engage only in behavior that you're prepared to stand by and defend. Be on your toes to be your best self at all times, even when no one is watching. Your character, to a large degree—perhaps more so now, in this age of social media—is most readily apparent from how you behave when no one is looking.

It's not automatically a bad thing that someone out there knows you almost as well as—maybe even better than—you know yourself. Think of those moments in a good relationship where you think you want something, and your partner tells you, lovingly, *No, sweetie, you don't.*

You: *I think I might invite my sister to just stay here with her kids when they're in town for Mom and Dad's anniversary party rather than getting a hotel.*

Loving Partner: *Do you think that's a good idea, with her daughter's allergies and the dogs? And remember last time they were here for a few days, you couldn't wait until they left.*

And after a moment, you conclude, *Yeah, you're right. I really don't want that.*

My professional experience gets me to the same place, if from the back end: I'm in the business of weaponizing intimacy, to dissolve marriages. Those who are in love and want to keep it that way should try to see the ability to weaponize intimacy not as a threat, but as proof of its power. Not just for ammunition on the witness stand. Power that can be used for good.

# Chapter 32

# ARGUE BETTER

I argue for a living. I've joked with my children, from time to time, when steadfastly refusing to allow them to engage in some typical teenage behavior, that I couldn't argue with them about it at home for free because "it wouldn't be fair to my paying customers."

One of the biggest lessons parenting has taught me: You can argue with someone and still love them very much. In fact, if you're committed to maintaining a long-term relationship with something as imperfect as a human being,* you're going to have arguments from time to time. Maybe the gap between "time" and "time" is mere hours. So it's a good idea to learn how to argue with someone you love (and plan to continue loving).

My clients are either monumentally bad at arguing or got bad at it over time. I hope that's not the case for you. If you need a primer, some thoughts:

1. *Make the holes you dig shallow, because the deep ones are hard to climb out of.* Married fights can be tricky. They start out about something benign, like how generous the pile of fried onions

---

* A dog might be a better choice. If you ever wondered who loves you more, your spouse or your dog, lock both in the trunk of your car, wait ten minutes, and open it back up. Which one is happy to see you?

should be on the top of green bean casserole or what's the best way to get to the Flatiron Building from the George Washington Bridge,* and the next thing you know you're airing out age-old quarrels that neither of you realized the other was still carrying around ("And three years ago on Christmas you let your brother say that horrible thing about me!"). Keep disputes focused; don't take current behavior and start extrapolating larger trends in the relationship because, in the moment, it might seem like a good idea to "get them out in the open" and "hash them out." Such leaps are dangerous, and they're dirty pool. When we lawyers are cross-examining even the skankiest people, we're restricted from jumping from the heinous behavior in question to other heinous acts not on the docket (even though we have elusive and allusive ways of connecting the dots, for juries and even for judges). If you're fighting about a specific issue, stick to that issue. You can bring up the old stuff later, after you've worked this one through and are both in a calmer state of mind. Or you may realize, in the interim, that it's best to let sleeping dogs lie. You are surely aware that you can never unsay things you say in arguments. You can apologize, but that doesn't take it back. To test this theory: Take a plate; throw it on the ground; now apologize to it. See what I mean?

2. *Identify the subject.* If you're arguing about a specific issue as an *example* of a larger pattern of behavior, focus the discussion on the larger pattern of behavior. (This may sound like the opposite of the previous point; I don't believe it is.) You're not mad that your spouse deleted the program you wanted to watch from the DVR after he finished it. Well, you *are*, but that's not what upsets you about it: It's that he was thinking only about himself in that moment and not thinking about what you might want. Of *course* that's the key issue—because, let's face it, if the DVR incident

---

* Correct answers: Very generous, so you get all the toasted crunchy bits; take the Henry Hudson to the exit for West Twenty-sixth Street and park before Seventh Avenue. The farther east you go, the crappier the parking.

was the first time he ever did something like that, you wouldn't be ready to bite his head off about it. You'd shrug it off. "It was an honest mistake," or "Things happen." But you didn't, because it's part of a larger body of disagreeable behavior. So get to that general principle first, and use the individual incident (or incidents) as supporting "evidence." Trial Lawyer says: Lead with the big picture, then provide the testimony and evidence to back it up.

3. *Don't start something that has no end.* If you married a guy who is short, don't argue with him about how much better it would be if he were taller. The argument is not going to end well. If you're arguing about something that's happened and can't be undone without the aid of a time machine, really make sure it's worth having the argument. Sure, there are times when your spouse did or said something stupid and they're likely to do it or say it again if the behavior is left unchecked. In those circumstances, it might be worth having the argument. The same is true if the behavior is indicative of a larger pattern (such as selfishness, rotten investment skills, an upsetting approach to parenting) that might come up again in different circumstances. If you're just holding a grudge and upset with your spouse about something unrelated and it's impossible to change or undo, tread lightly. We remember the complaints more vividly than the compliments. I would know: I listen to recollections of marital histories for hours and hours, fifty weeks of the year.

## Chapter 33

# GUT, HEART, AND HEAD

Fear and denial are not strategies. When a client and I are picking over the carcass of their relationship, it's commonplace that they will, at some especially unguarded moment, confess, "Part of me isn't surprised that this happened" or "I always knew this is how it would end."

Why is that? Because at some point, very early on, they knew there was a fundamental issue that remained unaddressed. Maybe addressing it would have ended things right there. And that's terrifying. But is it wiser to let the difficulty go untended? If we just ignore a potentially troubling medical report, is that a strategy? Will the next CT scan come back miraculously clean?

I'm guilty of this myself—actually, my ex-wife, MJ, and I both are. We got engaged when we were very young; then I broke off the engagement, ostensibly because right around that time my mother was diagnosed with cancer. Unsteadied by the news, I felt I needed to change everything—quit school for a semester, brood in my apartment, smoke even more pot than I already did. And break off the engagement.

A few months later, I gave MJ the ring again and we got re-engaged. I told myself, and her, that I had gotten unengaged only because of the freakout over my mother's illness.

Yet I always knew there was more to it. I knew we were too young.

I knew deep down that, much as I loved MJ, we weren't meant to be together long-term. I love many people whom I couldn't be married to for the rest of my life. MJ was one of those people.

And MJ? After we divorced, amicably, we revealed to each other lots of truths we hadn't before. We called it "post-gaming" the marriage. (In the intelligence community, it's called debriefing.) It was actually quite liberating. We had no incentive to lie to each other about anything anymore. Fuck it—we were already divorced.

She told me that on the day of our wedding, which took place in a small restaurant, she had a very clear thought as she climbed the stairs in her bridal gown to the dining room, which had been converted into a chapel where minutes later she would be walking down the aisle. She told me that the voice in her head was urging her, *You should really leave. This isn't going to work.*

At the time our younger selves were having these respective difficult thoughts, though, neither of us said or did anything. To be clear, neither of us regrets the marriage. Our beautiful sons would not be here if we had not married. Still, I can say from my experience as a divorce attorney—forget my experience personally—that the shockingly articulate voices in our heads; the wedding-eve dream that tells you so crystal-clearly to run, not walk, in the other direction; the feeling that you just know is more than cold feet even though everyone around you assures you it's *precisely* cold feet . . . all that stuff is probably not going away. It does *not* mean breakup is inevitable (though it may); but it *does* mean you had better address it.

Everything comes out, eventually.

I won't dispense some bullshit wisdom here about trusting your gut, or trusting your heart, or trusting your head. In fact, I believe you should not trust anything blindly, or anyone completely.* But if all three of those entities are shouting, *Holy shit—run!*, I think we can agree that you should maybe consider it.

---

* If your mother tells you she loves you, ask for references.

Do you need to Hit Send Now? Certainly you need to address the issue early and fully. It's not going away.

Once upon a time, when I was younger and I had bad news to deliver professionally, I did what almost everyone does: I looked for ways to put it off. I think of the story of Carlos, who thought both of his sons—four-year-old Hector and nine-month-old Cesar—were his, and he'd raised them as such, beautifully. Until it turned out that they were *not* his, biologically. Both boys had been fathered by Carlos's wife's lover. Carlos, profoundly upset and broken, left their home. The mother, an alcoholic, took the kids to go live with the boyfriend, also a drunk. Baby Cesar got dropped on a table. How'd it happen? The drunk mother went out for a pack of cigarettes, leaving the kids with the drunk boyfriend—sorry, the biological father—and the asshole dropped the kid. An accident, supposedly.

For months, Carlos tried desperately to regain custody of the boys he'd raised as his sons. Then, with all avenues exhausted, I had to tell him he didn't have standing to get them because he was not the biological father.

I waited. Who wants to be part of that moment?

"Carlos, *I* have as much standing as you do," I said when I played the scene over and over in my head, telling him as gently as I could. "Which is none whatsoever."

How exactly was I going to explain to him that the jackass drunk boyfriend, a guy who dropped a nine-month-old on the table, maybe even on purpose, maybe causing brain damage and certainly making the boy suffer, had custodial rights superior to Carlos's? How would I tell him that the absolute best case he could hope for was that the boys would be removed from their current home situation and put into state custody, where they would surely meet tremendous obstacles and face other suffering, at which point Carlos would *still* have no rights whatsoever to see them or be with them?

I went a whole day avoiding that conversation, then a second day, which made me miserable for those two days and made my family miserable for those two days because they had to be around my miserable self.

Delaying changed not a thing about the cruel message, of course. There would be no eleventh-hour reprieve, no spasm of justice. It was just me deluding, ignoring. Adults can play pretend, too. When I finally worked up the courage, and found myself sitting across from Carlos in a little conference room off the courthouse hallway, I explained to him what should have been inexplicable. He looked at me, as I knew he would, not comprehending.

I remember thinking that I had accomplished absolutely no good by waiting. No good, and some bad. I thought about when I was in college and volunteered at hospice. It turned out to be one of the most transformative experiences of my life. I saw that death—perhaps the one life experience about which we're even less honest and open than we are about love—is usually not the way we portray it to ourselves. It's messier. Dying people make weird noises and smells. If we want to make death a more integrated part of life, we need to be honest with ourselves about how it goes. I remember coming away from that experience thinking, *If everyone in the country were forced to do a week at a hospice, we would probably eradicate dishonesty and denial nationally.*

Your life, like every life, is going to have lies in it—probably many, some of them whoppers. But try your best not to lie to yourself. You deserve honesty from yourself. Listen to your inner dialogue and try to balance and interpret it all. You're probably smarter than you give yourself credit for.

## Chapter 34

# THE AUTHOR OF YOUR STORY

Almost all of us wake up each of the 365 days a year, 366 in leap years, and decide to be who we were yesterday. And who we were the day before that, and the week before that, and probably the year before that. This is a choice we make, not a default setting. Because every day we wake up, we *can,* at least in theory, say, "Fuck it, I'm done being that person; now I'm going to be someone else." That is a fucking superpower. That is liberating! Exciting! That is true freedom!

Yet virtually none of us does it.

Divorce is, for many people, an invitation to become a new person.

Do you know at least a few people who, post-divorce, got into new hobbies (yoga, travel, Brazilian Jiu-Jitsu . . . ), or made a new crowd of friends, or got a new tattoo, or changed their hairstyle, or decorated their new home in a completely different style? Divorce is an invitation to reinvent yourself. That's part of what makes it so terrifying but also exciting.

Staying married entrenches us more deeply in the habit of being ourselves.

I'm not saying that's a horrible thing. (If I haven't stated it explicitly yet, let me say it here: Being a partner in a good marriage is a fortunate, fantastic place to be, a place most of us want to get to. If it weren't, I wouldn't have written this book.) I'm just stating a fact. You *don't* wake up and completely change your life because, as a married person, you have made a very public contract with the universe. If I live alone and eat Cheerios for breakfast every day for many months, then suddenly decide to start eating scrambled eggs instead, there's no real discussion to be had. I make the change and the universe is none the wiser. If I'm married and I make a change like that, there's a whole shit show that comes with it. Suddenly I'm forced—or perhaps feel compelled, without having been asked—to explain that I've made this change. (The spouse and kids are going to notice the change in the shopping list, or the dishes, or the smell in the kitchen in the morning.) Maybe I even feel the need to proactively explain that I'm going to make this change, so as not to surprise my spouse who, reasonably, has become accustomed to waking up in a world where I generally do the same kinds of things on a daily basis and can be predicted to do the same kinds of things in the future.

Isn't marriage, to some degree, based on that premise?

But a marriage is a living thing, an organism. It survives when we repeat roughly the same conditions from day to day, but it thrives when it is truly nourished. There's a difference between waking up every day and not doing anything different (*It's Tuesday, we'll just continue the marriage . . . It's November, we'll just continue the marriage. . . .* ) vs. waking up every day, embracing what you have, and enthusiastically making a choice to continue it.

*I'm not just eating Cheerios because that's the only thing in the house or because that's what I had yesterday. I'm eating Cheerios because they're good for me and I like the way they taste.**

I'm not suggesting that if you experience anything short of daily euphoria, you should upend your married life. I am suggesting that divorced people can teach us a lot about reinvention.

In the days and months after a divorce, my client (and their ex, no doubt) is in a kind of shock. This was true for me after my divorce. It's hard to remember who you were, to remember who I was. The first

---

* No promotional consideration was paid by Cheerios for this example. I do, however, like Cheerios very much.

weekend after getting divorced, I remember, I was surveying the largely empty living room of my apartment, thinking not just *What kind of couch should I get?* but *I haven't had to think about what couch I would want for . . . almost forever.* And the choice of my first postmarriage couch became a far more profound matter than might sound rational. I felt as if I couldn't pick out a couch until I knew—or remembered—some very important things: What is important to me? What is beautiful to me (at least when it comes to furniture)? What colors do I like when I don't need to defend that color choice to someone with different color preferences? What message (if any) do I want to send with my couch choice? What will my couch say about me, whether I mean it to or not? Do I really even need a goddamn couch?

One truly rewarding aspect of being a divorce lawyer is that I get to see clients surprise themselves with their resiliency and sense of discovery. By the end of many a divorce, the client and I have been miles and miles (and miles) together; given the shared emotional journey, it's common for them to remain in touch for years after the divorce is finalized. I get countless holiday cards, emails, and bar/bat mitzvah and wedding invitations from former clients eager to share with me the joy of their post-divorce life, a life they credit me with having helped them create. This is just about the most beautiful aspect of the work I get to do.

Rebecca's husband had cheated on her, and she was sure she would never again be loved or able to trust. Yet here she is, three years later, inviting me to her wedding, engaged to Isaac, whom she describes as the "kindest and sweetest" man she's ever met. Gina, who had been married to Kyle, a dominant Type A hedge-fund guy, was certain that the two of them would "never be able to have a friendly relationship." Four years later, she checks in with an email telling me she's married to an amazing man, Kyle is married to a very nice woman, and not only do they share custody, they even throw joint birthday parties for the children each year, at which Gina and Kyle's new wife often "gang up" to make fun of him. To see my former clients build from the ashes of their broken marriages such beautiful, fulfilling lives and relationships is deeply gratifying, and motivates me to work hard for my current clients. On more than one occasion I have even asked a former client whether a new client who is feeling broken, hopeless, and vulnerable can speak to her, to hear that there is light at the end of the tunnel (and that the light isn't a train). I've been told by current and former clients that these exchanges are fulfilling and healing for both of them, both the Before and the After. Proof to the Before that there is still the chance of an ever-after that's happy; a rewarding reminder to the After of how far she's come.

It's hard to know what you're capable of. It's hard enough sometimes to remember who you are, even in the best of relationship circumstances. When the relationship is dysfunctional, it's harder still. So many of the broken marriages I handle have been nonoperative for so long that the individuals have forgotten who they are. That's scary: Can I still be that person? Do I want to be that person? Does it matter who I am?

Divorce forces you to examine who you are and who you want to be. Marriage, at its best, should be an invitation to do the same—with the huge added benefit of having at least one audience member who loves you and shares your desire to be happy (for yourself and for them). Don't wait until you're getting divorced to figure out who you want to be and how to go about becoming that person. Go get the best fucking couch your heart desires.

## Chapter 35

# WHO ARE YOU?

Once, I was in conference with Martin, a college professor I represented; his soon-to-be ex, Sylvia, a teacher; and her lawyer. There had been no adultery, no massive financial chicanery; nonetheless, husband and wife had grown wildly uncivil to each other, and it was difficult to get through a single deal point without some snarky comment from one of them.

While we were arguing, with an intensity more befitting the negotiation of a nuclear arms treaty with North Korea, whether Thanksgiving weekend visitation should extend from Wednesday to Sunday or only from Wednesday into Thursday evening, Sylvia's phone rang. Their daughter, Angela, was a flyer for her middle-school cheerleading squad, a position that entails being flung into the air, to be caught by a small group of other middle schoolers. One or more of them had apparently (though, at least to me, unsurprisingly) not been paying close attention. Angela fell, and the school was calling because she'd broken her arm. Before that moment, Sylvia and Martin had been seated across the table from each other, but now they stood, as one, the physical distance between them shrinking as if by magnetic pull, so they could huddle over the speaker on Sylvia's phone, talking to the nurse about who needed to do what.

Weapons had been sheathed; the same couple who moments ago had been unable to agree on minor scheduling issues were juggling who would go to the hospital and who would go get the other children after school, pick up Angela's books from the gym, and take their son to his basketball practice if the other was caring for Angela.

The woman who, moments ago, had expressed how little she trusted her soon-to-be ex-husband was now giving him a copy of her house key and suggesting that he hang out there with the younger kids and help them with their homework until she got back from the hospital with Angela, so he could see that she was okay and she could give him a hug. The same man who had just been arguing that he shouldn't have to spend an additional $10 to buy a second mouthpiece for their son's wrestling season and should instead require his soon-to-be ex-wife to make sure the mouthpiece travel with the son during visitation was now saying he would order Chinese food for the kids (it wasn't his night to feed them), and asking his estranged wife if she still liked moo shu shrimp, because "you're going to be hungry by the time you get back from the hospital with Angie." As they spoke, Sylvia even put her hand lightly on Martin's arm, and he responded by briefly rubbing her shoulder.

Then our session was aborted and they were gone. The whole interaction lasted maybe five minutes.

*Aha!* I remember thinking. *So it is possible for you guys to be kind and considerate toward each other! There's a shred of empathy between you, no matter how hard you try to deny it. Now all I have to do is secretly pray another child suffers a minor injury when this goes to trial.*

This always seemed nonsensical to me: Why, of all the people on the planet, would the person you married be the one you always have to be singularly critical of? Why hold the person with whom you signed a lifetime commitment to such a specific and unreasonably high standard? How come we're encouraged to give our friends a break and understand that from time to time they might not be their best selves—

yet we're not equally encouraged to give our spouses a similar level of leniency?

Buddhist philosophy has taught me a great deal about the human condition and made me a better lawyer, father, person. Among the many important questions I've learned to ask: "Who is this person in front of me?" Yes, I see it's my son Billy, or my best friend, Avram, or my secretary, Jaclyn, but who *is* he or she, really? Billy is not just my son; he's also Billy. What does it mean to be Billy?

When you talk to your partner, who exactly are you talking to? Who *you* think he is? Who *you* want him to be? Who *she* thinks she is? Who *she* wants to be?

The majority of divorcing parties have either stopped really looking at their partner, or have a painfully narrowed view.* When romance first breaks out, every word the other person utters is a revelation, not just in content but in presentation. We are learning what they have to say and how they say it. What do they sound like when they're joking? When they're holding back tears, or saying something painful and from the heart? After a period of time together, of course, the communication is no longer so new. We've learned to read our partner's tone; we know when they're just chatting, and when it's time to tune in and really listen. Eventually we reach the point where we've heard most of their best jokes and stories (and they, ours). Maybe we were present at many of the events they're prone to discussing, so we don't really need to listen as carefully.

Sure, there's some truth to the adages that "No man is a hero to his

---

* Or, worst-case, a totally demonized view, where one party imagines the other as a person who exists only in some fever-dream. Lance, owner of a gym, wanted me to dig for loopholes to get him out of paying child support to his ex-wife. Why? Because Donna had started dating after the divorce, and Lance was convinced she was using the money for things like sex toys, though he had zero evidence for such a suspicion, and she had zero history of being someone who would do that. "Lance, I'm guessing she's using the money to buy food and school supplies for the kids," I told him. "But what do I know? I'm a romantic."

valet" and "Familiarity breeds contempt." The more we learn about a person, the less fascinating they often become.

But that truth doesn't tell the whole story. The story doesn't end there.

I love a new suit, for example. The feel of it, the excitement of something different and untried. But the nicest new suit can't hold a candle to my favorite pair of jeans, the ones that just keep getting softer, the ones I've worn on countless adventures, the ones that slip on and fit in such a familiar and perfect way, as if the years together have molded their shape to me.

There's something beyond beautiful about shared experience. Familiarity breeds comfort as easily as contempt—much more easily, if there's genuine love. Strangers can offer us excitement—they have the potential to be fascinated and fascinating—but they can't offer us the insight born of common experience. Time together teaches us how to read our partner's communications, guiding us to speak most effectively not only to who they are but, perhaps more important, to who they think they are and who they aspire to be.

If I'm to be the most effective communicator I can be as a divorce attorney, it's imperative that I know my audience. Who is this person? What are her goals in this interaction? What does she really need from me at this moment? Those are three distinct questions whose answers help me to effectively communicate, so let's look at each one individually.

1. *Who is this person?* That is, who is she presenting herself as? Who does she want to be? The "want to be" is, in my view, the most important part. Who does she want me to think she is, and who does she want the world to see her as? Often when we speak to people, we speak far too candidly to who they are, not who they want to be. Want to persuade someone? Speak to who they aspire or imagine themselves to be, not to who they actually are.

   My twenty-year-old son, like most twenty-year-olds, has his head solidly planted up his ass most of the time. (I told him he was in the book, just not exactly how.) He's a great young man, but he's precisely that: a young man. He's prone to the impatience and impulsiveness of youth. He lacks the experience, in many situations, to provide himself with a much-needed frame of reference. So when I'm trying to persuade him of something important, I save my energy, and don't focus on the deficits in experience and wisdom (I will quickly hit a wall of youthful umbrage and denial) but on who he wishes to be—which, as with most twenty-year-olds, is this: mature, intelligent, credible, even worldly-wise. When I speak to those traits, I actually get somewhere, regardless of whether those traits actually, fully yet exist in him. (They don't. They will. He's awesome.) I believe it's okay to give credit where credit may not be due . . . yet.

2. *What are her goals in this interaction?* Is she hoping to persuade me? Does she need something tangible from me? Does she need my agreement to some course of action? Is she looking for me to push back so she can change her mind, or is she looking for me to push back so she can push harder and solidify her resolve? The sooner I know the answers to these questions, the sooner I can understand the true nature of our interaction and determine how best to proceed.

Example: My sister calls me frequently to recite, grimly, the worst-case scenario that could occur in each aspect of her life. (I also told her she would be in the book, just not how.) After years of this, I've figured out that things go one of two ways. I can disagree with her, point out how pessimistic she's being, and try to convince her that things will likely work out much better than she's speculating they will; to this, she will respond by arguing more fervently that I'm wrong and things are going to go terribly.*  Alternatively, I agree with her that everything that could possibly go wrong, will. To this, she responds that I'm being pessimistic and that it's at least as likely that everything will work out fine. I've come to understand that, when stressed, my sister needs to

---

* It's somewhat amusing that a Buddhist/nihilist/divorced divorce lawyer is advocating for optimism, but I love my sister and want her to feel better when she's stressed.

argue with someone in a way that's cathartic and helps her focus on the details of her real or imagined problems. Knowing that this is her goal in the interaction, I know how to proceed.

3. *What does she* really *need from me at this moment?* In some ways, this question is the most relevant, packed with subtext, but it's impossible to answer it without a clear understanding of the other two questions. (Simply put, it's a deeper version of the previous question.) We think in generalities, but we live in details. We have a specific set of tasks we need or want to accomplish on any given day; other people are, much of the time, simply part of our facilitating that agenda. By being brutally honest about what we ourselves and others really need at any particular moment, we can be much more effective in satisfying those needs.

For example, ask most people what their spouse needs or wants at a particular moment, and you'll get a relatively nonspecific answer:

"To be happy."

"To feel fulfilled."

"To lose weight."

"To feel less anxious."

But what are they *really* looking for? Specifically?

"To be happy" might mean "to accumulate lots and lots of nice material goods." Or it might mean "to spend more time engaging in activities that she enjoys, like surfing." Do you buy her a new necklace or drive her to the ocean?

"To feel fulfilled" might mean "to get over a specific traumatic event from his past." Or it might mean "to enjoy a less stressful job where there aren't so many people advancing competing agendas that he has to try to balance."

"To lose weight" might mean "to fit into clothing that has become really snug over the past few months." Or it might mean "to have more confidence and be regarded as more desirable." It's worth noting that in this third example, the actual goal and the stated goal are only superficially related to each other. There are countless ways to help yourself or your romantic partner feel more desirable that don't require a change in body composition.

I see this every day in court. If you ask someone what the "goal" of a judge is, they might say something like "the swift administration of justice" or "to see the guilty punished and the innocent freed." In my experience, the real, candid goals of most judges are, in no specific order, to move the cases along so they don't get backlogged, which would result in getting chastised by the administrative judge who over- sees their district; to put in as stress-free a day as possible from nine a.m. until four-thirty p.m., with room for a ninety-minute lunch, if possible; and to look and feel important, particularly in comparison with people who have the same educational background as they do but are making five to ten times as much money (lawyers). Justice isn't really anywhere in the equation or, if it is, it's a pleasant and not entirely unintended side effect. (To any judges I may work with in the future: I am not talking about you. You're brilliant and deeply devoted to justice. Also, you are very pretty/handsome. Have you been working out? It shows!)

There is no singular way to look at a person—or, if there is, then what you see may be as ephemeral as what Mark Twain supposedly said about New England weather: "If you don't like [it], just wait a few min- utes." Our needs and wants change all the time, often many times a day; it requires a sensitive partner to understand that. You're not going to be right all the time, which is why you'd better do some probing.

Early in my career, I did a lot of divorce mediation, a less oppositional path to divorce than litigation, and though the couples who elect that route tend to behave considerably more kindly toward each other than those in litigation, they *are* still divorcing, still prone to disagreement and in need of assistance.

William was a VP in a financial services firm and a workaholic, but he didn't regard all that time away from Nadine and family as him "try- ing to get away," as she put it; to him, it was a sign of responsibility, as well as modeling a work ethic for their two kids. Nadine, feeling ignored, frequently "interfered" in William's work (according to William).

She often wanted to get away, just the two of them, but William almost always said, "I've got too much work," and was often grumpy and stressed out (according to Nadine). Over time, she grew so resentful, and felt so cheated out of fun, that the flame went out. They had an eight-room Colonial and a big yard and a couple of Irish setters. The marriage collapsed after eighteen years.

We were at a late stage in the mediation, which had, at some point, devolved into shuttle diplomacy, with the parties in separate conference rooms and me going back and forth between them. I was alone with William, who was gazing out the window. It was a bleak scene— gray winter sky, bare trees—though given his pensive, depressed mood, it wouldn't have mattered had he been looking out at a splash of blue-birds singing Bobby McFerrin songs in a stand of cherry blossoms. "I could have done better," he said wistfully. "It's my fault." He was quiet for a few seconds. Then: "But Nadine . . . she could have told me she appreciated how hard I worked. And not just that, but that the work meant something to *me*. When she talked about vacation, it was always that she wanted to get away. She could have said she liked spending time away with *me*. I remember what it used to be like. She thought I was the funniest guy."

Looking at William in that moment, it occurred to me that during the marriage he wanted—needed—to be addressed as a different person from the one whose reflection looked back at him. He wanted to be approached by his wife as a person different from the one he thought, perhaps assumed (rightly or wrongly), she always saw. He had wanted to be addressed as his best self, or at least a better self; if not an angel, then at least someone capable of admirable, even occasionally beautiful things.

As I wrote in Chapter 1, I've never seen a broken marriage unbreak, so I'm not suggesting this was the one switch that needed to be flipped to produce a wildly different outcome. But just as a thought experiment: What *might* have happened if Nadine had framed her desire to get away with William in a different way? Suppose she'd told him, sincerely, "I appreciate so much the work that you do and I know how much you care about it. But I love spending time with you, and I also know you're so much more effective at work when you take a break and then you come back to it. So I'm really not saying that you work too much or that your work is not important. I know what we're like together, and I want that." What then?

"Frame," by the way, is not a euphemism for "manipulate." It's not "spin," or dishonesty. It means accessing another way to look at things—hopefully, a constructive, aspirational way. While it's meant foremost for the person being addressed, the speaker's role in this is crucial, too.\* When speaking to your partner's best self, you need to locate who you need to be for them in that moment. I have to do this all the time in my practice. After my consultation speech, where I tell the potential new client how I need them to be utterly candid with me (before capping it off with the offer of free candy), I can learn a huge amount from the first words out of their mouth after I say, "So, tell me about your marriage."

If the client says, "Oh, where do I start? That's such a giant question," already I can tell she takes a fairly rational approach, and needs me to share in that mind-set.

If her first words are "My husband's cheating," then she's pissed off (obviously), wants to go to war, and wants me to go to war with and for her.

If she says, "I heard you're a ruthless son of a bitch," she's even more pissed, and looking for me to posture about what a shark I am in the courtroom and how we're going to overpower her domineering husband and his lawyers. I will probably talk about Jiu-Jitsu.

If she says, "I'm not looking to fight here, I just want to be fair," it's possible that she's really rational—but far more likely, in my experience, that her husband has told her for so long that she's going to "get nothing" that she's internalized it, and will need to be convinced to take even the most basic assets, never mind what else she's entitled to. I will probably talk about Jiu-Jitsu.

---

\* It's impossible for real communication to be one-directional.

Once I can tell what the person needs from me, my voice changes, my demeanor changes. I shift to be what she needs me to be; *but I'm not lying.* Each version—the conciliator, the shark, the life coach, the devil's advocate—is an authentic representation of myself. It's not dishonest but human; in fact, it's humane, and good business.

During my college years, when I was a waiter at a restaurant named Steak and Ale, I would be a different person depending on the customer. If I was waiting on a table with a young man and woman obviously on a date, I aimed to make the man look good by praising whatever wine he selected as "an excellent choice" and whatever food he selected with it as "pairing beautifully with the wine." (Yes, a place with "Ale" in its name actually had a decent wine list.) A table of three middle-aged women in non-business attire? I would flirt or be playful with them. ("Uh-oh, this table looks like trouble. How are we tonight, ladies?") A talkative group of businessmen? I would be their buddy ("Who's ready for another round of Sam Adams? I heard this guy [pointing to the coolest-looking man] is buying!") and let them look more accomplished than their waiter. An old couple? I'd show them how to locate the best value on the menu and be as polite as humanly possible.

Call it stereotyping or profiling but it had less to do with the table's demographics and more to do with the energy coming off the people, with how their body language or expression invited me to interact with them. Their genders and ages were part of the equation, of course, but my assessment wasn't anywhere near as simple or reductive as that.

I do the same today. It's said that a good lawyer knows the law, while a great lawyer knows the judge. I don't mean that I "know" the judge—that I socialize with them (that kind of thing used to happen between lawyers and judges but almost never does anymore, at least not openly). But I do make it my business to know what the judge overseeing any given case of mine responds to. Judge Goodman, for example, loves sports, so I make sure to work in sports metaphors. "Your Honor, opposing counsel is trying to make an end-around here"; "Your Honor, this latest tack is just a Hail Mary." Judge Forsberg, a doting grandfather, always asks about the kids involved, so I humanize them even more than usual: "And the older boy is typically unavailable after school because he plays high school baseball—" "Oh, really? What position does he play?" Forsberg also refers to jeans as "dungarees" and demands more decorum in his courtroom than most, so I tell my client to make sure to button the top button. That sort of grace note costs me nothing, and may well help in some subtle way. I once spotted Judge Keller at a wine auction for charity, so I managed to work "If you're gonna make wine, Your Honor, you gotta smash a few grapes" into my presentation. Anything to connect. At a Japanese restaurant a couple towns over from one of my offices, I saw at the back of the room a judge dining with a woman I knew was not his wife. *Note to self: From now on, when arguing before Judge Weinberg, don't overdo it on the sin of adultery. None of this "Your Honor, the opposing party is running around with his girlfriend, withdrawing marital assets to lavish on her while his own children go hungry."*

To win an argument, regardless of the time, preparation, and passion I've invested in it, is much harder when the person receiving it is disinclined to respond favorably—or, worse, bristles at what I'm saying regardless of the merits. I try to aim my message at whoever the hearer thinks they are or aspire to be—or, in pop psychology–speak, the person's best self.

Is all this dishonesty, or is it giving people what they want and need? We all have so many selves. You're one way with your spouse, another way with your boss, yet another with your mother. It isn't necessarily phony to play the aggrieved party one night, the ball of mush the next. The key is to support your partner with the patience and engagement that they need—something that my clients, at that point in the relationship, are generally incapable of.

When you want and need to offer a criticism or apology or make a request or explain a decision or even make an overdue romantic entreaty, it's crucial not only to put it in terms that mean something to your partner, rather than just to you, but also to do so where and when your partner is best. When they are primed and ready to listen with their most receptive self. This could be just after working out, perhaps, or on Friday night, or after a glass of wine, or early in the morning before the kids are up, or, in the case of most men I know, just after sex. I'll be honest: I have promised many things after sex I would later regret.

So when and where were you planning on bringing up some issue? Is that really the most constructive setting for your partner to hear it? I marvel at stories from clients about how they tried to accomplish something *regardless of their spouse's readiness to receive it,* and how shocked and dismayed they were at being rebuffed or ignored. Seriously? Bringing stuff up on a Sunday night, say, when you know your spouse gets the back-to-work blues? Or right after work, when you're *both* exhausted? Or when they have just suffered a professional or medical setback? (*Seriously?* "Bad news about that CT scan, babe. Hey, can you start pulling your weight around the house some more?") I sometimes think of my job as getting people who are in desperate places to *not* make desperate decisions.

Similarly, you don't want the person you love to decide, respond, act in a way that is tainted by the less-than-ideal position they're in. If you haven't figured out where and when your partner is at their best, then get to figuring it out fast, file it, incorporate it. And then you can address them the way that's most likely to garner a good response. There's a reason we rub dogs, cats, and babies on their bellies or scratch the tops of their heads.

Here's an even more dramatic suggestion to force you to see your partner—or anyone—differently, to appreciate them more immediately. It's an exercise I myself have integrated into my thinking:

Imagine you're going to lose your spouse later today—that they're going to leave you today *because of something you've done to them.* How would you treat them then? Exactly as you think they would want to be treated, right? By the time I see couples, they've reached the point where it's almost impossible for them to remember that the person they're about to divorce was once the person they loved more than anyone in the world, the person whose happiness they would do anything to bring about. Solid couples who have hit a rough patch sometimes suffer a similar amnesia. If you conjure an image of your partner's best self and address *that* person, you can often defuse a fight or break an impasse.

This happened more than a decade ago.

During an ugly custody trial, Yvonne had spent the last three days describing, in detail, how my client, Sean, had been racist, homophobic, ill-mannered, and verbally abusive for the previous six years, and thus should be granted limited time with the parties' two-year-old son. I knew that some of the claims were simply not true, the rest overblown for dramatic effect: The judge was African-American, so by trying to paint my client as racist (among his other alleged faults), the opposing side was hoping to score some additional points (or at least shave some off my client's ledger).

When I cross-examined Yvonne, rather than start off slow and build to undercut, point by point, the allegations against my client, I took a different route. "Mr. Marson sounds like a truly awful person," I began.

Yvonne wasn't sure how to react. It wasn't really a question. And it can't have been what she had been prepared to expect from my cross-examination.

"I'm not sure what you mean," she said.

"I'm sorry. I'll try to be clearer. He sounds like an absolutely atrocious human being, based on your testimony. Is that fair to say?"

She paused for a moment and looked at her lawyer as if to get some guidance on where this was going.

"I don't know if I would say that he's atrocious," said Yvonne.

"You wouldn't?" I asked incredulously. "Come on. You just spent three days telling us how he's horribly racist, he hates gay people, he's verbally abusive, and he's an insensitive and inattentive father. I don't know how you define it, but that sounds pretty awful to me."

The judge let out an audible laugh, a good sign.

"Well. I guess so," she agreed—reluctantly, but it was impossible to disagree without losing credibility. "All the things I said are true, so, yes, I guess he is."

"And yet you married him."

She looked offended.

"Objection!" said opposing counsel.

"I'm sorry. I know. That wasn't a question. I'll withdraw it and rephrase. You knew him for three years before you married him, didn't you? You dated for three years. You dated this racist, homophobic, abusive, nasty idiot for three years and, at the end of that time, still liked him so much you signed on to be with him for the rest of your life, at least in theory. Isn't that correct?"

Yvonne had no idea how to respond. It was written all over her face.

"What did you like about him? What did you like to the point where you decided it was a good idea to marry him?"

She then spent ten minutes describing all his positive traits. For our side, it was a triumphant, albeit unorthodox, start to her two-day cross-examination, a surge of praise that undercut the credibility of her direct testimony and that forced her, in her own words, to frame for the court the occasional angels of my client's better nature.

The lesson here isn't "If you find yourself married to an abusive racist, remember what you liked about him when the relationship started." (If you find yourself in such a situation, divorce that person, quickly, and don't leave a forwarding address, if possible.) I *am* suggesting that when you're dealing with the day-to-day conflicts of sharing your mental and physical space with another human being, try to keep present, somewhere in your consciousness, a moment when you liked them very much, or when they were there for you, or when they were displaying the attributes that made their presence a comfort, not a chore. If Yvonne could do that, I figure it's a whole lot easier for someone *not* in the midst of a divorce to do the same, on a regular and willing basis.

One of the most recognizable features of a dead marriage is that the spouses find themselves in very different places—their level of anger, sense of loss, sense of accomplishment, readiness to move on—everything. If geology is the study of pressure and time, as Morgan Freeman's character surmises in *The Shawshank Redemption,* then maybe a failed marriage is the study of drift and time. With a married and/or in-love couple, the disparity between partners is not nearly as pronounced, but it's naïve to think that you and your partner are in the same place even most of the time, on most important matters. Some drift is fine, even beneficial. But to keep the vitality of true connection, communicate early and often, often and early, with the best version of the person whom—how great is this?—you already think so highly of.

## Chapter 36

# GRATUITOUS TIME-OUT: HOW NOT TO LET YOURSELF BE CROSS-EXAMINED

I had encouraged Jacob, the optometry store magnate who has appeared in previous chapters, to meet with me a week or so before his testimony to prepare him. I tell all of my clients who are unfortunate enough to see their case go to trial that I like to spend two days preparing for every one day of trial.* If you give me seven hours to chop down a tree, I'll spend six sharpening the ax.

But Jacob refused to meet with me to prepare for his testimony. This was entirely up to him, but I warned him that it was a colossally bad idea, with potentially disastrous and irreparable long-term consequences.

"I'm not paying you six hundred dollars per hour to practice asking me questions about things I already know about," he said (as I wrote earlier). "I don't need to study. I know my business. I know the truth. I don't need you to spend a few thousand dollars of my money teaching me how to talk. I didn't build a successful business by not knowing how to talk."

I told Jacob, again, that like every client, he had final decision-making authority on strategy related to his case. I warned him that the expense

---

* There's no real data out there on the number of cases that settle before trial, given the fact that many divorcing couples never set foot in court, but the popular consensus among divorce lawyers in New York is that 98 percent of divorce and custody cases are settled before a final decision is issued by a court.

of my hourly rate for a few hours of preparation was a very small invest-ment if it resulted in a more favorable outcome on the issues of child support, alimony, and the sale value of his business for the purposes of buying out his wife's share.

"You lawyers are always trying to find places to bill extra time. I'm not trying to insult you, Jim, but there's a reason people hate lawyers so much."

I repeated myself one more time and sent him an email a few days later, putting my advice in writing so it was clear and unambiguous.

Jacob took the stand a few days later, on a Monday morning, and after an uneventful direct examination was subject to cross-examination on Tuesday.*

"You testified on direct examination that your Brooklyn store is doing—and I'm going to try to use your exact words here—'really poorly,' is that right?"

Paul Walsh was my adversary on Jacob's trial. Paul worked for me for about five years early in his career, before he went out on his own—with my blessing—and opened a solo practice a few blocks over. We've remained friends and have lunch fairly often. He calls me to pick my brain on complicated issues, and I call him as well to hear his perspec-tive on things. He borrows my forms from time to time, I ask him to proofread my stuff. He's bright and talented but a little less aggressive and a lot less organized than I am.

I would never, however, underestimate his talents. That's a surefire way to get your legs chopped off. Jacob's trial was the third or fourth case I'd had with Paul as my adversary. You might think it's difficult to engage in this kind of combat with someone you're friends with outside the courtroom, but it's actually great. Years of boxing and martial arts have taught me the joy of punching my friends in the face and having them come at me just as hard. And afterward, you've got someone to

---

* Direct examination=the part where your lawyer asks you questions. The hard part for a lawyer, the easy part for a client. You remember when you were a kid and you set up a bunch of dominoes so they would fall in a cool pattern? The hard, time-consuming part was setting them up. The easy, way more fun part was knocking them down. Direct examination is setting up the dominoes. Cross is knocking them down.

laugh with about how the fight went, over drinks at the bar down the street from the courthouse.

"Yes," said Jacob. "That store has been doing badly for a long time."

"And why do you think it's doing so poorly?"

*Counsel must be feeling bold today, or have confidence in my client's stupidity,* I thought. Paul was breaking a cardinal rule of cross-examination: Don't ask open-ended questions that allow the witness to explain their answer. If the witness, on cross-examination, is saying much of anything other than yes or no, it usually means you're doing a shitty job. In Jacob's case, however, it meant that opposing counsel was confident in Jacob's ability to hang himself when given enough rope.

"Lots of reasons," replied Jacob. "People don't buy eyeglasses or contact lenses anymore, really. They get LASIK surgery and so I'm losing tons of customers who never come back because they never need glasses or contacts again."

*Technological innovation that renders a business obsolete. It's a classic. Well done, Jacob. Keep it together now. This is your time to shine. Let's wrap this one up!*

"Also, another shop opened only a few blocks away that offers some of the same styles and manufacturers that I do, so I've had to lower my prices to match or beat theirs. It's a chain store so they can sell the same stuff for a much lower price."

*Increased competition in the same geographic area. David versus Goliath. Mom-and-pop store versus Walmart. Tale as old as time. Puts him in a sympathetic light. Another beauty. Well played, Jacob. Don't fuck this up. Bring it home now.*

"And I lost some key employees over the past few years. The manager of that location quit abruptly, and ever since she left, the store hasn't been able to find its footing. It's hard to find good people. Without them you can't maintain a strong business."

*Boom goes the dynamite! The "Why my previously thriving business is suddenly a big pile of shit" trifecta is complete! And, for bonus points with our female judge, Jacob has managed to slip in that one of his stores was managed by a woman. Take that, patriarchy. Sisters are doing it for themselves. Jacob's wife better dust off her résumé. The location of the comma on the alimony check is moving to the left before our very eyes! Time to wrap this old party up!*

Paul paused for a moment as if to let this sink in. He shuffled some papers on his trial table to the right of the judge and the left of me, before returning to the podium to continue.

*Oh, no. I know this move.*

"That's very interesting, sir," said Paul. "But I've got a few questions about all those things you just said."

*Take your best shot, Paul. You're ready for this, Jacob. Just keep it together.*

"Now you just said, in sum and substance, that your shop in Brooklyn is failing for three main reasons: people getting LASIK, the opening of another store nearby, and losing a key manager. Did I get those right?"

*I'm loving this. It's a rookie mistake: reiterating the other side's arguments when it's your turn to state your case. Thanks for using what's supposed to be your time to shine to give me some free advertising and to repeat the precise points I was trying to get across to the judge earlier.*

"Yes. That's right."

"Okay. That's a lot to unpack. So let's look at those one at a time. . . . A large percentage of your customer base is Hasidic Jewish residents of Brooklyn, is that right?"

"I wouldn't say a large percentage, but yes, I have Hasidic customers. I'm proud to serve people from every community."

*Nice one.*

"You wouldn't say a large percentage? Isn't it a fact that you estimated, during an interview you gave to *Custom Eyewear* magazine in April of 2015, that close to ninety-six percent of your customer base is Hasidic Jews?"

"No. I don't believe I said that. I think you're misinterpreting what I said."

With that, opposing counsel handed the court reporter a glossy magazine.

"Your Honor, I would like to have this marked as Plaintiff's Exhibit Number Three for identification purposes and shown to the witness."

The reporter marked the magazine, and the court officer handed it to Jacob.

"I apologize if I misinterpreted what you said, sir, when I said that you estimated, during an interview you gave to *Custom Eyewear* magazine in April of 2015, that close to ninety-six percent of your customer base is Hasidic Jews. Could you please identify what's been marked as Plaintiff's Exhibit Number Three for identification purposes and handed to you just now?"

"It's the April 2015 issue of *Custom Eyewear* magazine."

"And could you turn to page twelve of that magazine, please, and read the second paragraph on that page?"

Jacob paused for a moment and scanned the page.

"'The Brooklyn eyewear scene is thriving in the religious communities of Greenpoint, Brooklyn, with Jacob Ashar, owner of Brooklyn Quality Optical, estimating that close to ninety-six percent of his customer base is religious Hasidic Jews."

*Shit.*

"So when you said that to the reporter, were you telling her the truth?"

*Well played, Paul. The old "Were you lying then or are you lying now?" trap. A classic on witness stands since before they started making them out of wood.*

"Yes. I just didn't remember the exact number. But yes. I guess that's about right."

"And sir, isn't it a fact that religious Hasidic Jews generally don't get LASIK surgery. In fact, it's not in keeping with their religious principles and practices to get LASIK, is it?"

"Objection! Calls for improper opinion testimony on the part of this witness. The defendant is an optometrist, not a rabbi, Your Honor. It's wrong for counsel to attempt to quiz him on the practices of a specific religious group of which he isn't a member."

(This objection was made in part because the question had some challengeable validity, but in larger part to throw off the momentum of the cross and give Jacob a second or two to think about a good answer. I would say a solid third of the objections I make at trial are totally invalid and designed solely to interrupt the flow of testimony, to frustrate opposing counsel after they've asked a particularly intricate or detailed question that they will now have to repeat, or just to be a dick because the other side is doing well. It's the equivalent, when you're in a fistfight, of shouting, "Hey, look over there!")

My adversary was ready for that one.

"Your Honor, I'm not asking some obscure tenet of Talmudic law. I'm asking a man who owns an eyeglasses business, for nearly twenty years, that he readily admits serves an overwhelmingly high percentage of a specific religious community, what the attitude of that religious community appears to be, from where he's sitting, on the specific items he sells."

"I'm going to allow it," the judge readily stated, turning to Jacob. "You may answer the question, Mr. Ashar."

Jacob looked a little annoyed.

"LASIK isn't particularly popular among Hasidic Jews. No."

Paul wasn't letting him off that easy.

"I'm sorry, sir, did you just say it isn't 'particularly popular'?"

"Yes. That's right."

"How many Hasidic Jewish customers have told you that they aren't coming back to your business because they recently had LASIK surgery?"

"I don't recall."

"You don't recall a precise number, or you don't recall any?"

"No. I don't recall any."

Paul smiled. That was the answer he wanted.

"Okay, so the first reason you offered for why your Brooklyn shop isn't doing well is, by your own admission, inapplicable to approximately ninety-six percent of your customer base for that store. Do I have that right?"

*Fuck.*

"Yes. I guess that's right."

*Okay. That wasn't ideal, Jacob, but you handled it well. You got caught and you didn't try to play around or be cute. You were candid. Forthright. It hurt your credibility a little, but it also bolstered your credibility a little when you didn't try to hide things. So let's hope that was a net neutral with the judge. She doesn't appear to be glaring at you. That's always a good sign with Judge Garvey. A lack of glaring. She tends to glare when she hates you. I know. She's glared at me more times than I care to admit. But we still got this, buddy boy.*

"So let's look at the second reason. You said another store opened up in the same neighborhood—you called it a chain store, I believe— and said they sell the same stuff you sell, but for a lower price. Is that right?"

*Thanks! Keep repeating it, Paul. Maybe the third time is a charm.*

"Yes. That's right. They opened a LensCrafters. They're a huge chain and they can operate at a much smaller markup than I can and make up for it in volume."

Counsel paused.

"Thank you for that. But I asked you a yes-or-no question. So if you could just answer the question I asked, I would appreciate it. You said the other store opened up 'in the same neighborhood' as your Brooklyn store and sells the 'same stuff you sell' but at a lower price. Now do I have that right? Yes or no?"

"Yes."

"Thank you. Okay. Now isn't it a fact that the LensCrafters you're referring to is, in fact, located in Sheepshead Bay, Brooklyn, not Green- point, where you maintain your shop?"

"It's also in Brooklyn. Same as my shop."

"That's not what I asked you, sir. Greenpoint and Coney Island are both in Brooklyn, as well. Does that make them 'in the same neighborhood,' in your view? Because, if it does, please don't tell my grandmother. It would ruin my excuse for not visiting her for dinner more often."

The judge laughed at this.

*Fuck. Fuck. Fuck. And Paul's grandmother lives in Queens. I know. I've met her. Ugh, and she's lovely. But that was a good one. Asshole.*

"And the brands that you claim your so-called competitor is able to offer at a discount—those are high-end designer frames from Gucci and Prada, isn't that right?"

"Yes. Among others."

"You discussed this in some detail in your deposition before trial, didn't you: Gucci, Prada, Ferragamo, Hermès. Those are the designers we're talking about here, right?"

"Yes."

I had to give Paul credit. When he was asking those questions in the deposition, I thought they were throwaway items, just to drag things out and get the witness talking. Now I see he was thinking more tactically than I gave him credit for. *See you at the bar, old friend.*

"And the 'discount' that LensCrafters is able to give. In reviewing your 'price matching' transactions over the past two years, it looks like it's about a one percent discount from your thirty percent markup. Do I have that right? Math was never my strong suit."

*Nice one. A little humility goes a long way. I taught him that line.*

"That sounds about right," Jacob admitted sheepishly.

"So, on a $400 pair of frames, that means the customer saves $4 and you make a profit of $116 instead of $120 on the pair. Is that right?"

"Yes. I guess that's right."

Paul stopped and began moving closer to the witness stand. He was far enough away that he didn't need to request permission to approach the witness, but close enough that it added to the dramatic flair of a confrontational question. Again, I'd like to think I taught him that move.

"So, it's your sworn testimony today that the Hasidic Jewish clientele that make up ninety-six percent of your business pay $5.50 to take a two-hour round-trip subway ride out of their home neighborhood so they can get a $4 discount on Gucci eyeglasses?"

*I've got to admit it. He's good. I might offer him his old job back.*

"I don't know. I just know business is down and they opened up. Maybe it's a coincidence."

"Maybe. Okay. So the third reason you gave was the abrupt departure of a key manager in the Greenpoint location. Is that right?"

"Yes."

"And you said that was a female employee, right?"

"Yes."

"Are you referring to Cheryl Miller?"

Jacob's pause would have been imperceptible to most people. It struck me immediately as a sign he was uncomfortable with where this was going.

"Yes."

"That's the manager you're referring to, correct?"

"Yes."

"The one who abruptly left the shop and threw it into its current state of disarray?"

"I didn't say abruptly."

"You didn't? I'm sorry. I thought you did. Should we have the court reporter read back your testimony from earlier?"

"No. If I said that, I was mistaken. It wasn't abruptly. But she left and it hurt the business."

"Right. You said that. So when she left, abruptly or inabruptly . . . Is that a word, 'inabruptly'?"

*Now Paul is really putting it on. I'm secretly a little proud of him: This is the kind of shit I'm notorious for.*

"If counsel needs me to Google that for him, just let me know," I chimed in.

*Don't try to outsnark me, Paul. Two can play at that game. I was charming the robes off judges while you were still in high school.*

"Withdrawn. So Cheryl Miller was the manager who left, the 'key' manager who left, and that hurt your business. Is that correct?"

"Yes."

Paul pulled something out of a folder on the defense table and handed it to the court reporter.

"I'd like this marked for identification purposes as Defendant's Exhibit Four and shown to the witness, please."

The reporter marked it and the court officer gave it to Jacob. Paul handed a copy to me and a second copy to the officer for the judge to review.

*Are you fucking kidding me?*

"Now, sir, I would respectfully request that you take a look at what's been marked for identification as Defendant's Exhibit Four and handed to you by the court officer. Do you recognize this?"

Jacob looked at the document for a moment and then looked at me.

*Don't look at me, pal. I can't help you right now. You're on your own at this particular moment, and you've got no one to blame for it but your-self.*

"Yes. I see it."

"This is a printout of the homepage for your Facebook profile, cor-rect?"

Jacob looked at it again with an expression that suggested he hoped it might have transformed into something else in the previous thirty sec-onds. "Yes."

"And does this printout fairly and accurately depict the Facebook homepage for your personal Facebook profile as it appears at the cur-rent time?"

"I would have to look at it closely."

"Please do. We can wait."

Jacob paused. Again. As if this was helping him somehow and not doing what it was actually doing: making him look like a deer in the headlights.

*This isn't helping, Jacob. Just take the hit like a man. You're slowing down the pace at precisely the time when opposing counsel wants you to slow down the pace. And I can't do anything to stop it. There aren't any objections to be made and I'm not asking for a bathroom break right now.*

"Yes. I guess that's it."

"You guess? Is there some ambiguity?"

"Objection!" I leaped out of my chair, happy to be able to do something, anything, to take the court's attention off this car crash.

"Basis?" asked the judge.

*Um . . . I want this to stop?*

"Asked and answered, Your Honor."

"Overruled," said the court. "Please answer the question, Mr. Ashar."

"No. No ambiguity. That's my Facebook profile. But I don't really use Facebook. I'm not very good with the computer."

*Don't try to be charming right now, Jacob. It makes you look guilty. The judge didn't even crack a smile on that one. If you were going to do the "Aw, shucks, I don't know how to use a computer" thing, the time to do it was much earlier, before you got yourself caught in the mousetrap.*

"And under your name and where you live, it has what they call your relationship status, is that correct?"

"Yes."

"And what does yours say?"

Jacob was visibly uncomfortable and answered hesitantly. "It says, 'In a Relationship with Cheryl Miller.'"

The judge was officially glaring at Jacob Ashar. This was very bad.

"So you're in a romantic relationship with Ms. Miller, is that correct?"

"Well . . . we have a relationship. We are friends and we spend time together."

*Don't do this, Jacob. Just take the hit. This is what I would have told you at my conference table if you had given me even half an hour to prepare you. Kill your credibility on the small issues and you're going to destroy it for the big ones. Don't do this. Even teenagers know "Facebook official" is akin to marriage in this day and age.*

"Oh . . . you aren't dating her?"

"I'm a forty-eight-year-old man. I'm not 'dating' someone. I'm not in high school. That's ridiculous."

He turned to Judge Garvey with a contemptuous look for opposing counsel, perhaps hoping for some sign of agreement. He did not get it.

She was still glaring. He was officially FUBAR and he was making a bad situation exponentially worse with every syllable that came out of his mouth.*

"So if we reviewed, for example, your American Express statements, we wouldn't find jewelry purchases at Tiffany's, lingerie purchases at La Perla, or charges for dinners at the Polo Club with Ms. Miller, would we?"

Paul was walking toward the defense table, to bring everyone's eyes toward the various folders he had there. He may or may not have had the actual credit card statements in there, and they may or may not have been certified copies that could be introduced into evidence, but I was hoping that Jacob wasn't going to gamble and find out.

"You might. She and I are very close."

Jacob looked as if he'd been punched in the gut a few times. He was broken now and, unfortunately, in that space where a defeated witness just starts agreeing with pretty much everything you ask him. It's a great place to be when you're the lawyer asking the questions. It's a shitty place to be when you're watching it happen to your client and you can't stop it.

"And it's your sworn testimony that she is, essentially, the third reason why your Brooklyn store isn't doing well? Isn't that right?"

"Well, it's not her fault entirely."

"I'm sorry, sir, wasn't your testimony earlier that the third and, with all due respect, only remaining potentially valid excuse for why your Brooklyn store isn't doing well financially was because Cheryl Miller, a 'key manager,' left abruptly and threw the business into chaos? Did you get her something from Tiffany's for a severance package?"

Jacob had taken the stand a cocky and overconfident business owner, determined to prevent his soon-to-be ex-wife from getting her fair share of his assets. He would likely have succeeded had he spent a few hours

---

* FUBAR—Fucked Up Beyond All Repair. While it's not a legal term, you'd be surprised how much divorce lawyers use it.

with me preparing. There were ways to address the vulnerabilities in his case, ways that required only a slight shift in focus and no perjury.

He left the witness stand a broken man. The case settled a few days later for several hundred thousand more than was on the table before the trial started.

But he saved a few bucks on trial preparation.

## Chapter 37

# WRITE A LETTER

Expressing intimacy is hard. Being vulnerable is hard. Advice that urges one approach for all people on how to do those things is idiotic. One size does not fit all. But here we go!

Suppose you wish to communicate better—to inquire about your partner's state of mind, to express your own before gripes harden—but you lack the skill to do it, or think you do. What if you feel inarticulate when speaking?

Write your loved one a letter.

If that sounds goofy: At times I've recommended that clients with children write letters to their soon-to-be exes after the custody agreement is in place, since they will be co-parents the rest of their lives. While there are certain things that, for legal reasons, I recommend they *don't* say (such as admitting fault that, in litigation, they have denied), I find that writing the letter can be a cleansing, positive experience for everyone.

In a texting world, a letter is romantic. For the purpose I'm suggesting—for any purpose, really—a letter is more deliberate and definitive, certainly more formal, and, dare I say, appropriately solemn. And why shouldn't it be? Given the subject matter, it *shouldn't* be an off-the-cuff quickie punched out with two thumbs in ten seconds. You can't express those emotions in emojis.

I won't presume to tell you what to say in this letter to your spouse. But I deeply believe that life is too short not to say what needs saying. When I recommend letter-writing to a client at the end of their marriage, I use the following as an example, because it covers a lot of ground:

> Dear Dina,
>
> Now that our divorce has been finalized, I just wanted to take a moment and apologize to you for the mistakes I made during our marriage. I know there were times during our marriage, and our divorce, when I could have been a better husband, father, and man. I can't take back anything I have said or done, but I can offer you my sincere apology for my mistakes and failings. I also want to let you know that I am deeply committed to being a good ex-husband to you and a dedicated father to our children. Although our marriage is over, I know how important you are to the children and how important you will always be to me because of that. Thank you for everything you have done for me and for them. I want, very much, to be a positive presence in our children's lives, and yours, as we enter this new chapter in our relationship. Thank you for the patience and affection you've shown me in the past.
>
> Rick

Granted, the letter above is formal. Would it be weird to write a letter to someone you've shared a bed with for years? Whom you see and talk to dozens of times a day? Even for those who can find the right words when speaking, writing things out may help you to better organize and hence understand what you really want to say—even if you end up not giving the letter to your partner. I know mediators who encourage their clients to come to the first meeting with a letter to their ex-to-be; it "lubricates communication," as one put it to me.

If at least some people in the midst of divorce can do that, it should be way easier for those in love, knowing that their partner is receptive to—maybe even hungry for—communication and intimacy. Anything that might ease communication in a divorce should apply far more effectively in a loving relationship.

Write a letter to your partner. List at least five things they do that you appreciate. Tell them a few things they do that upset you. Tell them what you are craving but not getting from them. Tell them a few things you *are* getting and are incredibly grateful for. Tell them a story from your shared history, in as much detail as you can, that you remember fondly. Maybe write a mini-chronicle of your marriage.

It's been said that the unexamined life is not worth living. My experience has taught me that the unexamined marriage is not sustainable. Write your spouse a letter. Make it simple or make it detailed. But make it authentic and honest.

You love her, right? You love him, right?

## Chapter 38

# YOURS, MINE, AND OURS:
# THE FINANCIAL SYSTEM
# THAT WORKS BEST

To put it mildly, Tara was upset at Cal.

It was hard to blame her. He had blown $350,000 the previous year, without her knowledge, playing blackjack in Vegas. That bonus he'd said his employer "decided not to give" for the last three years? It was being mailed to a post office box he never told her about. He lost it when he split tens against the dealer's eight (among many other losing hands). Cal was a better corporate financial analyst, apparently, than gambler.

When confronted with the specific evidence of his gambling that we discovered after sending subpoenas to most of the major casinos on the Vegas strip*—which we successfully argued as a "wasteful dissipation of marital assets," winning for Tara the value remaining in the parties' house—Cal got hot. "Do you know how much money she wastes on designer bags and shoes?" he shot back.

It didn't matter that Tara's spending didn't come anywhere near Cal's: Money makes people do and say crazy things. Except for infidelity, nothing causes more imbalance and eventual upheaval in a marriage than money. When a client bogs down a case and we can't move for-

---

* All of whom, I must say, are amazing recordkeepers. They literally watch and record everything you do there and, for a small photocopying fee, will send copies to your spouse's attorney when served with a subpoena that takes one of my paralegals thirty seconds to customize and spit out of the printer. Just a heads-up.

ward and hours are being wasted, I point out to them, "You can pay for your kids' college, or mine," and things straighten out. And it's simplistic to say that when money troubles lead to relationship troubles, it's because there just wasn't enough of it. The number-one root cause, in my experience, is lack of financial transparency.

If you're in a marriage or a shared-finances relationship that's not in trouble, what can you do to keep money from becoming a potentially debilitating issue? In so many marriages, bad and good, one partner, often the bigger breadwinner but not always, doesn't want the other to stress over money, so they keep that partner out of the loop. Most of the time this is done out of caring. But regardless of motive, it creates a transparency problem. The out-of-the-loop partner doesn't know what's going on and, more specifically, may not understand or appreciate how hard the other person is working, or how much stress they deal with to keep things running smoothly. And then, when the out-of-the-loop partner appears in my office, he or she has a totally unrealistic picture of how much juggling was going on ("All I know is we were doing very well and all the bills got paid"). In the effort to keep the engines churning, were they borrowing from Peter to pay Paul? Was something criminal going on? Are federal auditors readying a sting?

Anastasia was, by all signs, married to a very successful anesthesiologist. They enjoyed luxurious vacations. All five of their children attended religious private school. They drove nice cars and owned a stunning primary residence as well as a country home for which she had personally picked all the details, including the indoor infinity pool and far infrared sauna.

Two months into their divorce proceedings, I had to let Anastasia know that she was broke.

Her husband was part owner of three surgical centers, but he'd failed to mention to her that over the last few years he had leveraged his ownership interest against some speculative real estate investments that did not pan out; the notes came due, and he was forced to sell his interest to his partners. He could still work at the centers, at a good—not great—salary, but would no longer share in profits or the appreciation of the real estate or other assets of the business.

The fancy cars? Leased. The two homes? Mortgaged to the hilt, with primary mortgages that eclipsed nearly all the equity, the rest of which had been sucked out by home equity lines of credit that had gone to fund those luxurious vacations.

Anastasia still had some very nice Hermès bags and Christian Louboutin shoes, but you would be surprised how low the resale value of those items can be (particularly the shoes). I can't tell you how many people try to fund their retainer payment to my firm with some combination of high-end bags and jewelry. It's not surprising that my former office manager, when she quit working in family law, opened a consignment shop down the street from the courthouse.*

I was able to get Anastasia a reasonable child support award and sufficient alimony to cover her basic expenses. But it was clear that she was about to make an abrupt and wholly unexpected trip from the first-class cabin back to coach. The best I could do for her was to obtain a generous financial package that would, hopefully, be enforceable against any future income her ex might earn. But that was small comfort when she'd been blissfully ignorant for more than a decade about her husband's financial incompetence, unreasonable risk-taking, and, to a large extent, prolonged unspoken shame, the ramifications of which compounded about as fast as the interest on their credit cards.

People have great intentions, and things often get messed up despite that. After all, few actions that married people take, short of an affair, are at first perceived as something that could jeopardize the marriage. No, the damage happens gradually, until you wake up one morning and ask, "How the hell did we get here?"

You're having a rough month financially. To make matters worse, you just found out that, yes, your ten-year-old needs braces, and the first installment is due. This requires a mildly to moderately uncomfortable conversation about money or about how your son's teeth are going to be

---

* Elite Repeat, www.eliterepeatny.com. Great little spot. Tell Annmarie that Jim sent you.

weird his whole life . . . but who wants to have that talk? No one. So the talk is shelved. Ten months later, you look back and *wish* you had had that conversation, because it would have been so much better than the one you need to have now that there's an extra 0 in the orthodontist bill and you've got twenty thousand dollars in credit card debt.

Sometimes ignorance is bliss, and sometimes it's dangerous. For solid couples, simple financial models are often the best. What I call the Yours, Mine, and Ours economic system works best for most couples because *it's built precisely to maximize freedom while preventing lack of transparency.* It's a "business model" approach: It requires that you and your spouse, like salespeople with expense accounts, get each other's "authorization" for expenses exceeding a certain amount.

I know, I hear you: *Why should a married couple build a system of checks and balances into their finances? This isn't one partisan branch of government making sure the other one isn't up to its usual shenanigans. If you can't trust your spouse, you shouldn't be married to them! Married people shouldn't have rules, period, to manage their collective finances. It's unromantic to even suggest it.*

This isn't the first time I've been called unromantic.

In a perfect world, no system would be necessary. People would be able to trust themselves and their spouses completely when it comes to money (and every other issue). In a perfect world, we wouldn't need locks on our doors, or police, or calorie counts, or surgeons-general.

I've got Earth on Line One, so I'm going to return to the real world now.

I'm okay with being pragmatic rather than romantic; honestly, there's something romantic about pragmatism. I find reality way sexier than delusion.

For those currently in, and hoping to remain in, functional (ideally, happy) relationships, here's a brief overview of the Yours, Mine, and Ours Financial System.

Make three pools of money: Yours. Mine. Ours.

At the outset, agree with your spouse that anything in the "Mine" category is yours (well, "mine"), meaning assets and debts, and anything in the "Yours" category is your spouse's. (Or vice versa . . . I'm not sure who I'm talking to now.) Create bank accounts for each of these pools, funding them however you like (in equal amounts; in some portion from each of your earnings; in some portion from joint or separate savings . . . ). Create another account for the "Ours" category. Fund that pool with whatever sources you agree are appropriate (a portion of each of your earnings; proceeds from a joint asset you recently sold, and so on).

When an expense comes up that is inarguably for the benefit of the marriage (or, for example, the house you share, or the children), use the funds in the "Ours" account. Still, in the interest of transparency and clarity, you agree that when an expense exceeds a set threshold ($100 or $500 or whatever you choose), the one spending the money will notify the other, by email or text, of the expense. You might even consider a second, higher threshold that requires not just notification but the other partner's "preapproval."

What if you want to buy something for your spouse? What if you want to buy something for yourself without your spouse knowing about it? What if you want to buy something that your spouse thinks is frivolous, but you don't care because you're a grown-up?

That's where the "Yours" and "Mine" accounts come into play.

Each of these gives you some privacy, some autonomy, and some personal control over money, free from the reach or inquiry of the other but without totally separating your financial lives.

What are some of the perks of doing it this way?

1. *Preventing ignorance while maintaining privacy.* This system provides each party with insight into the collective financial picture without precluding one spouse from managing the "Ours" account should they happen to enjoy doing that. It also allows both parties to maintain some privacy in their individual accounts.

2. *It creates opportunities for autonomy (see also: permitted stupidity).* You want to buy a boat? Spouse thinks the boat is a stupid idea? Buy it with funds in your "Mine" account, or take a loan for it in

your name alone, and on some level it's no longer really your spouse's concern.*

3. *It can easily be converted into a legally binding system.* If you like, you can have an attorney prepare a simple document that, in essence, makes this approach the legally binding way of doing things in your marriage. So your spouse *really* doesn't have any obligation for your boat loan if you bought it with your "Mine" account.

(There's a fourth perk, but since that's only relevant if your marriage falls apart, it doesn't feel quite right to call it a perk.)†

If you're getting married, or if you're already married but don't have such a financial system in place, you'll want to understand how money intersects with your relationship. When Yours, Mine, and Ours works as it's supposed to, the system increases transparency, generates a sense both of sharing and of control/freedom, and decreases resentment. It keeps things running smoothly in your married financial life.

---

\* I acknowledge that that's the single most naïve thing I've written so far.

† You each have access to funds that the other can't "cut off"; this prevents the spouse who makes more from "starving out" the spouse with limited earnings; it prevents the lesser-earning spouse from arguing to a court that they need emergency access to funds because they are being "bullied" by the spouse with big earnings, preventing a temporary counsel fee application that could cost thousands of dollars.

## Chapter 39

# DESIGN, NOT DEFAULT

"We started off doing what we were doing; then we kept doing it; we made a left turn, then a right turn, then a left, a right . . . Oops! We found we weren't on the same road anymore."

I get it. It's hard to focus on the destination while also avoiding stumbles on the path to getting there. But marriage, perhaps uniquely, is both a goal *and* a tool for getting to that goal. It's the finish line *and* the technique for running the race. You get married to help you grow up, and getting married is a sign that you're grown up. Getting married helps you mature, but you need maturity to do it properly. Sound contradictory and complicated? That's because it is.

But what does a good marriage really look like? If love is, as the late great Amy Winehouse put it, a game, how do you gauge how well you're playing? I know—if you're in my office, most people would say you're losing. That's the easy part.

But what does it mean to "win" at marriage? As I've written, all marriages end: Death and divorce are the only two possible outcomes. You can't seriously, in modern times, conclude that the goal is simply "to stay married," as if it were noble to stay in a miserable marriage that stifles and harms both parties.

To "win" at marriage is, for most people, not only to remain married but also to find that the marriage brings joy, self-improvement, or some combination of the two that makes the benefits of staying married outweigh the burdens (as well as the lost potential benefits of remaining unmarried).

That sounds pretty unromantic, I know. But it's strange that so many of us have wagered all of our assets on a tool without ever articulating more clearly what we are looking for that tool to help us achieve.

Marriage doesn't mean depriving yourself of new experiences—a few of them, sure, like the experience of living a life free from attachment to another person, or, for most people in conventional marriages, the experience of dating people. Nor am I suggesting that serendipity and randomness play no role in life. Personally, I've found that life is characterized, in both the short and long terms, far more by the unexpected than the expected.

But unless you got married just to shut up your parents (in which case, you could have made it easier on yourselves and just ignored their calls), it's reasonable to conclude that you felt there was some logic to marrying. It's also reasonable to assume you might, ideally, still want to be together ten, twenty, thirty, or more years down the road. That's the goal. The long-term goal of marriage. To stay together. Happily, if possible.

If that's the case, then it's better to at least *try* to develop your relationship by design, not by default.

You married because you wanted to get someplace together, correct? Is there a map? Are using Waze and GPS the only times you explicitly go, together, from an agreed-upon Point A to Point B?

Ignoring the map is totally understandable. People need to just get through the day. It's hard to plan beyond tomorrow. At the office, you just want to make it to quitting time. Or to Friday. You spend fifty weeks of the year looking forward to the other two. Five days looking forward to two. If you run a business, it's *Please just make payroll through the month*. At home, maybe you're just trying to make it through the kids' midterm exams, or baseball season, or tax season, or the long cold winter months after which you can get back outside and breathe fresh air.

I get it. It's hard enough to make it through the day, and now I'm telling you you're doing it wrong because you don't have a research-and-development department set up in your living room? (The old Soviet Union famously created and followed one five-year economic plan after another after another, and look where that got them.) But in-the-moment living (admittedly, this isn't quite the kind of "in the moment" that Buddhists encourage) adds up: You're rarely checking in with your spouse about where she's going, or about whether you're both even pointing toward the same goal.

Most of my professional efforts are spent figuring out what "victory" looks like for my clients. Where does she want to be five, ten, twenty years from now? What can I do, in my representation of her, to maximize her chance of achieving that? Where does she want to live? In a house or in an apartment? Does she want to keep working? For how many years? During a divorce, it's critical to have candid conversations with yourself and with your attorney about what you want your post-divorce life to look like. Those conversations are an essential part of setting strategy and deciding what assets and support structure will make the most sense.

It's strange to me—sad, actually—that the first time people ask themselves these questions is, quite often, in my office, when they're in the process of crumpling up the future that wasn't. Isn't this inquiry something that married people should be doing on a regular basis? Individually, and *especially* together?

In simply talking things out with me—often brutally, but clearly and in detail—my clients gain a real sense of how they define generic, vague terms such as "success," "happiness," and "security," often for the first time in their adult life.

When is the last time you and your spouse discussed what it specifically means to be "happy" and how you each define that term? When was the last time you discussed, in specific terms, what a "satisfying" sex life is for each of you? These should be conversations you look forward to! They're about being happy and about fucking, for fuck's sake!

You're married. That means you're in the same car, driving on the same road. Logic says you should be headed toward the same destination. Are you? Who selected that destination? Is it where you both want to get? Is one of you crawling out the back window while the other plows ahead blindly?

(I know, I know . . . from the back of the car, one of the kids just whimpered, "Are we there yet?")

*Chapter 40*

# ACCEPTANCE:
# YOU HAVE TO LOVE
# THE BAD PARTS, TOO

In the movie *Boomerang*, Eddie Murphy's character is smitten with a beautiful woman until they sleep together and he gets a glimpse of her ugly toes.

A "Dear Abby" reader once wrote in about having found the nearly perfect partner—smart, attractive, kind, etc.—except for unsightly elbows.*

The huge question that individuals in a relationship must ask themselves isn't "Do I love every part of the other person?" It's *"Can I love every part of this person?"*

Lawyers face this question with each new client (though replace the word "love" with "tolerate for $600 per hour").† Teddy was an excellent father, and his ex was an absolute asshole regarding the kids, so Teddy wasn't hard to represent, right? Not necessarily. See, excellent parent though he was (and atrocious though his ex was), Teddy was the asshole when it came to child support–related issues: He let no opportunity pass to shortchange his ex, even if it meant shortchanging his children.

---

\* To Abby's credit, she reamed the advice-seeker for his shallowness.

† One can make an effective argument for almost every position—and an equally effective argument for the exact opposite of that position. It's what I was trained to do on the high school debate team and what I do now as a lawyer. If the spouse of a given client had walked into my office five minutes before my client did, I'd have made most of the same arguments for them that their lawyer did.

I represented him to the best of my ability. I "zealously advocated within the bounds of applicable law" to "achieve his lawful objectives" after the commencement of the attorney-client relationship. As with Louie the Pimp, I didn't learn about the less-than-noble aspects of Teddy's character until a few weeks into the case, by which time I was, once again, buckled up and duty bound to take the ride.

But that's professional obligation. It's not always easy, but you learn to put certain feelings aside.

With love, you'd think it would be less of a challenge to put such feelings aside. After all, this is someone you, well, *love*. You love being with them. You find their being lovable.

Nearly all of my clients, in telling their story, focus on what it is about their partner that they don't love. They refer to their spouse's "bad" parts— but what they *really* mean is "human" parts. Like elbows. So many of them portray the marriage, particularly its final chapters, as some sort of morality play, Obi-Wan Kenobi vs. Darth Vader. Rarely is that account accurate. None of us is a saint—not me, not you, no one. We all have our less-than-virtuous side.*

Too many of us want love à la carte: We want the good parts of marriage, of commitment, but not the tougher ones, the nuts and bolts. Love is a verb. It's about rolling your sleeves up and giving the effort. But this culture is premised on doing what you want. *Why should I have to do that?* Well, technically you don't have to. But then, technically, you probably don't get to enjoy the really deep, enriching stuff that comes only with a marriage or loving relationship of long standing. How about an amendment to "Be right or be happy": "Be happy right now, with these three or four easy-to-love aspects of your partner . . . or be happy longer, if you can love it all."

To love—really love—is to love the whole person. If you don't love the mundane or generic or less obviously lovable side, even the some-

---

* I'm not talking here about something as extreme as abusive/violent tendencies. I'm talking about routine personality issues and generally unlikeable traits. Domestic violence should not be tolerated by civilized society and nobody has the right to hit, abuse, threaten, or exert improper control over another human being.

times hateful side, then you don't love him or her; you love a person who doesn't exist. To see a fault, even a big one, even three big ones, as a possible gateway to the breakup—well, maybe it wasn't really love to begin with.

The romance in the movie *Titanic* is bullshit. I feel the same way about *Romeo and Juliet* and other such "tragic" love stories. At least one of the parties dies before they get to see and live for a while with the yet unexpressed, more annoying parts of their partner . . . which is when real love kicks in. Or doesn't. Anyone can love someone "forever" when that someone is really good-looking and hangs around for only a few days before drowning in the Atlantic. That's a vacation hookup.

Acceptance, perhaps the central plank of Buddhism, is not the same as compromise or surrender. Learning to love the flaws is not impossible, because *our virtues so often come out of our flaws.* In my case, a certain softness in my personality—I might even call it gentleness—was gradually snuffed out as I became a better lawyer and a more effective advocate for those who needed my help. Did that make me a worse person? A better person? Did it make me a slightly harsher father, but a more effective advocate for kids whose interests I represented in family court? Or was it all still just who I always was, but with different aspects of me brought more sharply into focus as I grew as a person? In his poem "In a Dark Time," Theodore Roethke asks, "What's madness but nobility of soul / At odds with circumstance?"

The more we know about our spouse, the fuller the picture we see. We experience their best parts and their worst. We see behavior that could cause damage to how we feel about them. Here's one I've heard a few hundred times during consultations: "My husband just shuts off. When we disagree on something he won't discuss it. He just gives me the silent treatment and won't share his feelings at all." Is that how one or both of his parents handle (or handled) conflict? Was he more open and talkative in his first relationship and had his trust betrayed?

I'm not suggesting some form of radical empathy that would require you to forgive or ignore atrocious behavior. I, of all people, believe that individuals who are incompatible on certain important levels should call it quits sooner rather than later. I do firmly believe, however, that if we know our partner's history—how he was raised, what she experienced in past relationships—it doesn't take a genius to reverse-engineer the origins of their current behavior.

Understanding the reasons for a bad behavior doesn't excuse it. Hurt people tend to hurt people. That doesn't excuse the harm, but it certainly helps to explain it. It helps us not take the bad behavior so personally, which in turn helps us look at our situation more honestly. That seems to me, in all settings, a consistently good thing.

Often, as time passes and life stress increases, the traits that drew us to our partner become the things about them that we can't stand. The way she was so unpredictable and spontaneous when you were first dating and you were working as an accountant in a boring office? You loved that about her. But now, thirteen years and two children later, she just seems irresponsible and chaotic. The way he took charge and picked the restaurant and managed your joint checkbook? You loved that about him. But now, five years later, it feels controlling and exclusionary.

So how do we deal with the flaws (if you want to call them that) or the parts of our partners that, even if once appealing, are now making them less appealing?

Maybe you've both outgrown old habits and patterns you fell into. Maybe your circumstances have changed, and what previously served you in those circumstances is now an outdated way of doing things and an impediment to your current reality.

For example, I've had countless clients (often women but, in the last few years, more and more men, too) tell me that their partner's status as a workaholic is in itself a major reason for the divorce or else is an underlying contributor to the behaviors that led to the divorce (for instance, neglected spouse looks to third party for attention/affection/sex, and marriage dissolves thereafter). When you talk to the workaholic spouse, they will frequently tell you that the work habits that led to dissatisfaction or estrangement from their partner were born in the early years of the relationship. "I always put in a ton of hours at the office! She knew that when we were first married. It's been that way forever."

It's a fair point—but a reasonable counterpoint is that the financial or professional conditions that required those hours are often no longer applicable, or they're seen by the other party as no longer inspired by service to the collective good. When the spouse was working eighty-hour weeks to make partner at the law firm or get a promotion to management so the couple could afford, together, a down payment on their first house, the long absences felt like an expression of devotion to the relationship. But now, having made partner years ago, or having put enough money in the bank to live comfortably, the still-working-eighty-hour-weeks spouse feels like an absentee landlord.

I can't help but wonder whether, if the allegedly workaholic spouse had taken a closer look at the actual demands of their professional and/or financial life, they might have simply pumped the brakes with the result that everyone would have ended up happier. Was the workaholic applying old habits to a new set of conditions that rendered the habits unnecessary and antagonistic to more important priorities?

The behavior is irritating and easy to hate, but its root cause may be easy to understand and forgive. Is she controlling about money because she came from poverty and as a result is insecure and afraid of failing financially? Is his sudden, unprecedented, and, in your view, entirely unwelcome desire to travel more (or get a motorcycle, or grow a mustache, or go out with new friends) rooted in the fact that your youngest child is leaving for college, so Dad is suddenly having a hard time navigating his role in the world? The behaviors may be irritating; the root causes may be nothing short of endearing. These are things that should be talked about.

Now and then people turn into irredeemable assholes. And the root causes of this descent into assholery appear to be intolerable, unforgivable, or inexplicable. Sometimes it's not worth trying to save something, because the saving requires you to be miserable. It's not worth doing CPR on a dead body. If it's dead, bury it.

But if it isn't dead . . . let's not bury it.

## Chapter 41

# THE SECRET THAT
# SHOULDN'T BE A SECRET:
# JUST GIVE A SHIT

To be clear: This is not an admonition that wives need to give their husbands more blowjobs.

Laura was calm and resolved; her divorce from Fred proceeded with minimal fanfare.* At one point, as we sat in the hallway of the courthouse where we were waiting to be called, I asked Laura that question I ask many of my clients, if it feels appropriate: Was there an unmistakable moment when you realized you needed to get a divorce? A lightbulb moment? As I wrote earlier, I'm interested in the psychology of that tipping point (if one can be identified) when a person realizes that this was no longer transient discord but, in fact, the end of a marriage.

"I don't know about one single moment," said Laura, "but I do remember that he just stopped noticing me, and I don't mean in the sense that he didn't look at me, or that he grunted when we talked, anything like that. I mean the little things. The things he used to do because I liked them—the foot rubs, the way he would knock the snow off my car in the morning." She got a little wistful at the memory. "There's this brand of flax granola I really like and it's only carried in certain stores, and whenever we used to run out of it, Fred would get it for me,

---

* I love doing boring divorces. While exciting divorces are more lucrative, and I love putting on a good show in the courtroom, I'd happily dispense with all the high-drama ones so long as I could still stay in business, obtaining the best results for my clients.

even if he had to try three stores. I ate it pretty much every morning with chopped almonds and soy milk. It always made me smile that he noticed I was out of it and wanted to replace it for me. That he knew this little thing about me that someone else wouldn't. This little silly preference. That he would do this small gesture of kindness for me without seeking anything in return or making a big show of it. It was sweet of him. A sign that he was paying attention in some way. I don't know. Maybe it's silly."

It didn't seem silly at all to me but very real and understandable.

She continued: "So a few years ago, I ran out of my granola. At first I didn't really think anything of it. Maybe he just didn't notice or something. I could get it for myself but, for whatever reason, maybe it was curiosity, maybe superstition, maybe it was just dumb, but I didn't. I wanted to wait until he bought it for me. He was going shopping a couple days later, so I left the empty box closer to the front of the cabinet, hoping he would notice it was empty and bring a new one home, like he always had before. But when he came back from shopping, he didn't have granola—that brand or any. And I remember thinking, very clearly: *I think this might be ending.*"

She didn't look mad or sad; their marriage had run its course and she was going to be better off, eventually, in her new life. Divorce—and marriage—are always more complex than we think, and rarely one-sided, and Laura seemed in a reflective mood, so I asked my usual follow-up question. "What about you? Is there something *you* stopped doing that Fred liked?"

"Yeah, sure, blowjobs," she said, without hesitation.

I nearly spat my espresso onto the hallway floor of the courthouse.

"I can't tell you the last time I gave him one. I used to do it a lot, and he was always so relaxed and mellow and happy the rest of the day."

There you have it.

Flax granola and blowjobs.

That may be all it takes. For Laura and Fred, anyway, but I suspect they're not alone.

Again: I'm not suggesting that anyone is "owed" a blowjob, or, for that matter, a never-ending supply of flax granola. But what *are* you entitled to? What is your spouse entitled to? After all, in a marriage, each partner has vowed not to go elsewhere for certain things (sex, most blatantly; genuine attention and affection, most fundamentally). So what constitutes an obligation, what's a concession, what's an act of love?

The biggest danger in a long-term relationship: slippage. Because—again—no one raindrop causes the flood. At some point, indeed at many, many points, you have to make it about the marriage or the relationship, even if just to recognize that things are pretty good. It can't always be about the things *around* the relationship—the kids, the careers, the house, the appointments, the unfinished basement, or the unfinished novel. It's trite to say, but nothing that you don't focus on—your abs, your stamp collection—will magically thrive. It will stagnate, then wither. Eventually. Why should your marriage be different? So many of my clients misspent their emotional resources on things *around* the marriage, until they became so depleted, there was nothing left *for* the marriage. They had stopped paying attention.

The line I use in my work more than any other is "I hear you." Not "You're right." I don't even need to agree. Just acknowledge.

*I hear you. I hear your frustration. I get it.*

Of course, that's with a client, not someone I love and want to make a life with.

Here's the secret revealed: Marriage is not hard work, as long as you don't consider paying attention hard work. It isn't rocket science. After all I've seen, it still amazes me how it's the simple gestures that work. Eye contact, physical touch, a response that suggests you've been listening very hard, some simple phrase or movement that shows you're still connected to the dialogue and the person you're with. Often it's as simple as that. We want to feel connected to the other person; verbal and nonverbal cues let us know we are. If that sounds too obvious and simplistic, try the opposite, as an experiment. When someone is trying to engage you in a conversation, stare into space and avoid eye contact. Walk away in the middle of their sentence. Or—more likely these days—don't look up from your stupid phone. It feels sadly disconnected, no? What about, alternatively, when you tilt your head slightly and make eye contact? We live in an increasingly disengaged and distracted time: Everyone's checking their Facebook feed, taking a photo for their Instagram, or simply walking around with their ear buds in, listening to something other than the sounds of where they are.

I can't help but wonder, in these conditions, how many of us miss our spouses even when they are sitting right across from us.

I'm skeptical of the argument that people are disengaged or disconnected in their relationships because the relationship is no longer making them happy. Did you stop paying attention because the relationship didn't make you happy, or did the relationship stop bringing happiness because you stopped paying attention to it? It might be worth figuring out this chicken-egg problem before you end up in that chair at my conference table.

How hard is it to be nice to your spouse? To show them some small kindness? Okay, maybe it's unfair to call a blowjob a "small kindness"; it seems, without question, to require agility, tenacity, and something that merits real appreciation. To be honest, it's a miracle. But the flax granola example? You can't tell me that's challenging. (If you feel it is: There's your answer right there.) Or buying flowers. Or leaving a little Post-it note with some word of affection. There's no risk, either. If it's ignored or not reciprocated, are you really that much poorer for the gesture? You haven't changed some fundamental aspect of yourself. And your conscience is clean for having tried.

Once you stop telling each other *that thing*—that thing you once upon a time just *had* to tell each other, early and often and in sweet and different ways—then things go downhill, though not always quickly. (It's usually with a whimper, not a bang.) Annmarie, one of the smartest, most romantic people I know, once matter-of-factly said to me about her husband, whom she adores—and who adores her—"I wouldn't put it past him to cheat on me if I stopped caring about him."

Making each other feel special. What if it's really that simple?

# AFTERWORD

## *Cannibals*

I said it at the start and I'll say it again: This is a how-not-to book, not a how-to.

Some might accuse me of pessimism about relationships, but after so many years of helping so many people navigate the demise of their unions, I still believe, deeply, in the power of love and connection. I still believe we can find ourselves, our authentic selves, most fully with the help of another person.

Most fully. But not most easily. My profession has made me a realist in that regard.

For someone who ends things for a living, it's surprisingly hard to know how to end this book. Do I end on a note of optimism? Tell some story of redemption? An anecdote of a couple who came back from the brink? Do I end it with a darker tone? With a grim warning of what can happen when you let someone like me, someone of my profession, into your life?

I'll end it with Trevor and Eileen. It feels like I spent most of last year dealing with them.

Don't look for a lesson here, unless that lesson is *Hate can eat away at you at least as much as it eats away at the object of your hate.* (Come to think of it, that's a pretty good lesson.)

Eileen was bitter, possibly the bitterest person I've ever met. (A joke among divorce lawyers: Q: Why don't cannibals eat divorced women? A.: They're bitter.) You know the look on your partner's face when they told you to make a left turn, and you argued that it wasn't *this* left, and they insisted that it *was* this left, and you passed the turn and realized a few minutes later that, yeah, it *was* the previous left?

Eileen had that look on her face all the time.

Eileen had learned of Trevor's affair in one of the three most predictable ways, his credit card statement.*

Eileen's hatred of Trevor was a hatred that saw for miles. A hatred that was all-consuming. A hatred that was bigger than so many other things, like the love she knew he felt for their children or his love for his money. I've never hated anyone or anything the way Eileen hated Trevor.

Eileen (and I come only halfheartedly to her defense) was exhausted and exhausting. She had tolerated Trevor's narcissism and myriad other shortcomings for several decades out of some sense of commitment and obligation that she mistakenly believed she and Trevor had agreed upon, for however long they both took breath into their equally miserable lungs. Maybe that was what first brought them together. "You hate everything? Me, too! Let's stay together until we hate each other!"

Then Trevor woke up one day and broke the contract. He decided he didn't want to be miserable anymore, and he realized that he had enough money to give away half of everything he had and still have plenty left to enjoy his life. This made Eileen furious. She was committed to ensuring that Trevor would be miserable without her, even if she had to make herself utterly miserable in the process.

What followed was three years of litigation over every single issue that two people in a divorce could litigate: custody, visitation, business valuation, alimony, real estate division, intangible assets, earning capacity, imputed income. I've often thought, if confidentiality weren't obligatory, you could teach a rather comprehensive class in family law by

---

* The other top two: cell phone bills and emails left open.

breaking down Eileen and Trevor's divorce, issue by issue and appearance by appearance.

The case would also make for a good class on how to have the most expensive and painful divorce possible. Three years and a little over $1.4 million in combined legal fees later, Eileen and Trevor were divorced.

Their children had, in the process, grown to resent them both and been scarred by their selfishness and by the loyalty binds that each of them had created.

The house was sold, the limited equity split equally. The vacation home and investment property were both sold to pay the legal fees.

There was no resolution. No catharsis. Neither Eileen nor Trevor felt any sense of closure when all was said and done. Each remained firmly convinced that the other was solely to blame for the whole mess.

What's the lesson here? To be honest, I'm not entirely certain.

Don't be Eileen and Trevor. That's one lesson. But I don't think even Eileen and Trevor set out to be Eileen and Trevor. So it's not terribly valuable, as lessons go.

Don't get divorced? That's not the lesson. That would be terrible for me from a professional standpoint and, ultimately, it would be bad advice for many of you. Sometimes getting divorced is the best thing to do. Sometimes it's the kindest thing to do. Sometimes, at the risk of seeming profane, it's the loving thing to do, for yourself and for your spouse (and children).

Perhaps the lesson to be learned from Eileen and Trevor is the harsh reality that divorce is, at best, a knife fight in a closet. And the kids are in the closet with you. And your most fragile and valuable possessions, they're in that closet, too. And the lights are off. And you've got two choices: You can start stabbing and take the risks, like Eileen and Trevor did, or you can stop to think and try to find a better way to fight the fight that might need fighting.

Or you can open the door. And let the light in.

It's not easy to maintain a connection to another person. It's painful, sometimes, to let go of options you would have had if you were alone, and to make the corrections necessary to not lose the plot of the story you're trying to write together.

Find a way to stay together happily or find a way to split up happily. As I see it, those are your two best options. Trevor and Eileen are your worst-case scenario.

I'm not sure of the best way to do it. But I know the wrong way when I see it. And believe me, I see it a lot.

So I hope I don't see you. I hope you take something from all this falling apart, that you find a way to shore up what you have and make it truly stronger. I hope you never sit in that chair in front of me—and that you stay away not because you're scared of ending something but because there's value in the keeping; not because you don't want to get divorced but because you want to be truly and deeply in your relationship. I hope you live happily ever after and you never end up in the world of courtrooms and lawyers I navigate.

But if I do: I hope I see the best you possible. The most rational you possible.

It's hard to end things. It's hard to keep things together.

I wish you so much more than luck in either path.

# ACKNOWLEDGMENTS

Thank you:

First and foremost, to my clients. I'm honored and humbled, every day, by the trust you place in me to protect what you value most.

To Andy Postman. None of this would ever have happened without you. "Thank you" feels terribly small.

To the attorneys and judges who helped shape me into the lawyer I am today.

To Richard Pine at Inkwell, for believing in this project and for being the best at what you do. Thanks to Eliza Rothstein for your great input and efforts.

To Serena Jones, my incredible editor, and to the entire team at Henry Holt.

To Alex Postman, for your helpful insights throughout.

To my dad, for all of your support and love along the way.

To my sister, Laurie "Beanbag" Forest. She's also an author, but her books are ridiculous and involve wizards. Don't buy them. It only encourages her.

To Avram, my brother. Write when you find work.

To Noah and Billy. I'm so proud of the men you are becoming. I love you both very much.

Finally, and most of all, to B, for everything. Literally everything.

## ABOUT THE AUTHOR

JAMES J. SEXTON is a divorce lawyer. He lives in New York City. He wakes up every day at four a.m.